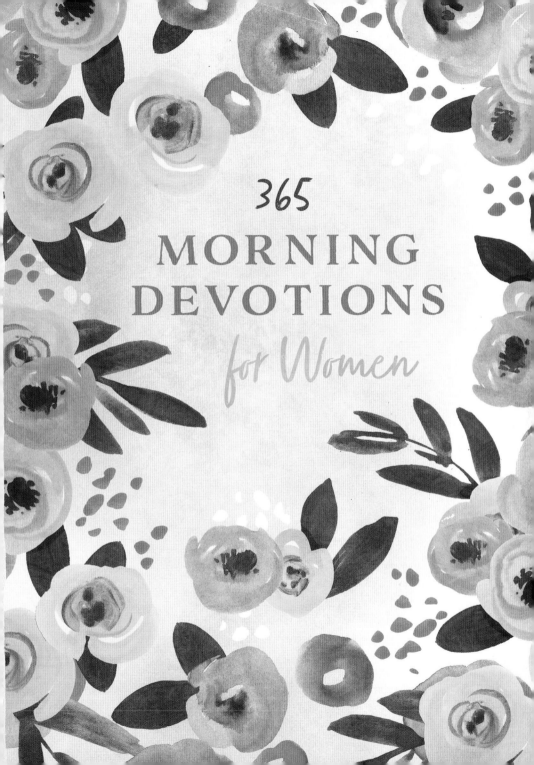

365
MORNING
DEVOTIONS
for Women

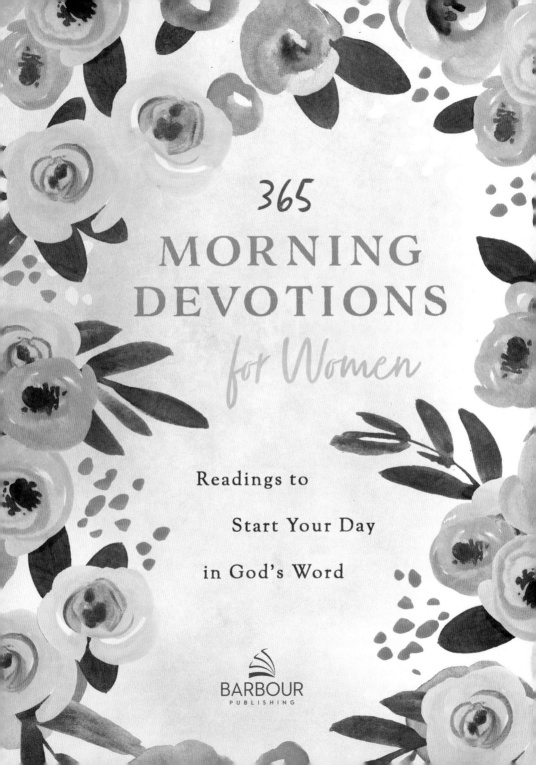

365

MORNING
DEVOTIONS
for Women

Readings to

Start Your Day

in God's Word

BARBOUR
PUBLISHING

Introduction

It seems like from the very moment we open our eyes we are on the go. We wake up, start the coffee, work out, check emails, rush to work, eat breakfast, check our to-do lists…the list is endless! We fall into a routine after so many mornings, so by the time our alarm sounds, we barely think about what we have to do before our days begin.

But our morning can have a huge impact on how the rest of our day goes. No, we won't be able to know about every obstacle or plan for every circumstance. Instead, our morning gives us the chance to prepare our attitudes to face whatever happens. What better way to prepare than to spend time with God in prayer and in His Word?

This collection, meant for busy or laid-back mornings, focuses on truths that your heavenly Father wants you to know before you start your day. So grab that cup of coffee and that comfy chair (or maybe snuggle into bed just a little bit longer!) and make a little time in your routine to spend with the Lord.

DAY 1

New Every Morning

Because of the LORD's great love we are not consumed,
for his compassions never fail. They are new
every morning; great is your faithfulness.
LAMENTATIONS 3:22–23 NIV

What's the first thing you do when you get up in the morning? Hop on the treadmill? Stumble to the kitchen for a mug of fresh-brewed caffeine? Walk blindly to the bathroom, not opening your eyes until a jet of hot water jolts you awake?

God starts out His day offering renewed compassion to His children. No matter what trials, difficulties, and sins yesterday brought, the morning ushers in a fresh experience, a brand-new beginning for believers who seek His forgiveness. All you have to do is accept the gift.

Are you burdened from yesterday's stress? Are the worries of tomorrow keeping you awake at night? Consider the dawning of the day as an opportunity to begin anew with our heavenly Father. Seek Him in the morning through studying His Word and through praying, embracing His compassion to be a blessing to others throughout your day.

Father, Your promise of never-ending compassion for me is amazing!
I never want to take for granted the grace You offer every day. I'm
so undeserving, but still You give and give and give. Please help
me to show mercy to others the same way You do to me. Amen.

DAY 2

Beautiful for the King

*Before each young woman was taken to the [king]. . .she was given the
prescribed twelve months of beauty treatments—six months with oil of
myrrh, followed by six months with special perfumes and ointments.*
ESTHER 2:12 NLT

Esther was just one of many women who had to take her turn at a full
year of beauty treatments before being taken to the king. What a regimen!

Sometimes just one morning with cosmetics at the bathroom mirror
can seem like forever, browsing through all the choices of creams,
colors, and scents. Although it is enjoyable to have these products, some
necessities—and maybe even a luxury or two—it's important to not
focus more on our outward appearance than we should.

Our King does expect His children to take care of our bodies. After all,
He created you. However, He doesn't expect everyone to be supermodels.
Despite unrealistic beauty images on television and in magazines and
movies impossible to live up to, all people are beautiful in the eyes of the
One who created the whole earth.

Aren't you thankful that the King of kings doesn't require that you
endure yearlong beauty treatments or be camera-ready for Him? He truly
loves you just as you are—created in His image and loved beyond measure.

*Lord, help me not to place too much emphasis on my outward appearance.
Thank You for creating me and for loving me just the way I am. Amen.*

DAY 3

Setting Priorities

Cause me to hear Your lovingkindness in the morning, for in You do I trust;
cause me to know the way in which I should walk, for I lift up my soul to You.
PSALM 143:8 NKJV

How easy it is to overcommit ourselves, become stressed, and let our lives get out of balance. We have work, sleep, relationships, recreation, and responsibilities of every sort vying for our attention.

One day at a time. That's what we get. Though we may often think we don't have enough hours for all we want to do, our Creator deemed one day at a time sufficient. How do we decide what to devote ourselves to during our one day?

The wisdom of the psalmist says to begin the one day by asking to hear the loving voice of the One who made you. You can lay your choices, problems, and conflicts before Him in prayer. He will show you which way to go. Psalm 118:7 (NIV) says, "The LORD is with me; he is my helper." Hold up that full plate of your life to Him, and allow Him to decide what to keep and what to let go.

Lord, make me willing to surrender my choices and activities
to You. Cause me to desire the things You want me to do.

DAY 4

Focus Time

In the morning, LORD, you hear my voice; in the morning
I lay my requests before you and wait expectantly.
PSALM 5:3 NIV

For any successful endeavor, preparation is key.

Throughout His earthly ministry, Jesus was an incredibly busy man. There were disciples to train, people to heal, and children to bless. No matter what He did or where He traveled, something or someone always seemed to need attention. However, despite the many demands placed upon Him, scripture tells us Jesus got up early in the morning, while it was still dark, and took time to meet His Father in prayer. Jesus was perfect, and yet even He knew this discipline was essential to ensure the effectiveness of His ministry.

Many of us hit the ground running in the mornings, armed with to-do lists miles long. Unfortunately, this means we try to take off in a hundred different directions, lacking focus and falling into our beds each night with a sense that we haven't accomplished anything at all.

While it doesn't ensure perfection, setting aside a short time each morning to focus on the Father and the day ahead can help prepare us to live more intentionally. During this time we, like Jesus, gain clarity, so that we can invest our lives in the things that truly matter.

Father, help me to take time each morning to focus
on You and the day ahead. Align my priorities so
that the things I do will be the things You want me to do.

DAY 5

Joyful Perseverance

Create in me a pure heart, O God, and renew a steadfast spirit within me.
Do not cast me from your presence or take your Holy Spirit from me. Restore
to me the joy of your salvation and grant me a willing spirit, to sustain me.
PSALM 51:10–12 NIV

Perseverance. Some days that word sounds so difficult. Maybe you dread Mondays, knowing that a full week of work and errands and demands await you. Maybe mornings in general are tough, each day holding burdens of its own.

Do not grow weary. Strive each day to keep a pure heart. Don't complain or dwell on small annoyances. Recognize your own worth in God's eyes, and recognize the worth of others, as well. Be joyful, even when you are not particularly happy.

This world will do all it can to pull you down, to tell you to give up. When you're tempted to grow discouraged, remember that you stand in the presence of God, and that He has given you the gift of His Spirit for times such as these.

Ask God for the power to press forward when your own spirit grows tired. Turn to other Christian believers for encouragement. Know that you are not alone—that you will never be alone. God craves your devotion. Turn to Him, and persevere.

Lord, I am feeling overwhelmed by the worries of this world.
Remind me of Your grace and salvation. Remind me of
Your love for me, so that I might better love others.

DAY 6

A Life of Joy

Satisfy us in the morning with your unfailing love,
that we may sing for joy and be glad all our days.
PSALM 90:14 NIV

Webster's dictionary defines joy as "emotion evoked by well-being, success, or good fortune." When was the last time you experienced joy? Was it last month? Last week? Today?

There are many joyful occasions: a birthday, an anniversary, a job promotion, a wedding, the birth of a baby. . .the list can go on. But do we need a big event to give us joy? Many ordinary moments can bring joy as well: getting a close parking spot at the mall, finding a ten-dollar bill in your pocket. . .again, the list continues.

First Thessalonians 5:16 (NLT) tells us to "always be joyful." That doesn't mean we need to take pleasure when things go wrong in life, smiling all the while. Rather, God wants us to maintain a spirit of joy, knowing that He has provided happy times and will carry us through the hard times.

Ever notice how a joyful spirit is contagious? When you're around someone who is full of joy, it's easy to find yourself sharing in that joy. Maybe you could be that person today, bringing smiles to others. When you find delight in the ordinary moments, they will catch the joy.

Heavenly Father, I thank You for being the source of my joy. Please help me
to share Your joy with those whom I come in contact with today. Amen.

DAY 7

The Same in a Changing World

"True, the grass withers and the wildflowers fade,
but our God's Word stands firm and forever."
ISAIAH 40:8 MSG

The world has changed so much in the past one hundred years. Electricity, indoor plumbing, airplanes and cars, computers, smart phones, and countless other technologies have created an entirely new world. Perhaps you have flipped through a yellowed photo album with pictures of your great-great-grandparents and then looked at perfectly preserved digital photos on an iPhone. Or maybe you remember a day when you paid much less for that gallon of gas or cup of coffee than you did yesterday morning. The world is changing, but our God is not.

God is the constant in our lives. He was, is, and will always be the same. It's amazing to think that while we cannot imagine life without electricity, someone hundreds of years ago read the Bible and was learning to trust in the same God just as we are learning to trust in Him. God's Word is for all people, regardless of the world they live in. God speaks to His people no matter where they are in life. Hundreds of years before the birth of Christ, Isaiah proclaimed that the Word of our God stands forever. Praise be to the Lord that we are still able to proclaim that same message today!

Dear Lord, thank You for Your unchanging Word. Thank
You for Your love and for the comfort of knowing that You
are the same yesterday, today, and forever. Amen.

DAY 8

It's About Time

There's an opportune time to do things,
a right time for everything on the earth.
ECCLESIASTES 3:1 MSG

Our schedules keep us moving from early in the morning until late at night. Every task—and often free time—needs to be penciled into our calendar.

What makes the top of your list of priorities? Is it spending time with friends? Working a second job? Going to the gym? What about reading the Bible? Spending time in prayer? Attending church?

While there is nothing wrong with doing anything listed above, we do, on occasion, need to step back and assess whether we have our priorities in order. We only have twenty-four hours in each day to eat, sleep, work, and do anything else that needs to be done.

Of course, God needs to be given first place. That doesn't necessarily mean that devotions should always be done first thing in the morning, but it does mean that devotional time should be set apart. After determining the best time for that, list your activities and prioritize them. You may find that you need to eliminate some things from your schedule in order to slow down the pace of life a bit. Pray about it—God will help you with the choices you need to make.

Dear Father, please be the Lord of my schedule. Give me
the wisdom I need in determining my priorities. Amen.

DAY 9

Rejoice

This is the day the LORD has made. Let us rejoice and be glad today!
PSALM 118:24 NCV

Heart shattered. Tears streamed down cheeks. Sitting in a chair late into the night, staring out the bedroom window at the pitch-black sky. We focus on the one thing we know for certain. The sun will rise in the east. And as it does, the reminder of God's faithfulness allows us to rejoice.

Have you ever experienced a time when you felt overwhelmed with sorrow? Life can be confusing and painful, and rejoicing with gladness is not always possible. Take heart. The Lord cares. He empathizes with our pain. With the birth of each new day, He reminds us that His mercies are new every morning. He provides sufficient grace and turns our weakness to strength as we trust Him.

Experiencing trials enables us to grow deeper in our relationship with the Lord. We realize that He is enough. Others may leave us, but He never will. He alone becomes the cause of our rejoicing and gladness. Let's worship our Creator, even in our darkest days.

Dear Lord, help me rejoice in You regardless of my circumstances. Amen.

DAY 10
The Blues

*Why, my soul, are you downcast? Why so disturbed within me? Put
your hope in God, for I will yet praise him, my Savior and my God.*
PSALM 42:11 NIV

It's hard not to be in a funk most days. From the moment we wake up in
the morning until we close our eyes at night, we can feel the burdens of
life. Newspaper headlines scream doom and gloom; gas and food prices
continue to rise; and the stress of job, family, and church ministries are
wearing you thin. Every burden in life seems unending, with no relief in
sight.

Everyone experiences times when frustrations seem to outweigh joy,
but as Christians, we have an unending source of encouragement in God.

That's great, you may think, *but how am I supposed to tap into that joy?*
First, pray. Ask God to unburden your spirit. Share your stress, frustrations, and worries with Him. Don't hold back; He can take it. Make a
list of the blessings in your life and thank the Provider of those blessings.
Choose to not focus on yourself; instead, praise Him for being Him.

Soon you'll feel true, holy refreshment—the freedom God wants you
to live out every day.

*Rejuvenate my spirit, Lord! You alone can take away the
burden I feel. You are my hope and my redeemer forever. Amen.*

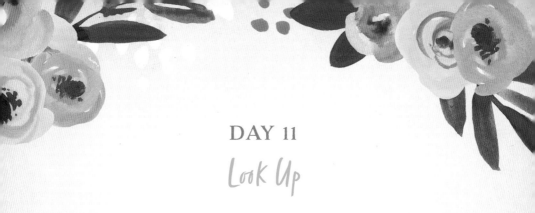

DAY 11

Look Up

In the morning will I direct my prayer unto thee, and will look up.
PSALM 5:3 KJV

"If you look at the ground, you'll be on the ground," the riding trainer says. Over and over the young girl hears this as she canters her horse and learns to jump fences of graduated heights.

"Steer with your eyes" is another expression she hears regularly from her teacher. As the horse and rider leap over one hurdle, her eyes are on the next fence ahead, giving the horse motivation to keep moving and go over it. It is this fixed gaze that keeps them moving together and springing over the fences.

The psalmist knows something about the importance of fixing one's gaze. "I will look up," he says. In the morning he directs his prayer to God and then watches and waits.

By going to God in prayer early in the day, we set our perspective for the entire day. Once we have given Him our problems and cares and listened for His voice to speak in our hearts, we have set our eyes for the day on Him as the place we are going for whatever we need.

Father, cause me to seek You early each day, to remember to
fix my gaze on You, and watch You work in my life.

DAY 12

A Heart That Sings

I will sing of your strength, in the morning I will sing
of your love; for you are my fortress, my refuge in times of
trouble. . . . I sing praise to you. . .my God on whom I can rely.
PSALM 59:16–17 NIV

Talk about trouble—David had a lion's share of it! Day in and day out, year after year, fueled by a king's jealousy, David was a wanted man: homeless, on the run and hunted by a bunch of lowlifes. Yet, amazingly, in Psalms we see that David's crying out to God turns into joyful music or praise. What an example he sets for us!

You too can be that real with God by telling Him your heart's burdens. Vent your hurts, disappointments, and struggles to Him. He can handle it. David didn't try to sound spiritual. He was genuine before the Lord. Once he cleared the air, his heart turned to thanksgiving and praise. He'd bring out the instruments, write a song or two, and regain his strength.

Playing God-focused music and joining in a song of praise can become a spirit booster. Humming along can help refocus a grumbling heart and brighten a dull day. Keep songs of praise and worship handy to maintain a cheerful heart.

Mighty Father, thank You for the wonder of music. Help me to sing Your
praises, to sing of Your strength and love daily, for You are my refuge. Amen.

DAY 13
Wear A Smile

Those who go to him for help are happy,
and they are never disgraced.
PSALM 34:5 NCV

Little Orphan Annie, dressed in threadbare hand-me-down clothes, gets the other girls in the orphanage to sing along with her. "You're never fully dressed without a smile."

We could all learn a lesson from Annie. Maybe we need to add it to our morning checklist: Make breakfast, pack lunches, apply makeup, and, oh yes—put on a smile.

Smiling does the heart good. Age will not dim our smiles, and they announce our happiness to the world.

But I'm not happy, you might argue.

Maybe we could choose another word and say we're joyful. Unlike happiness, joy depends on God rather than our circumstances. As the psalmist points out, God never disappoints anyone who comes to Him for help. He may not help us in quite the way we expect, but He will always give us exactly what we need.

When we wear a happy face despite our circumstances, we may find that our inward spirit changes to match the outward smile.

Dear Lord, let our smiles come from the inside out. Our
circumstances change, but You never do. Thank You, Lord!

DAY 14
All in Good Time

What a Day that will be! No more cold nights—in fact, no more nights! The Day is coming—the timing is GOD's—when it will be continuous day. Every evening will be a fresh morning.
ZECHARIAH 14:6 MSG

You've been praying for…a long time. As you begin to pray this morning, you may be asking yourself and God if continued prayer is even worth it anymore.

Through our tears, it can be hard to see the plan God has for our lives. If that plan means a better job, a physical healing, a new partner, kids, that will happen—but only in God's perfect time.

In today's Bible passage, Zechariah is talking about the Lord's return—but the lesson is applicable in a much broader context. God's timing is perfect. While our situations may seem hopeless, to God, they're just part of the bigger picture. Our job is to trust God's timing for every circumstance of life. God knows our situation, and He will not forsake us.

Dear God, help me to remember that Your timing is perfect. In every situation, whether looking for a partner or taking care of my family unit, I pray that You would help me to seek Your will and Your perfect timing.

DAY 15

Start Over

And Jesus said, "Neither do I. Go and sin no more."
JOHN 8:11 NLT

Ever wish our lives would give us the chance to do something over again? And again. And again. Until we finally get it right?

God gives us opportunities for daily "start overs." But not in the way we think He would.

One morning while teaching at the temple, Jesus was interrupted by some self-righteous Pharisees. They had dragged along a woman caught in adultery, insisting that she be stoned. "What do you say?" they asked Jesus.

Jesus quietly suggested that the man without sin had the right to throw the first stone. One by one, the accusers silently left. Jesus asked the woman, "Where are your accusers? Didn't even one of them condemn you?" (John 8:10 NLT).

She answered, "No one."

What was Jesus's response? "Neither do I. Go and sin no more." (John 8:11 NLT).

In other words, dear lady, start over.

Lord of second chances, thank You for not condemning me,
but for giving me daily opportunities to start over and do it right.

DAY 16

Sleep On It

It is of the LORD's mercies that we are not consumed,
because his compassions fail not. They are new
every morning: great is thy faithfulness.
LAMENTATIONS 3:22–23 KJV

Sleep on it.

Researchers have found that to be sound advice. They believe that sleep helps people sort through facts, thoughts, and memories, providing a clearer look at the big picture upon waking. Sleep also separates reality from emotions like fear and worry, which can cloud our thinking and interfere with rational decision-making. Scientifically speaking, sleep is good medicine.

For Christians, the biological effects of sleep are outweighed by the spiritual benefits of the new day God gives us. At the end of an exhausting day, after the worries and the pressures of life have piled high, we may lie down, feeling as though we can't take another moment of stress. But God's Word tells us that His great mercy will keep our worries and problems from consuming us.

Through the never-ending compassion of God, His faithfulness is revealed afresh each morning. We can rise with renewed vigor. We can eagerly anticipate the new day, leaving behind the concerns of yesterday.

Heavenly Father, thank You for giving me a new measure of
Your mercy and compassion each day so that my concerns don't
consume me. I rest in You and I lay my burdens at Your feet.

DAY 17

Weather "Face"

*"When I smiled at them, they could hardly believe it; their
faces lit up, their troubles took wing! I was their leader,
establishing the mood and setting the pace by which they lived."*
JOB 29:24 MSG

A dark and gloomy sky in the morning may set the tone for an unproductive and disappointing day. But a bright sunny sky can add hope and promise to the day's outlook.

So it is in the home.

Your face is the forecast for your day—and others' radars are always ready to take a reading. A gloomy face indicates hopelessness and an expectation of failure, but a cheerful face brings joy and eagerness to the day's outlook.

Attitude alone may not change our circumstances. But it can affect how we perceive things—and completely alter our final results. When we meet tough times with a cheerful, positive attitude, we can expect success and growth rather than failure and loss.

Perhaps we should examine our own habits. Do we mope around our homes with the "storm clouds" of long faces and gloomy dispositions? Or do we face each new day (and each new challenge) brightly with a sunshiny, eager confidence?

We set the forecast. May we reflect in our faces the kind of day that honors ourselves, our families, and our God.

*Heavenly Father, please help me to control my mood so that
I can cheerfully lead my family through the day. Let my face
reveal the hope and expectation I have in Your promises. Amen.*

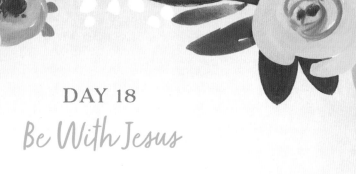

DAY 18

Be With Jesus

When they saw the courage of Peter and John and realized
that they were unschooled, ordinary men, they were astonished
and they took note that these men had been with Jesus.

ACTS 4:13 NIV

The third grader needs help with his multiplication tables, the spaghetti is boiling over, the phone is ringing, and the baby just threw applesauce on the wall. Not to mention the work emails and texts filling up your phone!

With all the concerns and distractions of our lives, it's easy to get so busy that we overlook our need to spend time with Jesus—reading His Word, praying, praising, and worshipping Him.

Don't let your time with Jesus slide! The "officials" of Acts 4:13 were amazed not by Peter and John's education, wealth, or status, but simply because it was obvious they had been with Jesus.

Others can tell when we've made time for Jesus. He'll give us bravery for our tasks, but also love, joy, peace, patience, kindness, goodness, faithfulness, gentleness, and self-control.

Each morning as we seek Jesus, let's not just give Him a list of our needs for the day. Let's listen to what He wants to tell us, and praise Him for who He is. The results will be amazing!

Dear Jesus, help me not to be so busy that I push You aside. I love You for
who You are. Shine through me today so others can be amazed by You.

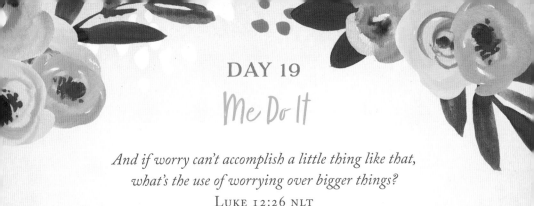

DAY 19
Me Do It

And if worry can't accomplish a little thing like that,
what's the use of worrying over bigger things?
LUKE 12:26 NLT

"Me do it!" Toddlers say as they struggle into their coats, hold their own cups, and waddle about—usually where we don't want them to go. We watch, sigh, and think how much easier it would be if they would only let us do it for them.

God must feel that way about us. He waits, letting us struggle and even fail, until we reach the point that we acknowledge our limitations.

Do we worry about food and clothing?

God provides for the ravens of the air and the lilies of the field (Luke 12:24, 27).

Do we struggle to be good Christians and role models?

God is pleased to give us the kingdom (Luke 12:32).

Do we cram as much as possible into each day, trying to add an hour to our lives?

Forget it (Luke 12:25).

Jesus reminds us that we can't do something as simple (to Him, that is) as adding an hour to our lives. Why do we think we can carry the world on our shoulders?

Instead, the Lord invites us to seek Him first. To take our worries to God in prayer and make that relationship our primary focus. Prayer is the treasure we should seek.

Almighty Lord, You can and do provide everything
we need. Teach me to take my worries to You in prayer.

DAY 20

A New Day

GOD, treat us kindly. You're our only hope. First thing in the morning, be there for us! When things go bad, help us out!
ISAIAH 33:2 MSG

There are days that start off wrong and finish worse. We say things we shouldn't say to our family or friends, using a voice that is too harsh or too loud. We experience days full of failure, tinged by sin. Wouldn't it be great to redo our bad days?

We have that opportunity. It's called *tomorrow*. Lamentations 3:22–23 tells us that by God's mercies, He gives us a fresh canvas every new day. Anger and pain don't have to be part of it. No matter how stormy the day before, each new day starts fresh. And He is there for us first thing in the morning and every step of the way in our day, even if things begin to go wrong—again.

Each day is a new day with God. We can focus on the things that matter most: worshipping Him, listening to Him, and being in His presence. No matter what happened the day before, we have a fresh start to enjoy a deeper relationship with Him. A fresh canvas, every new day.

Before I get out of bed in the morning, let me say these words and mean them: "This is the day the LORD has made. Let us rejoice and be glad today" (Psalm 118:24 NCV).

DAY 21

Small Beginnings

*"The people should not think that small beginnings
are unimportant. They will be happy when they
see Zerubbabel with tools, building the Temple."*

ZECHARIAH 4:10 NCV

Babies grow from just a bundle in their parent's arm. Magnificent sequoias start as a single seed. The world of Narnia began in the mind of C. S. Lewis, with the image of a faun carrying parcels and an umbrella.

The Israelites discovered that small beginnings are important too—when Zerubbabel arrived with tools to start building the second temple.

It's easy for us to put off family vacations or other adventures until we can afford something "big." We'd love to take our children to Disney World or to Washington, D.C. But until we can pull off that "big" event, we stay too busy to take advantage of the many smaller things around us.

We'd like to take our children to a professional ball game. They just want us to show up for their practices and games.

We'd like to go to a fancy restaurant. Our children enjoy grilling hot dogs and toasting marshmallows.

We'd like a weekend alone. But somehow, we don't enjoy the quiet that descends on the house once the children are in bed.

When we add up the small things, they become something big.

*Dear Lord, teach us to add up the minutes and not seek out
the hours. You are present in every moment of our lives.*

DAY 22

Steady Hands

*I keep my eyes always on the LORD. With him
at my right hand, I will not be shaken.*
PSALM 16:8 NIV

What shakes you? That list can be unending. An illness, a behavioral problem, or a pending eviction can shake the foundation of anyone, especially the one who lacks someone to turn to for help or encouragement.

Whatever the circumstances, remember that the Lord is at your right hand! In the Bible, the "right hand" symbolizes the kingship of God. He's the King of all kings, the ruler and ultimate authority over everything. And you know what? He holds your right hand and steadies your foundation.

Since God knows the beginning from the end, He's acutely aware of what we can handle. And He'll never allow even a smidgen more than we can take.

The Lord never said He'd take our hard times away. But at just the perfect time, He'll supply exactly what we need to get through the earthquakes of life. He'll lead us safely to a place that's solid and firm.

With Christ at our right hand, we need never be shaken.

*Jesus, please take my hand and steady my walk. When my
circumstances are shaky, be my firm foundation, Lord.*

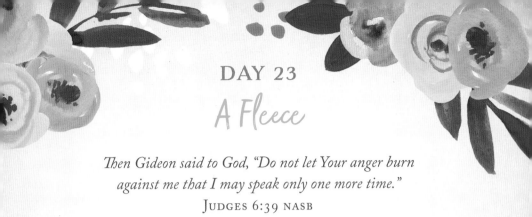

DAY 23
A Fleece

Then Gideon said to God, "Do not let Your anger burn against me that I may speak only one more time."
JUDGES 6:39 NASB

After seven years of judgment for doing evil in the eyes of the Lord, it was time for Israel to be freed from the Midianites. God chose Gideon, a mighty warrior, to lead the battle. He even promised Gideon that the battle would be won.

Gideon's response to this holy visit was to doubt the Lord's Word! Gideon wanted proof of victory, so God gave him a sign. Audaciously, Gideon asked for another. Gideon put a wool fleece out overnight and asked God to keep it dry from the morning dew. God complied. Then Gideon asked for a reversed scenario. Again, God complied. The story of Gideon's fleece is so well known that, even today, people refer to putting a fleece before God when they try to discern His will.

Amazingly, God wasn't angry with Gideon for his disbelief. God met Gideon where he was. Gideon's faith was growing; that's what mattered to God.

When we feel inadequate about qualifications for a job God has given us, we can take a page from Gideon's book. Gideon didn't hold back his fear of failure. He needed God's reassurance and patience in his faith walk, and God lovingly provided both.

He'll provide for us too—if only we'll ask.

Lord, the battles I face may not be like Gideon's, but the feelings I have certainly are. Be patient with me, Lord! I need encouragement today and a reminder that You are with me.

DAY 24
The Blessing of Peace

"The LORD bless you and keep you; the LORD make his
face shine on you and be gracious to you; the LORD
turn his face toward you and give you peace."
NUMBERS 6:24–26 NIV

These verses are the priestly blessing God told Moses to instruct the priests to give to the people. This beautiful gift from God is a taste of heaven to carry us through until we get there. The word *peace* here is the Hebrew *shalom*. Here *shalom* carries its full meaning of more than peace, but also rightness, well-being, and wholeness.

The repetition of the Lord's name leaves no doubt as to who is doing the blessing. And no doubt as to the One to whom we belong.

When God blesses us, He beams proudly at us like a father with his child. He wants us to have a close, personal relationship with Him. And when our relationship with Him is right, we have that all-encompassing peace, the peace Paul tells us in Philippians 4:7 passes all understanding.

When God blesses us, other people notice. How are we telling others of His goodness to us? How are we using His deeds to encourage other believers and point nonbelievers to Christ?

Heavenly Father, Your blessing us with Your peace is beyond
our ability to understand. You walk with us through all of life's
difficult circumstances. We thank You for Your goodness toward us.
Help us remember to share with others what You have done. Amen.

DAY 25
Powerful One

He who forms the mountains, who creates the wind, and who reveals
his thoughts to mankind, who turns dawn to darkness, and treads on
the heights of the earth—the LORD God Almighty is his name.
AMOS 4:13 NIV

Ever pondered the power of our Lord God Almighty? Meditating on God's power can soothe our biggest worries and calm our deepest fears.

The Word of God speaks often of His power—we know He created our universe in less than a week. But if that's too much to comprehend, consider the enormity of a single mountain or ocean. Those vast, mighty things came into being simply by God's voice—and they're only a tiny fraction of everything He made. What power!

The Lord opens the morning curtains to reveal the dawn and pulls the sky shades back at night to bring darkness. He plots the course of the wind, arranges for rainfall, and causes grass and trees to grow. If our Lord has enough knowledge and power to handle these jobs, surely He will look after us.

Problems that seem insurmountable to us are simply a breath to Him. Let's not be anxious today—God holds each one of us in the palm of His hand.

Lord God, You are my provider. Thank You for holding such power—and for
choosing me to be Your child. Please give me a greater understanding of who
You are, helping me to remember that You, the Lord God Almighty, love me.

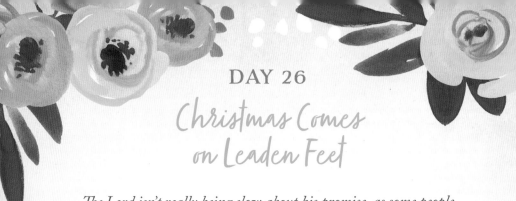

DAY 26

Christmas Comes on Leaden Feet

The Lord isn't really being slow about his promise, as some people think. No, he is being patient for your sake. He does not want anyone to be destroyed, but wants everyone to repent.

2 PETER 3:9 NLT

To a child, Christmas takes forever to arrive!

But to an adult, the calendar seems to flip to December every few months. It's exactly the same amount of time—but different viewpoints lead to very different perceptions.

In the first-century church, believers were growing impatient. Jesus had promised to return—but where was He? Like children waiting for Christmas, the early believers couldn't experience Jesus' second coming quickly enough.

God, though, sees time differently than we do. In His love and wisdom, He wants no one to perish. He's giving time to everyone to repent from their sins and truly know Him. It's an offer for every single person we love—even those we don't. His agenda, unlike ours, is always perfectly holy.

We have the promise of the Bible that Jesus is coming back. It may seem like a long time to wait—just as children feel about the arrival of Christmas. But one day, He will return, and our long wait will be forgotten.

It's a Christmas morning that lasts forever!

*Lord of the universe, You are coming back! May
I model patience and expectancy to my family,
never wavering in my belief that You will return!*

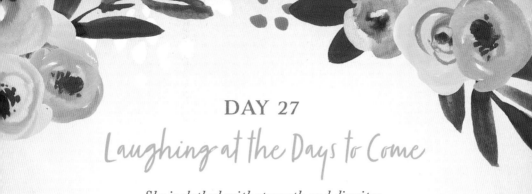

DAY 27
Laughing at the Days to Come

She is clothed with strength and dignity;
she can laugh at the days to come.
PROVERBS 31:25 NIV

You mean a woman of God can laugh at the days to come? Really? Wow! Most of the world wakes up each morning under a black cloud of regret and a debilitating fear of the future. That sounds more realistic, right? To laugh at the future is hard to imagine. To see hope instead of futility? Promise in the pain? What would that kind of woman look like? Sound like?

Perhaps a woman of God as described in Proverbs 31 doesn't necessarily have a lot of confidence in herself, but rather in God. Perhaps she trusts so implicitly in His divine plan and goodness that she can sleep deeply. She can wake up refreshed each morning.

And this woman of God knows some truths—that God will indeed work everything for good in her life. That He is watching over her comings and goings, and nothing will befall her that He can't handle. She knows that this earthly life is temporary. That heaven is not only for real but forever. Knowing these truths all the way to her soul gives her peace and joy, and it shows in her countenance. Yes, and even in her laugh.

Jesus, help me trust in You every hour of every day, and let me be
so full of peace that I too can laugh at the days to come. Amen.

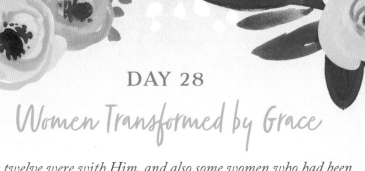

DAY 28
Women Transformed by Grace

The twelve were with Him, and also some women who had been
healed of evil spirits and sicknesses: Mary who was called Magdalene,
from whom seven demons had gone out, and Joanna the wife of
Chuza, Herod's steward, and Susanna, and many others who
were contributing to their support out of their private means.
LUKE 8:1–3 NASB

The scriptural account records that Jesus changed the lives of all who met Him. Some of these He changed simply by entering their world, and others were changed in more dramatic ways.

Of course, Mary, His mother, was the first woman whose life was radically altered by His incarnation. The sisters Mary and Martha knew Him as a frequent guest and friend. Other women contributed to His ministry and daily life through financial support; they followed Him, weeping, as He carried His cross and came with spices to prepare His body that misty third morning.

And these women: the woman at the well in Samaria, the woman caught in adultery and thrown at His feet, the widow whose son He raised from the dead, and the woman with the bleeding disorder who was made well from touching His robe. As Creator, Jesus understood the inner longings of a woman's heart and offered redemption for hurts and the promise of hope and healing. And He still does today.

Jesus, thank You for understanding me and for giving Your life
to redeem me. Please transform me with Your grace. Amen.

DAY 29
The Warrior Sings

"The LORD your God is with you, the Mighty Warrior who saves. He will take great delight in you; in his love he will no longer rebuke you, but will rejoice over you with singing."
ZEPHANIAH 3:17 NIV

What kind of picture does this verse create in your mind? The Lord is a mighty warrior who leads the armies of angels. Yet He is with us. One of Jesus' names is Immanuel, literally the "with us God." And He takes delight in us. He doesn't rebuke us. He rejoices over us with singing.

This verse from Zephaniah is like a sampler of God's attributes. Look them over again. How does each of these characteristics show up in your relationship with Him? What attribute do you need to know more about? Which do you struggle with?

We sing worships songs to God, but have you thought about His joy over you being so great He bursts out into song? Or maybe He sings you a sweet lullaby like a parent does to a small child. Next time you sing a worship song, think about what kind of song God would sing about you. Let that fuel your worship of Him and deepen your relationship with the One who loves you so greatly.

Heavenly Father, it is almost too much for us to comprehend that You, the Creator of the universe, could sing about us. We want to understand that, even in just the small way our minds can handle. Show us Your love and help us to love You more deeply. Amen.

DAY 30

Amazing Love

*"See, I have engraved you on the palms of
my hands; your walls are ever before me."*
ISAIAH 49:16 NIV

We do all sorts of things to keep reminders of our loved ones around us. Handprints and pawprints are memorialized in plaster or in paint. We keep letters and mementos tucked in drawers. Flowers are dried and pressed. But most often we put up pictures: on walls, on the refrigerator, on our computers, in our wallets, even on our phones.

Now think about how many times a day you look at your hands. We wear wedding rings and class rings to remind us of our connection to our loved ones in a most obvious way. When God says He has tattooed our faces on His hands, He is telling us we are never out of His thoughts. He thinks of us constantly.

The phrase "your walls are ever before me" refers to the walls of a city. In ancient times, a city without walls was vulnerable to attack. God's keeping an eye on our walls means that He is keeping us under His protection. He never takes His eyes off us.

As humans, there is a limit to our love, our attention, our protective eyes. But God's love is limitless. He loves us in a deep, amazing way with an attention that never strays.

*Dear God, we can't begin to fathom Your love for us. Help
us to see glimpses of it throughout our day and to smile
and thank You for Your amazing love. Amen.*

DAY 31

Encouragement from the Scriptures

For everything that was written in the past was written to teach us, so that through the endurance taught in the Scriptures and the encouragement they provide we might have hope.

ROMANS 15:4 NIV

You know those days when nothing goes right? And sometimes those days stretch into weeks and months? You don't get the promotion. Your car breaks down. Someone you love gets sick. Disappointment settles in and brings its brother, Discouragement. Things are not going according to your plan, and you may wonder if God even hears your prayers.

Looking at the heroes of the Old Testament, you'll see that God's plan for those people wasn't smooth sailing either. Joseph was sold into slavery, falsely accused by Potiphar's wife, and unjustly imprisoned. Moses tended flocks in the wilderness for forty years after murdering a man and before leading God's people out of slavery. David was anointed king but had to run for his life and wait fifteen years before actually sitting on the throne.

Those stories give us hope and encouragement. Our plans are quite different from God's plans, and His ways of doing things are quite different from what we would often choose. We see how things worked out for the people of the Old Testament. We can take encouragement from the fact that the same God is at work in our lives.

Heavenly Father, it can be difficult to have hope during trying times. Remind us to trust in You and cling to Your Word for encouragement. Amen.

DAY 32

Hope for the Soul

We have this hope as an anchor for the soul, firm and secure.
It enters the inner sanctuary behind the curtain.

HEBREWS 6:19 NIV

In just a few words, this verse paints a rich word picture to comfort us. "This hope" refers to the verses before where God secures His promise by swearing by Himself, giving us two trustworthy things to place our hope in, His Word and Himself.

Anchors are also a symbol of hope. During a storm, a strong anchor locked into a solid foundation keeps the boat from being blown off course or onto the rocks. Sailors' hope during a storm is the anchor.

"The inner sanctuary behind the curtain" would be familiar to these Jewish Christians—the audience of the book of Hebrews—as the Holy of Holies where the high priest went once a year, after the sin sacrifices were offered, to enter the presence of God. When Christ died on the cross, the curtain separating the two areas tore from top to bottom, symbolizing direct access to God for all believers. So instead of anchoring into solid rock, like a ship would, we anchor our hope directly to God.

Our hope is founded in the unshakable character of God, who loves us so much He sent His Son to die for us. His Word is true. He will do what He says He will do.

Heavenly Father, we are grateful for the sacrifice of Your Son,
making it possible for us to have a relationship with You. Remind us
we can trust You completely, and help us to rest in that truth. Amen.

DAY 33

Joy in Serving

Now John also was baptizing at Aenon near Salim, because there was plenty of water, and people were coming and being baptized.
JOHN 3:23 NIV

John the Baptist was single-mindedly focused on what God had told him to do. He went to a place that had the two things he needed to fulfill his mission: water and people wanting to be baptized.

Sometimes we make serving God more complicated than it needs to be. We don't need to wait for conditions to be right or to have more knowledge or experience or resources. We can serve right now where God has us. He will grow us into what He needs us to be.

John had joy because he was doing what he was supposed to be doing. He knew his mission had a reason. He was preparing to let someone else, Jesus, take over. It was not about John. It was about God.

What talents and interests do you have? What resources has God given you? How can you use what you have right now to serve Him? Be open to see what God brings your way. Serve God and find your joy.

Dear God, make us aware of talents and resources we can use to serve You. Open our eyes to the opportunities You have placed around us, and show us the joy in serving You. Amen.

DAY 34

Housekeeper or Zookeeper?

Noah was 600 years old when the flood covered the earth.
He went on board the boat to escape the flood—
he and his wife and his sons and their wives.
GENESIS 7:6–7 NLT

I know you may feel like your home is a zoo, but imagine what it was like for Noah's wife! She really did live in a zoo! There have been many women to whom God has given difficult assignments, but think about the details of life on the ark with the animals. We can only hope that Mrs. Noah was an animal lover…. Surely God gave her extra help to carry out her task.

Noah and his family cared for the animals and waited for the waters to recede. As the oldest woman on board, Mrs. Noah would have been the "mother" to whom they turned for nurture and counsel. She would have been a mentor to her sons' wives and Noah's confidante and helper. It was a tall order. Yet the Bible does not record her emotions, her actions, or even her name. It does indicate that she was faithful to fill her place, even if that meant sleeping in a zoo.

Where has God placed you today? What assignment has He given you to fulfill His plan? Whatever and wherever, you must rely on His strength and carry out His purpose; the end of your story has not yet been written. And who knows, you might end up loving your zoo!

God, I accept Your call on my life. Use me today for Your glory. Amen.

DAY 35

Taking Jesus at His Word

The royal official said, "Sir, come down before my child dies." "Go," Jesus replied, "your son will live." The man took Jesus at his word and departed.
JOHN 4:49–50 NIV

The royal official must have been desperate. He'd heard about a prophet the local Galileans called Jesus. Everyone was looking to see what miracles He would perform.

The official found Jesus and begged Him to come heal his son. But Jesus didn't do the expected. He didn't go to heal the man's son. Instead, He simply said that the son would live. The man may have had a moment of confusion at the unexpected turn of events, but he did take Jesus at His word. He believed that Jesus' word could heal his son, even though he'd expected that Jesus would have to touch his son to heal him. When he arrived home and found his son well, he and his whole household believed.

Sometimes we are like this official. We look to Jesus as a last resort, and then expect Him to act in a certain way. But as we look through the Gospels, we see that Jesus healed in a variety of ways. Still today He works any way He chooses, not just the way we expect.

Are you looking for Jesus to act in a certain way to answer a prayer? Ask God to open your eyes to the unexpected ways He is working.

Lord Jesus, thank You for being intimately involved in our lives. Remind us to trust You for everything. Amen.

DAY 36
Our Daily Bread

"Give us this day our daily bread."
MATTHEW 6:11 NKJV

A young woman gazed out her window as the morning sun just began to touch the snow-covered peaks of the mountains. Her thoughts could hardly be collected and organized, and so she just stared and prayed, "Lord, give us today our daily bread." She didn't know if her car would get her to work or not. Money was tight. Her grocery budget was minimal. Being new to the area, she had no one to turn to.

"Give us this day our daily bread."

Each day, the Lord answered this prayer. He gave her what she needed, whether it be patience, mental or physical strength, food, or faith. A bill never went unpaid. A stomach never went hungry. A body never went unclothed. The Lord provided all their needs.

Eventually, slowly, her situation began to improve. She was able to buy a new car, she picked up more hours at work, and eventually found a new job. A community began to form around her. Looking back, she remembers it as one of the best years of her life. It was a year she walked closely, intimately, with her Savior.

Father, I ask today that You would give me today's bread. Fill me with what I need to make it through the day, that I may praise Your name forever.

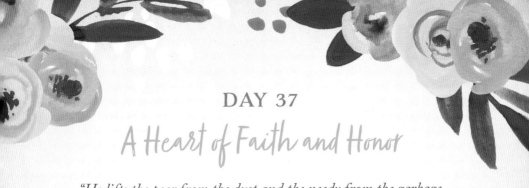

DAY 37
A Heart of Faith and Honor

*"He lifts the poor from the dust and the needy from the garbage
dump. He sets them among princes, placing them in seats of honor.
For all the earth is the LORD's, and he has set the world in order."*
I SAMUEL 2:8 NLT

This is just a part of the prayer that Hannah prayed as she left her son
to live with Eli the priest and serve the Lord all his life. Samuel was her
firstborn, a child she desperately prayed to God for, and she fulfilled her
promise and left Samuel in the care of Eli.

How hard it was for her to pray this prayer of praise to God. She finally
had a child, but she was committed to her promise to offer him in service
to the Lord. She would not be the one to raise him and experience all of
his "firsts" in life. And yet she prayed this prayer that does nothing but
honor the Lord. Even if there were moments when she wished she hadn't
made such a promise, she praised Him. "My heart rejoices in the LORD!
The LORD has made me strong" (1 Samuel 2:1 NLT).

We can learn so much from Hannah in the short space she is written about in 1 Samuel. She honored the Lord above all else and trusted
His ways. May God give you a heart of courage that honors Him and
strengthens you.

*Dear Lord, thank You for hearing my prayers
and remembering me in Your faithfulness. May I be
like Hannah, who fervently pursued and honored You.*

DAY 38

An Ever-Flowing Spring

"The LORD will guide you continually, giving you water when you are dry and restoring your strength. You will be like a well-watered garden, like an ever-flowing spring."
ISAIAH 58:11 NLT

It's easy to fall into the trap of looking to earthly things to restore us. Instead of immediately looking to the One who made us and knows every detail of what we need, we often look other places. The Lord is our water when we are dry. He restores our strength. As we look to Him, we will become like a lush, well-watered garden. Fruitful. Energetic. Growing.

This is one of those verses to keep close to your heart during a busy season. When it feels like your next day of rest is far off, this is a promise to cling to and draw strength from. Every day, as often as you can, make space for quiet moments with the Lord. A few moments can give you everything you need.

The Lord will restore you as you choose to take time to meditate on His Word and sit in His presence. When you are seeking out the right Source, you will find you can make it through even the most rigorous of weeks.

My eyes are set on You, and You restore me. As a gentle rain brings life to the driest soil, so Your very presence and love bring life to my soul.

DAY 39

The Ultimate Security

*"You will know at last that I, the LORD, am your Savior
and your Redeemer, the Mighty One of Israel."*
ISAIAH 60:16 NLT

Do you ever wonder what life would be like if we *knew* that the Lord was our Savior and Redeemer, the Mighty One of Israel? What would our lives look like if we believed this with every fiber of our being? Take a moment to think about that. How would your attitude about today change? This passage goes on to say, "I will make peace your leader and righteousness your ruler" (Isaiah 60:17 NLT).

It is a worthy goal to seek the Lord in everything we do, to get to know Him better with each passing day. What would our lives look like if we knew, really *knew*, that He alone is our Savior and Redeemer? Fear would be far from us, for we would understand that even mountains tremble before our God. Worry would drain away as we understood that He is the One who provides for every one of our needs. Even in the face of death, if that was what the Lord willed, we would be at peace, for then we would be even closer to meeting Him face-to-face. We would move forward in every opportunity with confidence. We would battle with courage, knowing our ultimate security is in God.

*Lord, may I know at last that You are the Lord, my Savior and Redeemer.
You are the Mighty One of Israel and forever my deepest desire.*

DAY 40
He Knows You

*How precious are your thoughts about me, O God. They cannot
be numbered! I can't even count them; they outnumber the grains
of sand! And when I wake up, you are still with me!*
PSALM 139:17–18 NLT

Did you know that you have a history with God? Your relationship is ever growing, ever changing, and He knows you. He knit you together in your mother's womb. He's watched as you've grown up. He's seen every good day. Every bad day. Not a moment passes that He's unaware of what you're up to.

And He still loves you. When you live in relationship with Him, covered by the sacrifice of Christ, He doesn't see the things you've done wrong. Don't walk into this day feeling the weight of your failures and imagining there is no way He could continue to love you. He does love you, even through the worst of times. Sending His Son while we were still sinners is proof of that love.

So instead of coming before Him this morning full of shame, come before Him in humble thankfulness and confidence that He loves you so much. When you come before Him, He is pleased to see His daughter—spotless and whole. He is willing—and desires—to have a deep and thriving relationship with you.

*Lord, I can never fully understand the grace with which
You love me. I am forever amazed and filled with joy. Let our
relationship grow deeper through this day and the days ahead.*

DAY 41

Remembering His Promises

Tell everyone about God's power. His majesty shines down on Israel;
his strength is mighty in the heavens. God is awesome in his sanctuary.
The God of Israel gives power and strength to his people. Praise be to God!
PSALM 68:34–35 NLT

Do you ever find yourself dreaming of a place of safety? A place where you can close your eyes, rest your head, and let go of the stress and angst that follow you around like a shadow? It rarely matters what kind of season you are in—busy or calm—you always seem to feel an inner longing to find a place where there is nothing but peace.

Before you move on to the next thing on the list for today, take a moment to close your eyes. Don't reach for a book. Refuse to look at your phone. Keep your thoughts from wandering away. And simply fix your heart on the One who loves you. Think about His compassion. Dwell on His promises. Consider His majesty, and the army of angels He commands. Have faith in the One sent so you can forever be with Him.

Whether you need comfort, encouragement, or protection, He is the answer. Look first in His direction for clarity and understanding. He is close and forever unchanging.

Lord, thank You for showing me that You are my everything.
Through every day, through every year, I need only to fix
my eyes on You—the author and perfecter of my faith.

DAY 42
Finding Joy

And now, dear brothers and sisters, one final thing. Fix your thoughts on what is true, and honorable, and right, and pure, and lovely, and admirable. Think about things that are excellent and worthy of praise. Keep putting into practice all you learned and received from me—everything you heard from me and saw me doing. Then the God of peace will be with you.
PHILIPPIANS 4:8–9 NLT

Your mind is powerful. The thoughts you choose to dwell on have the power to determine the outcome of your day. They can pave the way for a calm and grateful heart or set a course for cynicism and disbelief.

There is such a benefit to fixing your thoughts on things that are good, pleasing, and perfect. God was not being legalistic when He said to think on these things. He was giving us sound advice. He was showing us the path to peace. What makes your heart beat a little faster? What brings joy to your heart and a smile to your lips? What makes your eyes crinkle with laughter and your feet step a little lighter? Think about these things.

Life is meant to be enjoyed. Relish the simple things! He enjoys them, and He invites you to enjoy them too.

Oh Lord, You delight in every detail of my life! Surely that includes every wonderful moment and every bubble of laughter. May I fully indulge in the joy of life today.

DAY 43

Remember

"In the future your children will ask you, 'What do these stones mean?'
Then you can tell them, 'They remind us that the Jordan River stopped
flowing when the Ark of the LORD's Covenant went across.' These
stones will stand as a memorial among the people of Israel forever."
JOSHUA 4:6–7 NLT

After God did this miraculous thing for the Israelites, He instructed them to build a memorial so that what He did for them would be remembered for generations. Future generations would remember that God took care of His people. The memorial would serve as a symbol of His power and faithfulness and would give hope to those in the future.

What has God done for you? It is just as important for us to build memorials in our lives that declare the goodness of God. These things remind us that during hard times God is still there through it all. They remind us in times of plenty that it's because of His goodness we can shout and dance with joy.

There is no right way to remember what God has done. It can be through journaling or a photograph. It could be a vase sitting in your living room filled with little slips of paper full of the ways God has provided on a daily basis. They are all a way to remember the faithfulness of God.

You have been so good to me, Lord! As I go through today,
remind me. Remind me of the big and the little things,
that my faith in You may grow and my joy increase.

DAY 44
Beautifully Imperfect

*Yet I am confident I will see the LORD's goodness
while I am here in the land of the living.*
PSALM 27:13 NLT

Being in process is not pretty. In fact, sometimes it's downright ugly. When life gets too busy and overwhelming, oftentimes we snap. There is only so much our minds can sort through, and only so much our tired bodies can handle.

Remember—we must give ourselves grace. We must allow ourselves to be imperfect. Yes, we want to handle every situation with finesse and poise, but sometimes trying to achieve that goal only makes the situation worse. We are exhausted in every way and we cannot handle it the way we want. If we are completely honest, we only show our worst to one, maybe two people we trust. Everyone else gets the dressed-up version and the still-smiling face.

We are imperfect, so let's find some comfort in that. We can accept that we are broken and work from there. A lot of the time we stress ourselves out by trying to be flawless. But when we put that type of obsessive striving aside, we can sort through the pieces with a clear head because we're not hindered by trying to do it "just right." There is freedom in giving ourselves permission to be imperfect.

*Oh God, I am so thankful that I can be broken around You.
I will find comfort in Your perfect love as I give myself grace
for my imperfect self. Your love knows no limits. Amen.*

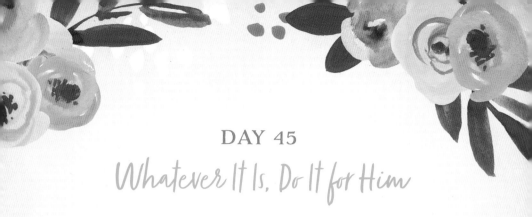

DAY 45

Whatever It Is, Do It for Him

So, my dear brothers and sisters, be strong and immovable.
Always work enthusiastically for the Lord, for you know
that nothing you do for the Lord is ever useless.
1 CORINTHIANS 15:58 NLT

Have you ever stopped to count how many small tasks you do each day? Laundry, dishes, bill payments, errands, meal preparation, grocery shopping. . . . Whether you work inside or outside the home (more than likely both), you work hard. But is this work really important?

It would be different if we were on the mission field, preaching the Good News to those who haven't heard it yet, or tutoring needy children, or teaching God's Word to our peers. But dishes? Laundry? Grocery shopping? It's tempting—especially when we're tired—to think of those things as useless. But God's Word tells us to be strong and immovable, working enthusiastically for the Lord. Even when our work doesn't seem important, it is never useless when we are doing it for Him. Colossians 3:17 says that whatever we do, in word or deed, we should do it for the Lord.

Father, help me to stop distinguishing between
important and unimportant work. Regardless of
what I do, help me to do it for You. Amen.

DAY 46
The Path to God's Will

All the paths of the LORD are faithfulness and truth to those who comply with His covenant and His testimonies.
PSALM 25:10 NASB

It's an age-old question: What is God's will for my life? It's easy to agonize over this question, pondering which path to take and fearfully wondering what will happen if we take a wrong step. But God's will is not necessarily a matter of choosing precisely the right step in each and every situation. This verse teaches that we should focus on God's covenant and His testimony. As we do so, the journey becomes part of the destination.

God doesn't always give us a clear road map, but He does clearly ask us to keep His covenant and His testimonies. When we do so, our individual steps will become clearer, and we will find ourselves more and more in step with His will. As He guides us closer to our destination, we will find much joy in the journey.

Lord, when I agonize over which way to take, help me to focus on Your covenant and Your testimonies. Help me to trust You to lead me on the paths You want me to take, knowing that when I follow Your Word, I am always in Your will. Amen.

DAY 47

No Worries

*"So don't worry about tomorrow, for tomorrow will bring
its own worries. Today's trouble is enough for today."*
MATTHEW 6:34 NLT

It has been said that today is the tomorrow you worried about yesterday. Isn't it true? And how much of the things you worry about actually happen? Worry robs us of joy in the moment and plants us firmly in the future, where we have absolutely no control. Instead of focusing on the problems that this day brings, we propel ourselves into an unknown tomorrow. In living this way, we miss out on all the little moments that make life precious.

The antidote to worry is to focus on today—this hour, this moment in time. What is happening now? Experience it with all five of your senses. Allow the wonder of today to touch your heart and settle it down. Sure, there is trouble today, and there are problems to solve, but Jesus is right here with us. We have the gift of the Holy Spirit who can counsel and comfort us and help us get through any and every situation. There is nothing you can't face without Jesus by your side. When you focus on what He can do instead of what you can't do, you will experience a deep and abiding peace that comes only from Him.

*Lord, worry is such a part of who I am! When I'm not worried,
I worry that I'm missing something. Please help me not to
worry about tomorrow. Help me to focus on today, on what is
happening now, and to let You take care of all my trouble. Amen.*

DAY 48

Truth in Love

Instead, we will speak the truth in love, growing in every way more and more like Christ, who is the head of his body, the church.
EPHESIANS 4:15 NLT

Sometimes it's difficult to say just the right thing at just the right time. Especially when we are hurt, confused, or angry, we tend to go to one extreme or the other. Either we blurt out whatever comes to mind, hurting others in the process; or we nurse our pain and keep silent, fearing how others might respond. Neither of these extremes is effective—or truthful. Instead, we can follow the example of Jesus, who demonstrated the perfect balance of speaking the truth in love. He was not afraid to confront others when they needed to hear the truth, but at the same time, He did so in gentleness and love. Jesus was hard in the right places and soft in the right places.

Keeping this balance requires maturity and work. We won't always get it right but speaking the truth in love will become more natural as we grow more like Christ. Becoming more Christlike means staying connected to His Body, the Church, and working through communication and conflict with a heart of love.

Jesus, sometimes it's hard for me to speak up, while others times I blurt out the wrong thing at the wrong time. Teach me to be more like You and to speak Your truth in love. Amen.

DAY 49
No Shame

Those who look to him for help will be radiant with joy;
no shadow of shame will darken their faces.
PSALM 34:5 NLT

Adam and Eve had the perfect home—a beautiful garden. Their perfect Father met every one of their needs. His rules were clear. All the garden belonged to them—except the fruit of the one tree. Adam was told plainly by God: Eat the fruit of this tree, and you will surely die (Genesis 2:16–17).

Of course, the one thing they couldn't have was the one thing that captured their attention. When the serpent presented an opportunity, Adam and Eve took the bait. What followed was a feeling known to all of us thereafter—shame. They hid their faces and their bodies from God, covered with the profound awareness that they had failed Him. In the cool of the garden, Adam tried to avoid God and hide from Him further. Yes, the consequences were severe, but God demanded Adam and Eve look to Him so He could remove their shame.

No matter how we disappoint God, we never have to hide from Him or cover our faces in shame. All we need to do is turn to Him and ask for His forgiveness, mercy, and grace. One look at the Father and our faces can be radiant with joy.

Father, when I have disappointed You, the last thing I want is to look to You for help. I know it's because I can't comprehend Your mercy and Your love for me. Thank You for freedom from the shadow of shame. Amen.

DAY 50

My Morning Prayer

Let me hear Your faithfulness in the morning, for I trust in You;
teach me the way in which I should walk; for to You I lift up my soul.
PSALM 143:8 NASB

Do mornings excite or depress you? Do you say "Good morning, Lord!" or "Good Lord, it's morning!"? When David wrote Psalm 143, he probably dreaded the sun coming up because that meant his enemies could continue pursuing him and persecuting his soul.

What did David do when he didn't know which way to turn? He turned to the Lord. He stayed in prayer with God and meditated on God's faithfulness and righteousness, God's past work in his life, and His loyal love. He also took refuge in God and continued serving Him. All this he wrote in Psalm 143.

No matter what our day holds, we can face it confidently by practicing verse 8. Let's look for God's loving-kindness and keep trusting Him no matter what. Ask Him to teach and lead us in the way He wants us to go. We have the privilege of offering up our souls (thoughts, emotions, and will) to Him anew each morning. Have a good day.

Good morning, Lord. You are my loving Father, secure
Refuge, and trustworthy God. Deliver me from my enemies
and show me Your loving heart as I trust in You. Help me to
please You today in my decisions and goals, in my attitudes toward
circumstances, and in the way I respond to people around me.

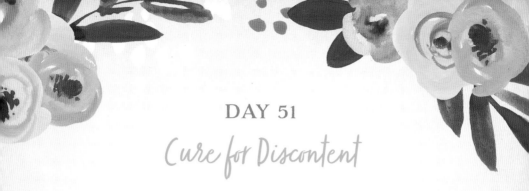

DAY 51

Cure for Discontent

*Always giving thanks for all things in the name of
our Lord Jesus Christ to God, even the Father.*
EPHESIANS 5:20 NASB

Do you struggle with being satisfied with your current situation in life? Discontent is a heart disease that manifests in comparing, coveting, and complaining. What is the cure? The habit of gratitude. Thanking God for everything—the good and the bad—means we accept it as His will, even if we don't like it.

Sometimes we receive a gift we have no desire for, but we still thank the giver. God is the good giver of every perfect gift (James 1:17).

When God asks us for thanksgiving, He is not mandating our feelings but rather our submission. Because thankfulness changes our attitude and outlook, it does affect our feelings. Discontent and resentment cannot coexist with humble acceptance of what happens to us. Therefore, thanking God must become our lifelong habit. When we wake in the morning, we can prepare to thank God for each event—good and bad—because He is good. We can be satisfied with that.

*Bountiful Father, I'm sorry I often rebel against Your sovereign
plan for me. Thank You for doing all things well. Your essence
is love, and every mark You make in my life is a love mark,
conforming me to Christ. I accept Your will and Your ways.*

DAY 52

God Sees and Hears

"You shall call his name Ishmael, because the LORD has heard your affliction. . . ." Then she called the name of the LORD who spoke to her, You-Are-the-God-Who-Sees.

GENESIS 16:11, 13 NKJV

Scripture gives the account of a woman who was marginalized, who had no voice, who was used for her body and treated harshly. Yet God met her in the wilderness. He spoke to her and let her speak. Then He told her what to do and she obeyed. Who was it?

Hagar—a maid servant, an Egyptian not a Hebrew, and yet she was the first person in scripture to whom the Angel of the Lord appeared. He sent her back to the place of her suffering but gave her promises regarding her unborn son: he would become a great nation; he would be free and independent, hold his own in conflict, and live in the presence of his brethren. Believing what God said and knowing that Ishmael would not be a servant like she was gave her courage to face her conflicts back home.

She obeyed because of who God was. He was the *Ishmael*—God-Who-Hears—and the *El Roi*—God-Who-Sees. Other Bible people named the place where God encountered them; Hagar alone gave God Himself a new name.

When we are stuck in undesirable circumstances and wish we could run away, we can endure suffering because God has promised never to leave us or forsake us.

My ever-present God, in my wilderness places, thank You for seeing all my needs and hearing all my pleas.

DAY 53

Clothed

She is clothed with strength and dignity;
she can laugh at the days to come.
PROVERBS 31:25 NIV

You, as a daughter of the Most High, are clothed with strength and dignity. In those moments when you feel particularly vulnerable and naked, just remember—you are clothed with the strength that God gives you and with the dignity of being His image bearer.

Many things and people in this life can belittle you. But no matter what the circumstance, you are valued as one of God's children. You bear your heavenly Father's image. You clearly belong to Him and are loved by Him as part of His family. The value and dignity that God places on you are more significant than whatever society or anyone else tells you your value is.

Even when you feel totally beaten down and think there is no way you can continue, all you need to do is ask for God's strength. He will clothe you in it to cover up all your vulnerability and brokenness.

No wonder the woman in this verse could laugh at the future. She knew that in God she had limitless strength and a dignity that no one could take away. Nothing in her future, or yours, could change that.

Lord, thank You that I am clothed with strength and dignity.
Nothing on this earth can take away the dignity I have as
Your daughter or break the strength that You offer me.

DAY 54

Daughter

And He said to her, "Daughter, your faith has made
you well; go in peace and be cured of your disease."
MARK 5:34 NASB

The woman in this passage had suffered greatly from an affliction that made her ceremonially unclean; she was an outcast, not able to participate in society. In an act of desperation, she pushed through the thick crowd to Jesus and touched His garments. When Jesus turned around and asked who had touched Him, she fell in fear and trembling at His feet and told her whole story. This woman had probably been in shameful hiding for many years and now, in front of a large crowd, recounted her humiliating story. Probably some of the spectators were repulsed by her story, and yet Jesus, in front of the whole crowd, called her "daughter." Can you imagine how it must have felt to this rejected and shamed woman to hear herself called "daughter"—a term of belonging and love?

You also have been adopted and called a daughter of God. Don't hide your shame and struggles from Him. In circumstances where you can hardly stand up under the weight of your burden, fall at His feet as this woman did. You will not be rejected or shamed by Him. He calls you daughter. He loves you and is able to heal you.

Lord, may I have the same faith that this woman had.
Thank You that You have made me Your daughter.

DAY 55

Watch Expectantly

But as for me, I will be on the watch for the LORD; I will wait for the God of my salvation. My God will hear me.
MICAH 7:7 NASB

In this verse Micah has prayed to God and is now waiting expectantly for what He will do. How often do you pray without really thinking that God hears or cares? Or maybe you think your prayers are just too big (or too small) to matter to Him.

You pray to the sovereign and all-powerful God who loves you. This means you can pray big and often and you can expect God to act. Obviously, we don't know how God will answer a prayer, because His ways are far above our ways. So watch expectantly to see how He will act in ways beyond your imaginings.

Wait for God. Too often we become impatient after we pray, wanting a quick fix or an obvious and direct answer. In this verse we find that Micah was willing to wait for God to answer. While you wait, praise Him for what He is already doing in your life.

Your God will hear you. Be confident in this. God does not turn away from His children. He hears you and desires to give you good things. As you pray throughout today, be confident that the Most High God is listening.

Lord, thank You that You hear every one of my prayers.
I wait expectantly to see in what ways You will answer me.

DAY 56

Peace

Let the peace of Christ, to which you were indeed called
in one body, rule in your hearts; and be thankful.
COLOSSIANS 3:15 NASB

You are to let the peace of Christ rule in your heart. The peace that hinges on the fact that He died in your place, that you are redeemed, blameless, and inseparable from God's love and salvation. Nothing in this world can snatch you out of the loving care of your heavenly Father. Your life is watched over and cared for by the almighty God. You can come to Him with all of your cares and concerns and He will listen. He is for you and loves you in a way that can't be comprehended.

How different would your life be if you truly believed in this peace? It would rule and sway every decision you make. It would assuage the pain and suffering you endure in this world. And it would give you the courage and perseverance you need to face even the most daunting and fearful of circumstances.

Let these truths wash over you, rest in them, and let them take authority in your heart and mind. Be thankful for the immense gift that Christ has offered you—to live a life free from the anxiety, fear, and restlessness of the world.

Lord, may I be grounded in Your peace. I ask now
that You would dethrone anything else that has taken
authority in my life so that You can rule unchallenged.

Good Gifts

Every good thing given and every perfect gift is from
above, coming down from the Father of lights, with
whom there is no variation or shifting shadow.
JAMES 1:17 NASB

Take this morning to thank God for the good things and blessings in your life. At times it's easy to get in the pattern of only requesting things *of* God as though He were your divine servant, without recognizing all the beautiful and bountiful blessings He has already lavished on you. This verse says that *every* good thing is from God. Think through all the good things in your life—each one is from God. They are tokens to remind you of His care and love for you. Don't take them for granted. Be grateful for the perfect gifts that He loves to give His children.

God is described as the Father of lights in this verse. Since He is a source of light, there is no shadow or variation with Him. He does not manipulate. He does not change. He doesn't try to hide behind something He is not. He doesn't give gifts to you to try to earn your allegiance or love. He gives to you purely out of His love. There is no guile in Him. He expects nothing in return. So accept His gifts freely and with a thankful and humbled heart.

Lord, thank You for all the good things in my life. Thank
You that You know how to give perfect gifts. Keep me
from taking anything You've given me for granted.

DAY 58

Perfection

For I am confident of this very thing, that He who began a good work among you will complete it by the day of Christ Jesus.

<small>PHILIPPIANS 1:6 NASB</small>

You are a work in progress! He has started a good work in you that has not yet been completed. Take this truth to heart and don't be unduly discouraged when you fall into the same sin patterns—God is working in you. If you ever feel that you must not be saved because you're struggling with things that you shouldn't struggle with as a Christian, be encouraged that no matter how it feels to you, from the moment you were saved God started working in you. On the days when it doesn't feel like God is working at all, remind yourself of Philippians 1:6.

God will perfect the work He has started in you. Even if there are road bumps along the way, He *will* complete and perfect His work in you. He won't abandon you if you don't perform up to some standard. He perfects the good work in you because He desires that you be more like Him and that you walk in closer relationship with Him. So be encouraged and try to recognize the areas in which God has already been perfecting His work in your life. You are on a good and perfect trajectory.

Lord, thank You that You are working in me even when I don't feel it. Thank You that You will not abandon the work that You have started in me no matter what.

DAY 59

Let Your Fire Burn

Our God is a consuming fire.
HEBREWS 12:29 NKJV

The Holy Spirit is often referred to as a fire. Each believer's heart carries that flaming light of God. Just as heat boils out the impurities in elements such as gold, so the Spirit burns in our hearts both to refine and to fuel the work He has called us to do.

Paul admonishes believers not to quench the fire (1 Thessalonians 5:19), but many restrict it from growing so there is barely a glow in the coals of their bellies. They fear that the flames might actually spread and purify their hearts, compelling them to give up their darling sins—the ones that aren't hurting anyone, the ones that stay hidden.

So when the heart is convicted of sin or called to mission work or challenged to change, it's easier to smother the Spirit with logic and justification and keep the coal neither hot nor cold, but comfortably lukewarm.

Is it time to remove the bushel that has hidden your light so long and trust the winds of God's Spirit to fan the flames? Fuel the fire with prayer, obedience, and meditation, and watch in amazement as God transforms you into what He's always wanted you to be.

Father, let the fire of the Holy Spirit blaze and spread
among Your people so that we burn with passion for
Your Word and the coming of Your kingdom.

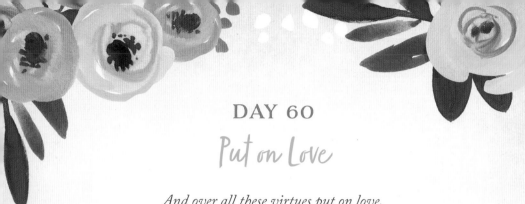

DAY 60
Put on Love

And over all these virtues put on love,
which binds them all together in perfect unity.
COLOSSIANS 3:14 NIV

How many mornings have we stood in our closet, looking hopelessly at its overstuffed contents and thinking we have nothing to wear? What we're really thinking is that we have nothing to wear that makes us feel cute or pretty or sporty or professional—or whatever look we're going for that day. We want to look attractive. We want others to be drawn to us. And sometimes, no matter how many blouses we have to choose from, nothing feels right.

But there is one accessory we all have available to us that always fits. It always looks right, is always appropriate, and always makes us more attractive to others. When we wear it, we are beautiful, no matter how faded or dated our wardrobes may be.

What is that accessory, you ask, and where can you buy it?

It's love, and you can't buy it anywhere. But it's free, and it's always available through the Holy Spirit. When we call on Him to help us love others, He cloaks us in a beautiful covering that draws people to us and makes us perfectly lovely in every way.

Dear Father, as I get dressed each day, help me to remember the
most important accessory I can wear is Your love. Amen.

DAY 61

Promises of God

*"For the LORD your God is living among you. He is a mighty savior.
He will take delight in you with gladness. With his love, he will
calm all your fears. He will rejoice over you with joyful songs."*

ZEPHANIAH 3:17 NLT

Look at all the promises packed into this one verse of scripture! God is with you. He is your mighty savior. He delights in you with gladness. He calms your fears with His love. He rejoices over you with joyful songs. Wow!

What a bundle of hope is found here for the believer. Like a mother attuned to her newborn baby's cries, so is your heavenly Father's heart for you. He delights in being your Father. He knows when the storms of life are raging all around you. He senses your need to be held close and for your fears to be calmed. It is in those times that He is for you a Prince of Peace, a Comforter.

He rejoices over you with joyful songs. Can you imagine that God loves you so much that you cause Him to sing? God sings over you. And the songs He sings are joyful. He loves you with an unconditional, everlasting love. Face this day knowing that your God is with you. He calms you. And He sings over you. You are blessed to be a daughter of the King.

Father, thank You for loving me the way You do. You are all I need. Amen.

DAY 62

I Forgive You

Smart people know how to hold their tongue;
their grandeur is to forgive and forget.
PROVERBS 19:11 MSG

Great power comes in these three little words: *I forgive you.* Often they are hard to say, but they are powerful in their ability to heal our own hearts. Jesus taught His disciples to pray, "Forgive us our trespasses as we forgive those who trespass against us." He knew we needed to forgive others to be whole. When we are angry or hold a grudge against someone, our spirits are bound. The release that comes with extending forgiveness enables our spirits to commune with God more closely and love swells within us.

How do you forgive? Begin with prayer. Recognize the humanity of the person who wronged you, and make a choice to forgive. Ask the Lord to help you forgive them. Be honest, for the Lord sees your heart. Trust the Holy Spirit to guide you and cleanse you. Then step out and follow His leading in obedience.

By forgiving, we can move forward, knowing that God has good things in store for us. And the heaviness of spirit is lifted, and relief washes over us after we've forgiven. A new sense of hope and expectancy rises. *I forgive you.* Do you need to say those words today?

Father, search my heart and show me areas where I might need
to forgive another. Help me let go and begin to heal. Amen.

DAY 63

A Choice

I'm singing joyful praise to GOD. I'm turning cartwheels of joy to my Savior God. Counting on GOD's Rule to prevail, I take heart and gain strength. I run like a deer. I feel like I'm king of the mountain!

HABAKKUK 3:18–19 MSG

Many days, life seems like an uphill battle, where we are swimming against the current, working hard to maintain our equilibrium. Exhausted from the battle, we often throw up our hands in defeat and want to quit. That's when we should realize we have a choice. We can choose to surrender our burdens to the Lord!

What would happen if we followed the advice of the psalmist and turned a cartwheel of joy in our hearts—regardless of the circumstances—then leaned and trusted in His rule to prevail? Think of the happiness and peace that could be ours with a total surrender to God's care.

It's a decision to count on God's rule to triumph. And we must realize His Word, His rule, never fails. Never. Then we must want to stand on that Word. Taking a giant step, armed with scriptures and praise and joy, we can surmount any obstacle put before us, running like a deer, climbing the tall mountains. With God at our side, it's possible to be king of the mountain.

Dear Lord, I need Your help. Gently guide me so I might learn to lean on You and become confident in Your care. Amen.

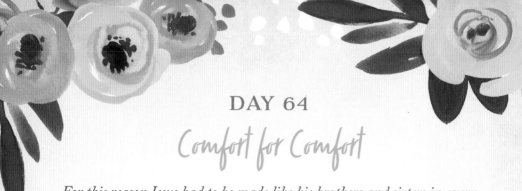

DAY 64

Comfort for Comfort

*For this reason Jesus had to be made like his brothers and sisters in every
way so he could be their merciful and faithful high priest in service to God.
Then Jesus could die in their place to take away their sins. And now he can
help those who are tempted, because he himself suffered and was tempted.*
HEBREWS 2:17–18 NCV

God chose to come to earth to be made like us. To understand what it's
like to be human. To be able to fully take our place and remove our sins.
Because He was fully human while being fully God, He can help. The
Bible says that He "comforts us in all our troubles, so that we can comfort
those in any trouble with the comfort we ourselves receive from God"
(2 Corinthians 1:4 NIV).

It's so encouraging that Jesus was just like us! Our God is not one who
wants to remain as a distant high king, out of touch with the commoners.
He wants a very personal relationship with each one of us. He lowered
Himself to our level so that we could have personal and continuous access
to Him. His glory knows no bounds, yet He desires to be our Friend. Take
great comfort in that.

And then when people around you are troubled, you can step in. You
can wrap your arms around someone else who needs a friend because of
what Jesus has done for you.

*Dear Jesus, thank You for the great gift of Your friendship. Allow me the
opportunity to be a friend and comfort to those around me in need. Amen.*

DAY 65
Stay Teachable

When Apollos wanted to go to Achaia, the brothers and sisters
encouraged him and wrote to the disciples there to welcome him.
ACTS 18:27 NIV

Apollos was a powerhouse for the Lord. The scriptures describe him as "a learned man, with a thorough knowledge of the Scriptures. . .he spoke with great fervor and taught about Jesus accurately" (Acts 18:24–26 NIV).

So it's interesting that even with those credentials, Priscilla and Aquila, having heard him, invited him to their house for additional teaching. Afterward, Apollos desired to preach in Achaia, and the couple encouraged him to do so. They immediately contacted the disciples there to welcome him. The result? Apollos won a public debate, proving that Jesus was the Messiah while helping the apostles at the same time (Acts 18:27–28).

We all have room for spiritual growth and godly knowledge no matter how long we have known the Lord. The Bible encourages us to encourage one another. What would happen to advance the kingdom if every believer, despite their position or spiritual seniority, exercised the humility of Apollos? Though scholarly, he accepted more instruction from other believers who, in turn, encouraged his ministry. Jealousy, pride, or one-upmanship didn't exist.

We are to encourage one another, just as God encourages us.

Lord, keep me teachable so that I can become more effective
for You to encourage others in their ministries. Amen.

DAY 66

No Harm

Love does no harm to a neighbor.
Therefore love is the fulfillment of the law.
ROMANS 13:10 NIV

Love does no harm. Ever. That is a powerful statement.

If love does no wrong to a neighbor, that means love never utters cruel words. Love never gossips. Love is never violent, never impatient, never easily angered. And love certainly never plans out mean, vicious actions.

Love does only good to the people around us. Only good.

Unfortunately, none of us loves perfectly—yet. And we won't love perfectly until we're made perfect by our Creator, when we stand before Him. Until then, we will mess up. We will act in unloving ways sometimes.

The key is to make love a habit and admit when we've not acted in love. When we catch ourselves thinking unkind thoughts, we need to get our thoughts in line, for unkind thoughts lead to unkind actions. When we let our tongues slip and we say cruel things, we should apologize. And we need to continually examine our hearts and our motives, to see if we're being ruled by love.

Love always builds up, always points people to the Source of love—God. And since God's love for each and every one of His children is perfect and complete, we must work to deliver that kind of love as well.

Dear Father, forgive me for the times I have been cruel or thoughtless and have not acted in love. Help me to make love a way of life for me. Amen.

DAY 67

The Lord Is Close

*Everything the LORD does is right. He is loyal to all he has made. The
LORD is close to everyone who prays to him, to all who truly pray to him.*
PSALM 145:17–18 NCV

Do you ever feel like you go to God in prayer with the same things over
and over again? Is your prayer life in need of a little lift? To find a road
map for prayers and promises, look to the Psalms that are full of prayers
and truth.

The authors of the Psalms knew the truth of this scripture—that the
Lord is close to those who pray to Him. They expressed their honest
emotions to God—their joy, their fears, their praise. They understood
that God loved them and wanted to have a personal relationship with
them—just like He does with us.

If you're struggling with how to pray to God or what to pray about,
use the Psalms as your guide. Pray through a psalm every day. Add your
own personal thoughts and feelings as you pray. You'll realize that you
have begun a personal friendship with the Creator of the universe.

*How amazing that You, Lord, Creator of heaven and earth,
want to know me intimately! Thank You for loving me and showing
Yourself to me through Your Word and Your creation. Thank You for
being close to me so that I can know You and live for You. Amen.*

DAY 68

When You Can't Pray

And the Holy Spirit helps us in our weakness. For example, we don't know what God wants us to pray for. But the Holy Spirit prays for us with groanings that cannot be expressed in words. And the Father who knows all hearts knows what the Spirit is saying, for the Spirit pleads for us believers in harmony with God's own will.

ROMANS 8:26–27 NLT

Sometimes we literally cannot pray. The Holy Spirit takes over on such occasions. Go before God; enter into His presence in a quiet spot where there will not be interruptions. And just be still before the Lord. When your heart is broken, the Holy Spirit will intercede for you. When you have lost someone or something precious, the Holy Spirit will go before the Father on your behalf. When you are weak, the Comforter will ask the Father to strengthen you. When you are confused and anxious about a decision that looms before you, the Counselor will seek God's best for you.

You are not alone. You are a precious daughter of the Living God. And when Christ ascended back into heaven, He did not leave you on this earth to forge through the wilderness on your own. He sent a Comforter, a Counselor, the Holy Ghost, the Spirit of Truth. When you don't know what to pray, the Bible promises that the Spirit has you covered.

Father, please hear the groaning of the Holy Spirit
who intercedes on my behalf before Your throne. Amen.

DAY 69

Ask in Faith

But when you ask God, you must believe and not doubt. Anyone who doubts is like a wave in the sea, blown up and down by the wind.

JAMES 1:6 NCV

What does it mean to ask God for something *in faith?* Does it mean we believe that He *can* grant our requests? That He *will* grant our requests? Exactly what is required to prove our faith?

These are difficult questions. Many who have prayed for healed bodies and healed relationships have received exactly that, this side of heaven. Others who have prayed for the same things, believing only God could bring healing, haven't received the answers they wanted.

There is no secret ingredient that makes all our longings come to fruition. The secret ingredient, if there is one, is faith that God is who He says He is. It's faith that God is good and will use our circumstances to bring about His purpose and high calling in our lives and in the world.

When we don't get the answers we want from God, it's okay to feel disappointed. He understands. But we must never doubt His goodness or His motives. We must stand firm in our belief that God's love for us will never change.

Dear Father, I know that You are good and that You love me. I know Your love for me will never change, even when my circumstances are hard. Help me cling to Your love, even when You don't give the answers I want. Amen.

DAY 70

He Carries Us

*In his love and mercy he redeemed them. He lifted
them up and carried them through all the years.*
Isaiah 63:9–10 NLT

Are you feeling broken today? Depressed? Defeated? Run to Jesus and not away from Him.

When we suffer, He cries. Isaiah 63:9–10 (NLT) says, "In all their suffering he also suffered, and he personally rescued them. In his love and mercy he redeemed them. He lifted them up and carried them through all the years."

He will carry us—no matter what pain we have to endure. No matter what happens to us. God sent Jesus to be our Redeemer. He knew the world would hate, malign, and kill Jesus. Yet He allowed His very flesh to writhe in agony on the cross—so that we could also become His sons and daughters. He loved me, and you, that much.

One day, we will be with Him. *"Beloved,"* He will say, *"No more tears. No more pain."* He will lift us up and hold us in His mighty arms, and then He will show us His kingdom, and we will, finally, be whole.

*Lord Jesus, thank You for coming to us—for not abandoning us
when we are broken. Thank You for Your work on the cross; for Your
grace, mercy, and love. Help me to seek You even when I can't feel
You; to love You even when I don't know all the answers. Amen.*

DAY 71

Linking Hearts with God

"You will receive power when the Holy Spirit comes on you;
and you will be my witnesses. . .to the ends of the earth."
ACTS 1:8 NIV

God knows our hearts. He knows what we need to make it through a day. So in His kindness, He gave us a gift in the form of the Holy Spirit. As a Counselor, a Comforter, and a Friend, the Holy Spirit acts as our inner compass. He upholds us when times are hard and helps us hear God's directions. When the path of obedience grows dark, the Spirit floods it with light. What revelation! He lives within us. Therefore, our prayers are lifted to the Father, to the very throne of God. Whatever petitions we have, we may rest assured they are heard.

We can rejoice in the fact that God cared enough to bless our lives with the Spirit to direct our paths. God loves the praises of His people, and these praises revive the Spirit within you. If you are weary or burdened, allow the Holy Spirit to minister to you. Seek the Holy Spirit and His wisdom, and ask Him to revive and refresh your inner man. Place your hope in God and trust the Spirit's guidance, and He will never let you down.

Father God, how blessed I am to come into Your presence.
Help me, Father, when I am weak. Guide me this day. Amen.

DAY 72

High Expectations

"They found grace out in the desert. . . . Israel, out looking for a place to rest, met God out looking for them!" GOD told them, "I've never quit loving you and never will. Expect love, love, and more love!"

JEREMIAH 31:2–3 MSG

Grace out in the desert. What a refreshing thought. Have you been in a desert place, lost, lonely, disappointed, feeling the pain of rejection? Often our immediate response is to berate ourselves, look within to see how we have been the one lacking, plummeting our self-esteem. Dejected we crawl to that desert place to lick our wounds.

Behold! God is in our desert place. He longs to fill our dry hearts with His healing love and mercy. Yet it's so hard for us—with our finite minds—to grasp that the Creator of the universe cares for us and loves us with an everlasting love, no matter what.

Despite their transgressions, God told the Israelites He never quit loving them. That is true for you today. Look beyond any circumstances and you will discover God looking at you, His eyes filled with love. Scripture promises an overwhelming, unexpected river of love that will pour out when we trust the Lord our God. Rest today in His Word. Expect God's love, love, and more love to fill that empty place in your life.

Father, we read these words and choose this day to believe in Your unfailing love. Amen.

DAY 73

Love Made Perfect

*There is no fear in love. But perfect love drives out fear, because
fear has to do with punishment. The one who fears is not
made perfect in love. We love because he first loved us.*

1 JOHN 4:18–19 NIV

It's good to fear God, isn't it? God is awesome and fierce in His power. Yet, while we need to have a healthy respect for God, we don't need to be terrified of Him. At least, not if we really love Him.

Those who truly love God with all their hearts and souls have nothing to fear, for we know He loves us even more. We know that although He may allow us to walk through some difficult things, His plans for us are always good. When we love God, His love is made perfect in us. Our love for God causes His love for us to reign.

It's only when we choose not to love God that we need to fear Him, for though God's patience is long, He is a just God. He will not let the guilty go unpunished. When we love God with our lives, there's no need for punishment. When we love God with our lives, we love others and put their needs ahead of our own. And that, dear friends, is how His love is made perfect in us.

*Dear Father, thank You for loving me. I want to love You
with my life and honor You with my actions. Amen.*

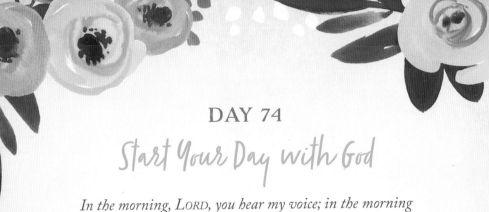

DAY 74
Start Your Day with God

*In the morning, LORD, you hear my voice; in the morning
I lay my requests before you and wait expectantly.*
PSALM 5:3 NIV

God wants to be the very center of your life. He doesn't want to be at the top of your priority list—just another box to check off each day. He wants your heart and attention morning, noon, and night. You won't get more points with God if you read ten Bible verses before your morning cup of coffee.

So how can you start your day with God even if you haven't gotten up hours earlier for devotions? As you wake up in the morning, thank the Lord for a new day. Ask Him to control your thoughts and attitude as you make the bed. Thank Him for providing for you as you toast your bagel. Ask that your self-image be based on your relationship with Christ as you get dressed and brush your teeth. Continue to pray as you drive to work or school. Spend time in His Word throughout the day. End your day by thanking Him for His love and faithfulness.

God wants a constant relationship with you, and He is available and waiting to do life with you twenty-four hours a day.

*Dear Lord, thank You for the gift of a new day. Help me
be aware of Your constant presence in my life. Amen.*

DAY 75
Rest for Your Soul

*"Come to me, all you who are weary and burdened, and I
will give you rest. Take my yoke upon you and learn from me,
for I am gentle and humble in heart, and you will find rest
for your souls. For my yoke is easy and my burden is light."*
MATTHEW 11:28–30 NIV

Jesus says, "Come to me." Just as He invited the little children to come
to Him, Jesus calls us to come to Him and bring all of our burdens and
lay them at His feet. He wants to help. He wants to relieve the load we're
carrying.

A yoke is a harness placed over an animal or set of animals for the
purpose of dragging something or carrying heavy equipment. Jesus liked
to use visual imagery to get His meaning across. Can't you just picture
all the burdens you are carrying right now strapped to your back like an
ox plowing a field? Now imagine yourself unloading each one onto Jesus'
shoulders instead. Take a deep breath.

Jesus tells us many times throughout the Gospels not to worry. Worrying about something will never help you. Worry makes things worse
and burdens seem larger. Worry clutters up your soul. Jesus wants us to
find rest in Him. Hear His gentle words rush over you—"Come to me."
Find rest for your soul.

*Jesus, thank You for taking my burdens. I give them fully to You. Help me not
to take them back! I want the rest and peace that You are offering. Amen.*

DAY 76

Relax

*"You will not have to fight this battle. Take up your positions;
stand firm and see the deliverance the LORD will give you."*

2 CHRONICLES 20:17 NIV

Why do we always feel we need to fight our own battles?

Oh, God wants us to use common sense and stand up for others and ourselves when it's appropriate. But sometimes, it's best not to defend ourselves at all. Sometimes when we know we've done no wrong, when we know we stand innocent before God in whatever situation we find ourselves, it's good just to remain still and calm and let God be our defender.

Truly, the more we defend ourselves, the guiltier we sound sometimes. But when we can stand before God with clean hands and a pure heart, God will deliver us. It may not be in the way we want. It may not happen as quickly as we'd like. But when we decide to stand firm, to continue living godly lives, to continue seeking His approval in our words, thoughts, and actions, we can trust Him.

Let's remember today to rest in His goodness, despite the battles that rage around us. We don't have to live our lives fighting. We can relax. Our Father is the judge, and He will deliver us.

Dear Father, thank You for being my defender. Thank You for delivering me from all sorts of trouble. Help me to relax and let You take care of me. Amen.

DAY 77

Create a "Smile File"

The best that people can do is eat, drink, and enjoy
their work. I saw that even this comes from God.
ECCLESIASTES 2:24 NCV

A woman's job—whether she's a mom, physician, schoolteacher, CFO, or artist—can be tiring and discouraging. Workplaces can be competitive, and children and husbands aren't always appreciative.

Be honest: Don't you, at times, feel trapped beneath the weight of expectations, to-do lists, and fatigue? To avoid burnout, it's important to regularly take note of your successes—especially when others don't notice your tireless efforts.

An aspiring songwriter decided that for every rejection she received, she'd note in her journal three productive things she had done that same week to hone her craft. An administrative assistant created an email folder specifically for affirming notes she received from her boss, kids, and husband. And an executive director of a nonprofit keeps a hanging file of silly cartoons, jokes, and pictures. When she is stressed or overwhelmed, she takes a moment to read something fun. It never fails to lift her spirits.

Why not keep a "Smile File" of your own? Take a simple shoebox or organizing bin and place encouraging cards, emails, and photos inside. You never know when it might come in handy.

Dear Lord, help me to not feel the full weight of difficulties
in my work. Give me ideas on how to avoid burning out;
and thank You for the encouragement others give. Amen.

DAY 78
Making Allowances

Always be humble and gentle. Be patient with each other,
making allowance for each other's faults because of your love.
EPHESIANS 4:2 NLT

This verse contains such a simple, forgotten truth, doesn't it? God wants us to be holy. He wants us to be righteous and good and godly. But He knows we'll never get it exactly right until we're made perfect in His presence. Until then, we all have our faults. Numerous faults, if we're honest with ourselves. And God doesn't want us standing around, whispering and pointing self-righteous fingers of condemnation. God is the only One who is allowed to wear the judge's robe.

And He doesn't condemn us. Instead, He pours His love and acceptance into our lives, with a gentle admonition to "go and sin no more" (John 8:11 NLT). In other words, "It's okay. You messed up, but it's been taken care of. The price has been paid. I still love you. Just try not to do it again."

Why do we find it so hard to extend grace to others, when so much grace has been shown to us? As we go through each day, let's make it a point to live out this verse. Let's be humble, gentle, and patient, making allowances for the faults of others because of God's love.

Dear Father, help me to be gentle and loving with others.
Remind me of the grace You've shown me, and help
me show the same love to those around me. Amen.

DAY 79
The Simple Things

In him our hearts rejoice, for we trust in his holy name.
PSALM 33:21 NIV

Think about the simple pleasures in everyday life—that first sip of coffee in the morning, waking up to realize you still have a few more minutes to sleep, or putting on fresh, warm clothes right out of the dryer on a cold winter morning. Perhaps it's a walk along the beach or a hike up the mountains into the blue skies that give you a simple peace.

God knows all the simple pleasures you enjoy—and He created them for your delight. When the simple things that can come only by His hand fill you with contentment, He is pleased. He takes pleasure in you. You are His delight. Giving you peace, comfort, and a sense of knowing that you belong to Him is a simple thing for Him.

Take a moment today and step away from the busyness of life. Take notice and fully experience some of those things you enjoy most. Then share that special joy with Him.

*Lord, thank You for the simple things that bring
pleasure to my day. I enjoy each gift You've given me.
I invite You to share those moments with me today. Amen.*

DAY 80
Love God, Love Others

Jesus answered, "'Love the Lord your God with all your heart, all your soul, and all your mind.' This is the first and most important command. And the second command is like the first: 'Love your neighbor as you love yourself.'"
MATTHEW 22:37–39 NCV

It was Saint Augustine who said, "Love God and do what you will," meaning that if we're truly loving God, everything else will come together as it should (Romans 8:28). We'll make the choices He wants us to make as He guides us. The entire Word of God is summed up in Jesus' response to the Pharisee who asked Him to tell which commandment was greatest. That's simple. Our purpose and mission in life is this: love God and love others.

If you're obeying God's command to love Him above all else and to love others, then you are fulfilling all the rest.

How can you live a life of love? Ask God to be the very center of your life. Get to know Him on a moment-by-moment basis. Both His power and presence are constantly available to you. As you relate to others, remember the preciousness of each person. Even the difficult ones. They are created and loved by God.

Jesus, thank You for summing up Your Word for me so simply. Expand my love for You and allow me to love others like You want me to. Amen.

DAY 81

Much, Much More

With God's power working in us, God can do much, much more than anything we can ask or imagine. To him be glory in the church and in Christ Jesus for all time, forever and ever. Amen.

EPHESIANS 3:20–21 NCV

Think back to a time when something happened in your life that you never saw coming. Something that happened out of the blue and absolutely amazed you. When God's power is at work within you, the possibilities are beyond your imagination.

The NIV says that He can do "immeasurably more" than what you could imagine. Whatever problem you are facing right now—big or small—God cares. As you pray about it and seek God's will, don't put Him in a box thinking that there's no way out or that there is only one right answer. His response just might be beyond your understanding and your wildest imagination.

Remember that things aren't always what they seem. When you feel disappointed in God's answers to your prayers, look outside the box. God is always, always working everything out for your good. God sees all. Trust that God can do much more than anything you could ever ask or imagine!

Heavenly Father, help me trust You with my whole heart. When I'm disappointed, help me to see outside myself and what I think are the best answers for my life. Thank You for working everything out according to Your great plan. Amen.

DAY 82

Praying the Mind of Christ

*We demolish arguments and every pretension that sets
itself up against the knowledge of God, and we take
captive every thought to make it obedient to Christ.*

2 CORINTHIANS 10:5 NIV

As Christ-followers, we are learning to become like Him in our thoughts, words, and deeds. Part of becoming Christlike is also in mastering our minds. Sometimes it is hard to pray because other thoughts interfere with our ability to listen closely to what God is saying. This is a favorite trick of the enemy's. . .getting us to think about our to-do list instead of what God is trying to tell us.

By reading and praying scripture and using positive statements in our prayers that claim what God has already said He will do for us, the mind of Christ is being activated in us. By taking captive every thought, we learn to know what thought is of God, what belongs to us, and what is of the enemy. Recognize, take captive, and bind up the thoughts that are of the enemy, and throw them out! The more we commune with God, fellowship with Him, and learn from Him, the more we cultivate the mind of Christ.

*Lord, help me identify the thoughts that are not Your thoughts
and purge them. I know that soon Your thoughts will be the
ones that I hear, and not the enemy's. In this way, I will hear
You more clearly so I may be an obedient disciple. Amen!*

DAY 83
The Battle Is His

"Do not be. . .discouraged. . .the battle is not yours. . . .
Stand firm. . . . The LORD will be with you."
2 CHRONICLES 20:15–17 NIV

It can be difficult to see your job as a ministry and where God has placed you as your mission field. Every day, wherever you may go, it can feel like you are girding for battle as you prepare for work. And in some ways, you are. When you receive a paycheck, after all the cuts, you may wonder if all your effort is worth it.

But you just want to work. You want to live. You are tired of fighting without seeing any worthwhile results.

Joshua was also discouraged by the battle he faced. God had called him to fight a seemingly unbeatable enemy with meager resources. The man of God had no idea how his small army would prevail.

Then God said, "This battle isn't yours; it's mine. Don't be afraid. . .just stand still, and see what I will do." God, not Joshua and his men, won the battle that day. And He will win our battles for us, if we will allow it.

God, help me to see my daily struggles as opportunities for You to
show Your power, instead of unmovable obstacles. Thank You for
promising that You are always with me and will fight for me. Amen.

DAY 84

Hurt Happens—Love Anyway

"I have loved you even as the Father has loved me. Remain in my love."
JOHN 15:9 NLT

Do you ever feel like Jesus overcame life's challenges more easily than you because He was God? It's important to realize that Jesus lived His life as a man—empowered just as you are today as a believer. He relied on His relationship with God and the Holy Spirit working in Him to do all that He did. He too was human. He suffered pain, hurt, and disappointment just as you do.

Imagine His feelings when brothers, sisters, aunts, uncles, and cousins refused to believe He was the Messiah or discounted His words of truth because He was family. How painful it must have been to have those closest to Him reject Him. Jesus knew that Judas would betray Him and Peter would deny Him. Jesus must have felt that hurt deeply—and yet He loved them anyway. In the face of the cross, He asked God to forgive those who put Him there.

When faced with pain or disappointment, it's easier to become angry, defend yourself, or even sever the relationship. The same Spirit that empowered Jesus to live His faith can empower you. When hurt happens—choose to love anyway!

Lord, You have shown me how to respond in love. Give me strength by Your Holy Spirit to love others in the face of pain, disappointment, and hurt. Comfort me and provide ways for me to show love to others. Amen.

DAY 85
Mission Impossible

And he said, The things which are impossible
with men are possible with God.
LUKE 18:27 KJV

As capable as we may be, some things will always remain impossible for us. No matter how much education we get, how determined we are, or how much money we have, some things are out of our control.

Yet just because something is impossible for us doesn't mean we don't have any hope. Where we can't, God can. The God who created the universe, who set the moon and stars in the sky, who placed the sun in place, and who brought Lazarus back to life after four days in the grave is a God who knows no limits.

Whatever we face, we can face with confidence. God, who loves us more than anything, will move heaven and earth to fulfill His purpose. And He is a God who likes to show off, who likes to take things to the limit before acting, just so He can get the glory. He is an amazing, all-powerful God, and He cares deeply about each and every one of His children.

It may seem like we are facing the impossible. And left up to us, it may be impossible. But we must never, ever forget. Nothing is impossible with God.

Dear Father, thank You for being a God of miracles.
Help me to trust in Your ability to accomplish Your
purpose, even when it seems impossible to me. Amen.

DAY 86

The End of Your Rope

Do not be far from me, for trouble is near and there is no one to help.
PSALM 22:11 NIV

You can feel the desperation in David's prayer as you read Psalm 22. He feels utterly rejected and alone as he cries out to God.

Have you been there? Have you ever felt so alone and helpless that you are sure no one is there for you? Jesus meets us in those dark places of hopelessness. He calls to us and says, "Do not let your hearts be troubled and do not be afraid" (John 14:27 NIV). "I will never leave you nor forsake you" (Hebrews 13:5 NKJV). You are never alone.

The late youth evangelist Dave Busby said, "The end of your rope is God's permanent address." Jesus reaches down and wraps you in His loving arms when you call to Him for help. The Bible tells us that He is close to the brokenhearted (Psalm 34:18).

We may not have the answers we are looking for here in this life, but we can be sure of this: God sees your pain and loves you desperately. Call to Him in times of trouble. If you feel that you're at the end of your rope, look up! His mighty hand is reaching toward you.

Heavenly Father, I feel alone and afraid. Surround
me with Your love and give me peace. Amen.

DAY 87

Online Encouragement

And now, dear brothers and sisters, one final thing. Fix your thoughts on what is true, and honorable, and right, and pure, and lovely, and admirable. Think about things that are excellent and worthy of praise.
PHILIPPIANS 4:8 NLT

Negative thoughts cross our minds on a daily basis. Social media and TV don't help either. Even Christian friends jump on the bandwagon and post thoughts and ideas online that make us cringe.

Instead of running away from connecting with people online because you've had enough, make it your goal to be a light in what can be a very dark, negative atmosphere. Encourage one another. Comment, post, and share God's love with your friends as much as possible.

For the next thirty days, why not plan to post, text, or write at least one encouraging comment every day? Post encouraging scripture; text a friend a note to make her smile; tweet your favorite quote; share sweet stories about your husband and kids on your blog.

Before you grumble or complain about something online, stop and fix your thoughts on what is true, right, and pure. Then see if your comment is still valid.

Father, help me not to run from online interaction but to see it as a mission field. Help me be an encouragement to everyone I communicate with online. Amen.

DAY 88

Difficult People

"You have heard that it was said, 'Love your neighbor and hate your enemy.' But I tell you, love your enemies and pray for those who persecute you, that you may be children of your Father in heaven."
MATTHEW 5:43–45 NIV

It's easy to thank God for the people we love, who bring joy and peace and laughter and all sorts of other good things to our lives.

But what about those people we don't like? What about the people who are all-stress-and-no-bless? Are we supposed to thank God for the people who put knots in our stomachs, who make us cry, or who leave us fist-clenching, smoke-breathing angry? We know we're supposed to pray for our enemies, but do we really need to thank God for them?

Well, yes. God wants us to love our enemies, and it only stands to reason that we'd thank God for the people we love. It is through the difficult people in our lives that we grow and stretch, for they often test our faith in ways the easier relationships can't. Even though we may not see a lot of good in some people, God looks at every person and sees someone He loved enough to die for. And apart from Christ, we can be difficult people too.

Dear Father, thank You for the easy, happy relationships in my life. And thank You for the difficult people too, for they stretch me and push me toward You. Help me to love the way You do. Amen.

DAY 89

Jungle of Life

*God's word is alive and working and is sharper than a
double-edged sword. It cuts all the way into us, where the
soul and the spirit are joined, to the center of our joints and
bones. And it judges the thoughts and feelings in our hearts.*
HEBREWS 4:12 NCV

Since the time Adam and Eve disobeyed God, the consequences of sin
have often stood between us and God's best for our lives. Choosing a life
of faith can feel like we are lost in a jungle, tangled in the underbrush.
But God has given us a powerful tool that will cut through the debris of
life in a fallen world.

When you take the Bible and live according to His plans, obeying
Him, God's Word cuts like a machete through the entanglements of life.
When you choose to use the Sword of Truth, it clears a path and can free
you from the weights of the world that try to entrap and ensnare you.

No matter what the challenges of life are saying to you today, take
His Word and speak His plans into your life. Choose His words of encouragement and peace instead of the negative things the circumstances
are telling you.

*God, I want to live in Your Truth. I want to believe what You
say about me in the Bible. Help me to speak Your words today
instead of letting the problem speak to me. Help me believe. Amen.*

DAY 90
Lead Us, Lord

I know, GOD, that mere mortals can't run their own lives,
that men and women don't have what it takes to take
charge of life. So correct us, GOD, as you see best.
JEREMIAH 10:23 MSG

So many changes would happen in our lives if we lived Jeremiah's words. If we really believed God was in control. We would be able to release our worries and problems in a prayer of thanksgiving and then wait. And that's the difficulty that trips us up. In our frenzied world, we feel we need immediate answers, and we rush to solve situations our own way. Sometimes that works; however, often we become enmeshed in less than desirable circumstances.

The last line of the scripture entreats God to correct us, and that's certainly not a desirous thought. Not many hope to be straightened out. But when we yield our lives to Him and trust Him implicitly, understanding full well that our Creator God wants the best for us, then our prayers of thanksgiving and trust fall more easily from our mouths. Adoration and praise should fall from our lips before our requests.

A prayer of total surrender gives glory to God the Father and pleases Him. It allows Him to work in our lives in ways we often don't understand.

Lord, I bless You and give You my heartfelt praise.
Thank You for all You do to work on my behalf. Amen.

DAY 91

Humiliating Moments as Raw Clay

*All the LORD's ways are loving and true for those
who follow the demands of his agreement.*
PSALM 25:10 NCV

Did you know that God wants to use even our humiliating experiences to transform our character?

In *The Message*, the psalmist says, "I learned God-worship when my pride was shattered" (51:16). The Creator is an artist. If He can't redeem our worst moments, there will be a lot of material that goes unused. God wants to take our failures and lovingly, like a potter sculpts raw clay, mold them into something beautiful.

As our sin-bearer, Jesus endured one of the most painful, visible humiliations the world has ever seen. And yet—through His death, eternal life became available to us. And as human beings with many faults, we will experience visible and painful humiliations, either through our own sins, others' poor choices, or our foolish decisions. But whatever the cause of our embarrassment, when we surrender to God, He can turn it into a tool for our transformation.

*Lord, help me to see those times I am humiliated
(at least in retrospect) as moments You can use to
change me into the woman You want me to be. Amen.*

DAY 92

Why Praise God?

Though he slay me, yet will I trust in him.
JOB 13:15 KJV

"How can I praise God when everything in my life is falling apart?" Who hasn't pondered that question in moments of defeat, despair, or grief?

In the book of Acts, Paul and Silas, under Roman law, were publicly stripped and severely beaten for their faith. Afterward, they were jailed. Yet with bloody backs and shackled feet, they sat in a dirty cell undefeated. Rather than question God's intentions or apparent lack of protection, the scriptures state that around midnight, "Paul and Silas were praying and singing hymns to God" (Acts 16:25 NIV).

The power of prayer and praise resulted in complete deliverance. The prison doors flew open, and their chains fell off. What's more, the jailer and his family accepted Christ, and these ardent believers were able to witness to other inmates.

It's difficult to praise God when problems press in harder than a crowd exiting a burning building. But that's the time to praise Him the most. We wait for our circumstances to change, while God desires to change us despite them. Praise coupled with prayer in our darkest moments is what moves the mighty hand of God to work in our hearts and lives.

How can we pray and praise God when everything goes wrong? The bigger question might be: How can we not?

Jesus, help me to pray and praise You despite my circumstances. Amen.

DAY 93

His Steady Hand

*The L*ORD* makes firm the steps of the one who delights in him; though he*
*may stumble, he will not fall, for the L*ORD* upholds him with his hand.*
PSALM 37:23–24 NIV

The wonderful thing about our mighty God is He knows our hearts. There are days when we succumb to responding or acting out in the flesh. But praise God, He loves us so much and is faithful even when we as human beings are unable to be. Just as a parent grasps a child's hand, He will take ours in His and help us along our pathway.

The Lord knows there are times when we will stumble. We may even backslide into the very activity that caused us to call on the Lord for salvation in the first place. But His Word assures us His love is eternal, and when we cry out to Him, He will hear.

Do not be discouraged with those stumbling blocks in your path, because the Lord is with you always. Scripture tells us we are in the palm of His hand. Hope is found in the Lord. He delights in us and wants the very best for us because of His perfect love.

Lord God, the cross was necessary for sinners like me. I thank You that You
loved me enough to choose me, and I accepted the free gift of salvation. Amen.

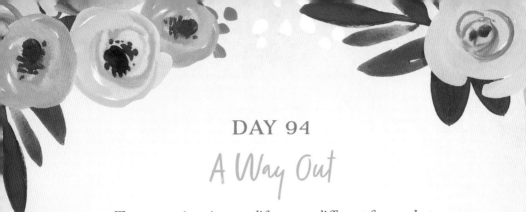

DAY 94

A Way Out

The temptations in your life are no different from what others experience. And God is faithful. He will not allow the temptation to be more than you can stand. When you are tempted, he will show you a way out so that you can endure.

1 CORINTHIANS 10:13 NLT

Is there a hang-up in your life that is hard to get over or get rid of? Temptation comes in all shapes and sizes, so what might be tempting to you isn't a problem for someone else. The opposite is also true. The comforting thing is that everyone has been there. We all make mistakes, and whatever is tempting you, you can bet that it has also tripped up many others too.

It's so easy to get discouraged when we mess up. Especially when we mess up in the same area over and over again.

Here's the encouraging thing: whenever you face temptation, God promises to provide a way out. Look for it! In every moment that you are tempted, look for it! Pay attention to the interruptions that occur during temptation and grasp hold of them. They may just be "divine appointments" there to lead the way out!

Dear Jesus, I cry out for grace and mercy and praise You that Your love has covered my sin completely. Help me find the way out in every temptation. Amen.

DAY 95

The Winning Team

If God is for us, who can be against us?
ROMANS 8:31 NIV

We always *know* God is for us, but it doesn't always *feel* that way. Even though we know the end of the story, even though we know we are on the winning team, sometimes it feels like we're losing battle after battle.

We can make sure God really is on our team, in the little battles, when we conduct ourselves in a way that honors Him. If we've been in the wrong, we can't claim that God is on our side in that battle. But when we love God with all our hearts, when we serve Him and serve others, when we keep our promises and make the people around us feel loved and valued and cherished, we can know God is pleased. We can know that He will stand behind us, defend us, and support us.

And ultimately, no matter how many battles we may feel like we're losing, if we stand with God, we will stand victorious. The other team may score a few points here and there. But when we're on God's team, we know we're the winners.

*Dear Father, thank You for being on my team. Help me
to live in a way that represents Your team well. Amen.*

DAY 96
The Right Focus

Turning your ear to wisdom and applying your heart to understanding—indeed, if you call out for insight and cry aloud for understanding, and if you look for it as for silver and search for it as for hidden treasure, then you will understand the fear of the LORD and find the knowledge of God.

PROVERBS 2:2–5 NIV

If you've ever lost something—your keys, your glasses, or an important document—you've no doubt searched everywhere. Sometimes when you finally find it, you realize that, in your haste, you simply overlooked the very thing you were frantically searching for.

It's all about focus! Even when you're looking in the right direction, you can still miss something because your focus is slightly off. This can be the challenge in our relationship with God. We can ask God a question and be really intent on getting the answer, only to find that His response to us was there all along—just not the answer we expected or wanted.

Frustration and stress can keep us from clearly seeing the things that God puts before us. Time spent in prayer and meditation on God's Word can often wash away the dirt and grime of the day-to-day and provide a clear picture of God's intentions for our lives. Step outside the pressure and into His presence, and get the right focus for whatever you're facing today.

Lord, help me to avoid distractions and keep my eyes on You. Amen.

DAY 97

Full Redemption and Love

Israel, put your hope in the LORD, for with the LORD is
unfailing love and with him is full redemption.
PSALM 130:7 NIV

Jesus offers each of us full redemption: complete freedom from sin because of His great love for us. God doesn't want us to carry around our list of sins, being burdened by our past mistakes. He wants us to have a clear conscience, a joy-filled life!

The Bible tells us that God removes our sins as far as the east is from the west (Psalm 103:12) and that He remembers our sin no more (Isaiah 43:25, Hebrews 8:12). It's so important to confess your sins to the Lord as soon as you feel convicted and then turn from them and move in a right direction. There is no reason to hang your head in shame over sins of the past.

Turning from sin is tough. Especially when it has become a bad habit. Find an accountability partner to pray for you and check in with you about your struggles, but don't allow the enemy to speak lies into your life. You have full redemption through Jesus Christ!

Dear Jesus, I confess my sin to You. Thank You for blotting out each
mistake and not holding anything against me. Help me to make
right choices through the power of Your Spirit inside me. Amen.

DAY 98
Hang in There

Let perseverance finish its work so that you may
be mature and complete, not lacking anything.
JAMES 1:4 NIV

Perseverance can't be rushed. The only way to develop perseverance is to endure pressure, over a long period of time. A weightlifter must gradually add more weight if he wants to build up his muscles. A runner must run farther and farther, pushing past what is comfortable. If these athletes want to grow and improve, they must persevere through pressure, over time.

The same is true for our faith. If we want to grow as Christians, we have to endure pressure. God allows difficult things into our lives to help build our strength and endurance. Just as the athlete who gives up at the first sign of hardship will never improve at her sport, the Christian who abandons her faith during times of distress will never reach maturity.

No one ever said the Christian life was an easy one. In fact, Christ told us we'd endure hardships of many kinds. But He also said not to get discouraged. When we stick it out and follow Him no matter what, we will become mature and complete, perfectly fulfilling God's plan for our lives.

Dear Father, help me to persevere when life gets hard. Help me
cling to You and do things Your way, even when it feels like I
can't go on. I trust that You won't give me more than I can
handle and You're working to make me mature. Amen.

DAY 99
Seek God

"I love all who love me. Those who search will surely find me."
PROVERBS 8:17 NLT

Did you ever play hide-and-seek as a child? Sometimes it was easy to find your sibling or friend. A foot sticking out from behind the couch or chair was a dead giveaway! Other times, a playmate may have selected a better hiding place. She was harder to find. You searched high and low. You looked behind doors and beneath beds. You lifted quilts and moved aside piles of pillows. But you didn't give up. Not until you found her!

Scripture tells us that God loves those who love Him and that if we search for Him, we will surely find Him. One translation of the Bible says it this way: "Those who seek me early and diligently will find me" (AMP).

Seek God in all things and in all ways. Search for Him in each moment of every day you are blessed to walk on this earth. He is found easily in His creation and in His Word. He is with you. Just look for Him. He wants to be found!

Father in heaven, thank You for Your unfailing love for me. Help me to search for You diligently. I know that when I seek, I will find You. Amen.

DAY 100
Teach Me Your Paths

Show me your ways, LORD, teach me your paths. Guide me in your truth and teach me, for you are God my Savior, and my hope is in you all day long.
PSALM 25:4–5 NIV

This psalm is a great prayer to memorize and keep close in your mind each day. The Bible tells us that God's Word is a lamp for our feet (Psalm 119:105). As we read, study, and hide God's Word in our hearts, the Holy Spirit will bring those words to mind to guide us and show us the way that God wants us to go. If you want to hear God's voice and know His will for your life, get into His Word.

Hebrews 4:12 tells us that the scriptures are living and active. Just think about that for a moment. God's Word is alive! As busy women, it can be difficult to find the time to open the Bible and meditate on the message—but it's *necessary* if you want God to teach you His path for your life.

Instead of giving up on finding time for Bible reading, get creative. Download a free Bible application on your phone. Have a daily scripture reading and devotion emailed to you from heartlight.org. Jot down a few verses on a note card to memorize. There are many ways to get in the Word of God and be trained by it. Start today!

Lord, I believe Your Word is living and active. I want to know Your will for my life. Help me get in Your Word more and understand Your plan for me. Amen.

DAY 101
Love Without Limits

Your love, LORD, reaches to the heavens,
your faithfulness to the skies.
PSALM 36:5 NIV

God's love and faithfulness have no bounds. They reach to the heavens. They stretch to the skies and beyond. This is hard for us to understand. As humans, even our very best attempts at love and faithfulness are limited. God's love is limitless. When God created you, knit you together in your mother's womb, and brought you into this world, He loved you. He loves you just as much today as He did when you were an innocent babe. He is incapable of loving you any less or any more than He already does. His love is not based on what you do or don't do. It is not here today and gone tomorrow due to any mistake or failure in your life. He is faithful even when we are faithless. If it seems that you are not as close to God as you once were, He is not the one who moved. Draw close to your heavenly Father. You will find that He is there, faithful and true, ready to receive you back unto Himself. Thank the Lord today for an unfailing, unfathomable sort of love. What a blessing is the love of our faithful God!

Thank You, God, for loving me with a love that reaches to the heavens.
You are faithful even when I am not. I love You, Lord. Amen.

DAY 102

Continue in His Love

"As the Father loved Me, I also have loved you; abide in My love."
JOHN 15:9 NKJV

What does it mean to "continue" or "remain" in Christ's love? Since His love is perfect, and was shown in the flesh, remaining in His love means staying connected to the person of Jesus Christ through the priceless gift of His Spirit.

Throughout your day, ask God to give you creative ways to stay connected to Jesus. Here are a few examples:

When you get up and walk to the coffeepot to turn it on, pray that God will pour His love into you so that you can pour it into others.

During your shower, ask God to cleanse you of your sins.

As you put on your makeup or brush your hair, meditate on His beauty and goodness. Ask Him to make you aware of the beauty He gives through creation and other people throughout the day.

As you eat meals, praise God for the food He gives us in His Word. Take time to meditate on scripture, even if it's just for a few moments, as you eat. If you eat with others, pray for opportunities to talk about Him.

Jehovah God, I praise You for being my Creator, Redeemer, and Friend. Thank You for giving me the love of Jesus, and help me to remain in that love every day. Amen.

DAY 103
Strength in the Lord

The LORD is my light and my salvation—whom shall I fear? The
LORD is the stronghold of my life—of whom shall I be afraid?
PSALM 27:1 NIV

Even when it seems that everything is piling up around you, Christ is there for you. Take heart! He is your stronghold, a very present help right in the midst of your trial. Regardless of what comes against you in this life, you have the Lord on your side. He is your light in the darkness and your salvation from eternal separation from God. You have nothing to fear.

At times, this world can be a tough, unfair, lonely place. Since the fall of man in the garden, things have not been as God originally intended. The Bible assures us that we will face trials in this life, but it also exclaims that we are more than conquerors through Christ who is in us! When you find yourself up against a tribulation that seems insurmountable, *look up*. Christ is there. He goes before you, stands with you, and is backing you up in your time of need. You may lose everyone and everything else in this life, but nothing has the power to separate you from the love of Christ. Nothing.

Jesus, I cling to the hope I have in You. You are my rock, my stronghold,
my defense. I will not fear, for You are with me always. Amen.

DAY 104
Thankful, Thankful Heart

I will praise you, LORD, with all my heart.
I will tell all the miracles you have done.
PSALM 9:1 NCV

If you live from the perspective that 10 percent of life is what happens to you and the rest is how you respond, then every situation has a side—positive or negative. Say you're late to work, every stoplight on your way is a red one, and you feel like you just can't make up the time. Instead of complaining, consider the delay was one that God appointed to keep you safe.

When you choose to approach life from the positive side, you can find thankfulness in most of life's circumstances. It completely changes your outlook, your attitude, and your countenance. God wants to bless you. When you are tempted to feel sorry for yourself or to blame others or God for difficulties, push PAUSE. Take a moment and rewind your life. Look back and count the blessings that God has given you. As you remind yourself of all He has done for you and in you, it will bring change to your attitude and give you hope in the situation you're facing. Count your blessings today.

Lord, I am thankful for my life and all You have done for me. When life happens, help me to respond to it in a healthy, positive way. Remind me to look to You and trust You to carry me through life's challenges. Amen.

DAY 105
Love Your Enemies

"Love your enemies, do good to them, and lend to them without expecting to get anything back. Then your reward will be great."
LUKE 6:35 NIV

These words, spoken by Jesus, are some of the hardest words we have to consider. Love our enemies? Really?

The thought of loving those who do us harm just doesn't sit right. The thought of giving kindness in return for malicious intent makes no sense and causes our stomachs to knot up, our shoulders to tighten. Love our enemies? Please, God, no.

Isn't it enough to avoid our enemies and do them no harm?

Sometimes. Maybe. But most of the time, God calls us to a love so brave, so intense that it defies logic and turns the world on its side. He calls us to love like He loves.

That means we must show patience where others have been short. We must show kindness where others have been cruel. We must look for ways to bless, when others have cursed.

Something about that just doesn't feel right to our human hearts.

But God promises great rewards for those who do this. Oh, the rewards may not be immediate. But when God promises great rewards, we can know without a doubt that any present struggle will be repaid with goodness and blessing, many times over.

Dear Father, help me to love those who hate me, bless those who curse me, and show kindness to those who have been cruel. Help me to love like You love. Amen.

DAY 106

Love Covers a Multitude

And now these three remain: faith, hope and love. But the greatest of these is love.
1 CORINTHIANS 13:13 NIV

He leaves the toilet seat up and forgets to shut the drawers on a regular basis. He sometimes uses the wrong toothbrush, leaving dried toothpaste on her brush. He drops coffee grounds in the silverware drawer and leaves all but one pan dirty in the kitchen when he cooks. But he will text to say he loves her.

His balled-up, sweaty socks that need to be unraveled before washing or drying are usually full of grass or dirt. He leaves bikes and things behind parked cars, where he forgets about them. But he keeps working hard to support her and the kids.

He can't remember the dinner event she has told him about three times this week, and he has lost his phone again. . . .

Then she remembers how patient God is with her many shortcomings. God never stops working, and He clearly loves her. God says in His text how He died for her and will never give up on her.

Love covers a multitude. Indeed.

Lord, thank You for the way You love us without fail, even with our many flaws. Thank You for helping us to love others the same way. Amen.

DAY 107

Praying for Our Loved Ones

Therefore I tell you, whatever you ask for in prayer,
believe that you have received it, and it will be yours.

MARK 11:24 NIV

One of the best things we can do for our friends and family members is pray for them. And while there isn't one single formula for prayer in the Bible, we can take cues from the prayers of people in the scriptures.

Are we Pharisee-ical as we talk to our heavenly Father, asking Him to change others—but neglecting to ask Him to change us? Do we take responsibility for the hurts we have caused, like David did in the Psalms? Do we pray with thanksgiving, like Mary did after Gabriel came to her?

Do we beseech God with faith, believing that He can do anything, as Hannah did? Or do we pray in hesitation, lacking conviction? We could also learn a lot from the prayers of Paul in his letters to the churches he ministered to. Many of his prayers can be prayed verbatim for those we love.

We also find help and hope when we sit in silence, listening in prayer. God, through His Holy Spirit, can give us wisdom, endurance, and insight we would never come up with on our own.

Though we can't always see it, He is at work. . .in our loved ones' hearts—and in ours.

Lord, thank You for Your concern for those I love.
I know You love them even more than I do. Amen.

DAY 108

Rejoice!

Rejoice in the Lord always. I will say it again: Rejoice!
PHILIPPIANS 4:4 NIV

Paul wrote these words from prison. Considering his circumstances, it doesn't seem like he had much reason to rejoice. Yet he knew what many of us forget: when we have the Lord on our side, we always have reason to rejoice.

He didn't say, "Rejoice in your circumstances." He told us to rejoice in the Lord. When we're feeling depressed, anxious, or lost in despair, we can think of our Lord. We can remind ourselves that we are so very loved. We are special to God. He adores us, and in His heart, each of us is irreplaceable.

Perhaps the reason we lose our joy sometimes is because we've let the wrong things be the source of our joy. If our joy is in our finances, our jobs, or our relationships, what happens when those things fall through? Our joy is lost.

But when God is the source of our joy, we will never lose that joy. Circumstances may frustrate us and break our hearts. But God is able to supply all our needs. He is able to restore broken relationships. He can give us a new job or help us to succeed at our current job. Through it all, despite it all, we can rejoice in knowing that we are God's, and He loves us.

*Dear Father, thank You for loving me. Help me
to make You the source of my joy. Amen.*

DAY 109
Unshakeable Love

"For even if the mountains walk away and the hills fall to pieces, my love won't walk away from you, my covenant commitment of peace won't fall apart." The GOD who has compassion on you says so.
ISAIAH 54:10 MSG

As modern women, anxiety seems to stalk us. Our newsfeeds mention uprisings, terrorist attacks, market fluctuations, and hurricanes. Fear is a very common reaction to the world's instability, and it can easily cloud our mind and turn us into quaking, terrified children. The question is, do we want to dissolve into frightened, anxious women who rarely step outside our comfort zones, or do we desire to be bold, unashamed, fearless women of the Most High King?

God doesn't want us to cower beneath the weight of uncertainty. Instead, through the scriptures, other believers, and the indwelling Holy Spirit, He encourages us to be bold, passionate, and faithful. But how do we bridge the gap between our emotions and His desires for us?

The answer: love. We must rest in God's wild, unbending love for us. He promises in Isaiah that no matter what happens, He will never remove Himself from us. When we believe Him wholeheartedly and rest in His love, we will be filled with fear-busting peace and adventurous faith. That faith allows us to dream big dreams and conquer the worries that keep us chained.

Lord, thank You for Your love, which never leaves me.
Help me to rest in Your love above all else. Amen.

DAY 110
Fully Equipped

*His divine power has given us everything we need for a godly life through
our knowledge of him who called us by his own glory and goodness.
Through these he has given us his very great and precious promises,
so that through them you may participate in the divine nature,
having escaped the corruption in the world caused by evil desires.*

2 PETER 1:3–4 NIV

As Christians, we are fully equipped to live a godly life on earth. We don't have to live in a state of constant confusion. We don't have to stress about what to do or how to live. God has given us everything we need to be able to follow Him daily.

Second Corinthians 1:21–22 (NIV) tells us that "He anointed us, set his seal of ownership on us, and put his Spirit in our hearts as a deposit, guaranteeing what is to come." When we accept Christ as our Savior and Lord of our life, God gives us *His Spirit*! He places *His very own Spirit* in *our* hearts! Isn't that amazing? Take some time to fully reflect on that!

John 15:26 calls the Holy Spirit our "Helper." We are never alone. God's Spirit is right there with us as we make decisions, as we go about our day, as we face trials, and as we enjoy His blessings. We have a constant Helper everywhere we go!

*Heavenly Father, I'm amazed at what You've done. Thank You for placing
Your Spirit in my heart. Help me to listen as You lead and guide me! Amen.*

DAY 111
Wonderful You

For you created my inmost being; you knit me together in my mother's womb. I praise you because I am fearfully and wonderfully made; your works are wonderful, I know that full well.

PSALM 139:13–14 NIV

Many of us look at ourselves and find something we want to change:

"I wish I had her figure. I hate my hips."

"I love her curly hair. Mine is so straight and hard to manage."

"Maybe I will color my hair auburn. Brown looks mousy."

And yet, many of the very things we may not like are what make us unique. The psalmist says that we are fearfully and wonderfully made. That means that we are made in such a way to produce reverence and inspire awe. Our bodies are complicated and wondrous in the way they work and heal.

By looking at ourselves the way God looks at us, we can see that our differences are reason to praise Him and acknowledge that it is right to honor, love, and be grateful for all of His creation, including us. Even though we may not understand why He gave us the physical attributes that He did, we can praise Him since we know He took great love and pleasure in creating us.

Loving Father, I praise You for making me the way You did. I am deeply impressed by how You put me together, making me so unique; there is no one exactly like me. I love You! Amen.

DAY 112

Mary's Prayer

*And Mary said, Behold the handmaid of the Lord; be it unto
me according to thy word. And the angel departed from her.*
LUKE 1:38 KJV

Imagine Mary's excitement and delight as she accepted Joseph's marriage proposal. A young bride-to-be with her entire life before her is suddenly approached by an angel with a different proposal. Seeing an angel in the first place was certainly a shocking surprise; then to be told that she had been chosen to carry God's Son—to become a mother without ever knowing a man. Imagine the thrill and also the concern! What would Joseph think, finding her pregnant before their wedding day? She certainly must have thought about that.

Yet Mary told the angel she would accept God's assignment—"Let it be done in me as you have said." She was willing to accept God's will by faith. She had to believe God would take care of all the details. . .and He did. He took Joseph aside and assured him that Mary had not been with another man, but the child was God's own Son.

What has God put in your heart? Are you willing to allow His perfect will to be done in you at the expense of what others might think?

*Lord, give me a heart for Your purpose and plans. Help me to believe
that You will take care of all the details as I step out in faith. Amen.*

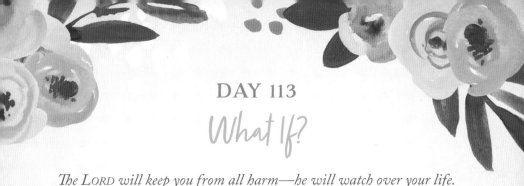

DAY 113
What If?

The LORD will keep you from all harm—he will watch over your life.
PSALM 121:7 NIV

"Mommy, what if the sun falls down? What if an earthquake swallows our house? What if. . .?" When the world appears scary to children, they run to their parents with questions. They look to their mothers and fathers for comfort, reassurance, and peace.

Grown-ups are no different. They run to Father God with their what-if's. "What if I have cancer? What if I lose my job? What if there is a terrorist attack? What if. . .?"

Psalm 46 provides the answer to all these questions. It says, "God is our refuge and strength, an ever-present help in trouble. Therefore we will not fear, though the earth give way and the mountains fall into the heart of the sea, though its waters roar and foam and the mountains quake with their surging. . . . The LORD Almighty is with us; the God of Jacob is our fortress" (NIV).

Feeling safe and secure rests not in the world or in other human beings but with God alone. He is a Christian's help and hope in every frightening situation. He promises to provide peace to everyone who puts their faith and trust in Him.

What are you afraid of today? Allow God to encourage you. Trust Him to bring you through it and to give you peace.

Dear Lord, hear my prayers, soothe me with
Your Word, and give me peace. Amen.

DAY 114

A Friend of God

*Instead, be filled with the Holy Spirit, singing psalms and hymns
and spiritual songs among yourselves, and making music
to the Lord in your hearts. And give thanks for everything
to God the Father in the name of our Lord Jesus Christ.*
EPHESIANS 5:18–20 NLT

In John 15:15, Jesus says that we are His friends. He has given us His Spirit so that we can know His heart and His ways. A great woman of God said that when she spends time with God, He always makes her feel like His favorite daughter. It's so true. You're His favorite daughter too, and He wants to be your best friend.

This same woman of God has a very special relationship with her heavenly Father. She sings songs of praise to God throughout the day. If you were to have a conversation with her in the hallway at church, she would likely break into song as God prompted her. Her heart is so full of thanks to God for His faithfulness to her. You wouldn't know by the joy oozing from her that she had many heartbreaking moments, including her husband being taken from her by a freak strike of lightning as he was standing beside her on vacation. She pressed into God during that time instead of pushing Him away. She has allowed God to guide her every step and heal her brokenness. She is always pointing others to the one true God.

Will you be God's friend in joy and sorrow?

*God, please strengthen my faith in You. Show me Your love
and faithfulness in a personal and powerful way. Amen.*

DAY 115
Making Good Decisions

Trust in the LORD with all your heart, and lean not on your
own understanding; in all your ways acknowledge Him,
and He shall direct your paths. Do not be wise in your
own eyes; fear the LORD and depart from evil.
PROVERBS 3:5–7 NKJV

Everyone goes through tough times, and having to make important decisions during those dark days only adds to the pain and frustration. Marilyn wanted to do the right thing in regard to a failing relationship, but she worried she would make a mistake she'd regret. She went to an older Christian friend for advice. He listened and talked with her, but in the end, he said, "You need to make a decision, but only you can do it. No one can make it for you."

Marilyn knew her friend was right. She began praying earnestly about the situation, relying on God for wisdom and courage. Some days were still hard and she didn't know which direction to take, but she continued to trust God and wait for His help. When the resolution came, Marilyn knew God had intervened and worked things out for the best.

When we learn to trust the Lord and not our own limited understanding, He will direct our paths. The secret is to trust Him with all our hearts and acknowledge Him. God is personal for each of us. He wants to be included in our decisions and our daily lives. No matter what we face, He knows how to resolve it. Whatever you need, trust Him.

Father, give me Your wisdom and understanding.
Help me to rely on You and not myself.

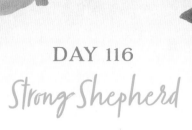

DAY 116
Strong Shepherd

Behold, the Lord GOD shall come with a strong hand, and His arm shall rule for Him; behold, His reward is with Him, and His work before Him. He will feed His flock like a shepherd; He will gather the lambs with His arm, and carry them in His bosom, and gently lead those who are with young.

ISAIAH 40:10–11 NKJV

Have you ever watched lambs play? They skip and bounce with newfound joy. It is hard not to smile as you watch their little jig. Today's passage from Isaiah shows some of God's characteristics. He is mighty, and not the fake bodybuilding mighty but a power and strength that is timeless and has no limit. We have only glimpsed the Lord's power in rainstorms and wind. He uses this might and power to lead His flock. What an oxymoron. The God of the universe uses His infinite strength to care for His flock, to "carry them in His bosom, and gently lead those who are with young."

His is not a passive shepherding. Throughout the verses we see God come with might; we see Him rule, tend, gather, carry, and lead. He is our Protector. Why would we ever want to stray from this shepherd? Unlike man, God does not abuse His power. Throughout scripture and history we see dictators rise and fall, kings and queens take advantage of the poor; yet our God is just. He rules and leads His flock and nothing is outside His control, not even the heart and soul of a dictator.

Father, thank You for being a diligent and mighty Shepherd. Help me to take these truths to heart so that I may trust You more each day. Amen.

DAY 117

Fearless

God is love. Whoever lives in love lives in God, and God in them. . . .
There is no fear in love. But perfect love drives out fear, because fear has
to do with punishment. The one who fears is not made perfect in love."
1 JOHN 4:16, 18 NIV

It sounds simple enough, but fear can creep in when we consider what it means to show God complete devotion. Putting Him first in our lives might cost us more than we expect—in our relationships, in our jobs, in how we spend our money or time. We might worry about what others might think of us or fear that we can't accomplish what God calls us to do.

God's unconditional love frees us from fear—the fear of punishment, failure, or harsh judgment from others—because His opinion of us matters most. Through everything, He has promised to be with us and strengthen us. We may feel ashamed of our fear, but God is not angry. Instead, He gives us exactly what we need to strengthen our faith, whether it's the sign of a damp sheepskin (Gideon, Judges 6) or the invitation to touch His wounds (Jesus to Thomas, John 20:24–29).

Do not fear. Christ shows us the vastness of His love to drive out our worries and anxieties. When we rely on Him, we can accomplish *anything* He asks of us.

Father God, I want to step out in faith and do what You command.
Banish my fears by showing me how perfectly You love me. Amen.

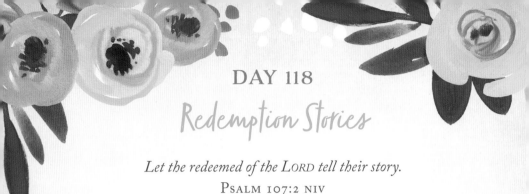

DAY 118
Redemption Stories

Let the redeemed of the Lord tell their story.
PSALM 107:2 NIV

For just about as long as the entertainment industry has been around (or longer), redemption stories have been the basis for popular movies and novels and plays. Everyone loves to follow the story of the bad guy turned knight in shining armor, the down-on-his-luck everyman who receives big blessings, the orphan in rags who gains a family and great riches all at once.

If you are a follower of Christ, there's a good chance you've had to exchange something for the path to eternal life. You've had to let something go or give something up. Or perhaps you've been changed in some significant way. No one encounters Jesus Christ and comes away exactly the same.

Let these words encourage you today to tell your story. If you have not told it before, start now. Pick a few small details to share, or give the whole general outline. Tell a loved one. Tell a coworker. Tell your pastor. Tell a friend. Tell a stranger on the subway. Tell anyone who will listen.

You never know how your story might impact someone else. You will never know the strength and love and hope you have to give until you open your mouth and let your truth out.

Everyone loves a redemption story. Why not give them yours?

Dear Redeemer, thank You for dying for us,
for saving us, and for preparing a place for us in heaven.
Help me to have the courage to share my story of You. Amen.

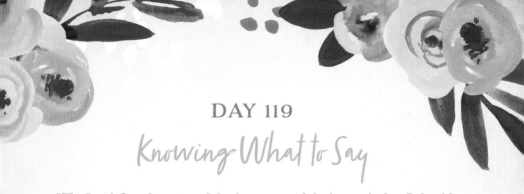

DAY 119
Knowing What to Say

"The Lord God has given Me the tongue of the learned, that I should know how to speak a word in season to him who is weary. He awakens Me morning by morning, He awakens My ear to hear as the learned."
ISAIAH 50:4 NKJV

Sometimes it's hard to know what to say to a friend or loved one when tragedy strikes their family. We all know the usual trite lines like 'Everything will turn out for the best,' or 'I'm sorry for your loss.' And even though these aren't bad words, they do little to comfort someone in pain.

We are limited in our ability to comfort. We can sympathize with others, but unless we have experienced what they are going through, we cannot feel the depth of their pain or how it is affecting them. It's in these times that we need God's Spirit to help us be a comforter.

Isaiah writes that the Lord gave him a tongue so he would know how to speak the right word to someone who was weary. We can apply this scripture to our own lives and ask God to give us the right word to speak to the one needing comfort. If we allow Him, God will awaken our ears to hear His voice every day. Then we can speak God's words and bring a measure of comfort to a hurting individual. When we give His Word to someone, it will be the right one.

Lord, open my ears to hear Your message
of hope and speak it to someone in need.

Hold Your Temper

A hot-tempered person stirs up conflict,
but the one who is patient calms a quarrel.

PROVERBS 15:18 NIV

For the third time in a week, Jane called her Internet provider hoping for a solution to her problem. Internet service had been sporadic for several days and she hoped to reach someone who could give her some answers.

The person on the other end of the line sounded young and inexperienced, but Jane decided to give her a chance. As they discussed the problem, the technician tried several ideas to get the service working again, but to no avail. She finally offered a solution that would require Jane to pay a fee of one hundred fifty dollars. Jane felt angry the company would require a large fee in light of the fact she was already paying a monthly fee and not receiving good service. The longer they talked, the more stressed and upset she became. But in spite of the frustration she voiced to the other person, the girl remained polite and helpful.

Jane felt like giving the service technician a piece of her mind, but knew it wouldn't solve anything. With God's help, she remained calm in spite of the stress she felt. They ended the call by wishing each other a good day despite the failure to resolve the situation. Even though Jane still didn't have an answer to her problem, she was glad she had not spoken in haste and made the situation worse.

Lord, keep me calm in the face of anger and trouble. Help me
not to quarrel even when I feel justified in doing so.

DAY 121
He Makes All Things New

Create in me a pure heart, O God, and renew a steadfast spirit within me.
Do not cast me from your presence or take your Holy Spirit from me. Restore
to me the joy of your salvation and grant me a willing spirit, to sustain me.
<small>PSALM 51:10–12 NIV</small>

King David committed adultery and had the woman's husband killed in battle (see Psalm 51). Talk about guilt! Yet the Bible says David was a man after God's own heart. David truly loved God, and being a king with power, he messed up royally!

David had faith in God's goodness. He was truly repentant and expected to be restored to God's presence. He could not stand to be separated from God. He recognized that he must become clean again through the power of forgiveness.

Perhaps there have been times when you felt distant from God because of choices you made. There is no sin that is too big for God to cover or too small to bother Him with. He is willing to forgive, and He forgets when you ask Him. He expects you to do the same. If you don't let forgiven sin go, it can become a tool for torture for the enemy to use against you. God sent Jesus to the cross for you to restore you to relationship with Him.

Heavenly Father, thank You for sending Jesus to pay for my sins.
Forgive me and make me new. Fill me with Your presence today. Amen.

DAY 122
Making It to the Top

I once thought these things were valuable, but now I consider them worthless because of what Christ has done. . . . I press on to reach the end of the race and receive the heavenly prize for which God, through Christ Jesus, is calling us.
PHILIPPIANS 3:7, 14 NLT

The world believes who you know can take you far in life. You need the right contacts with clout to make it to the top. You need to run with the right crowd to be successful. You may even be expected to do unethical or immoral things to move up in the company. Women are sometimes asked to have affairs with their superiors. You may be asked to lie for your boss, dress a certain way, or flirt with potential customers. This lifestyle is degrading and results in unhappiness and tragedy for many.

God's Word teaches a different example. Knowing Christ is the best decision we can make as we go through life. He will never ask us to do anything immoral but will give us a pure heart and teach us to respect ourselves and others. It may mean we don't run with the popular, successful crowd. We may get passed over for a promotion or a raise, but knowing Christ gives us hope for the future. As we press toward the mark for a higher calling in Him, we find peace and wisdom in our daily lives.

Father, show me the path I'm to walk and give me wisdom
to take each step, knowing You will walk beside me.

DAY 123
Dwelling on the Important Things

Set your mind on things above, not on things on the earth.
COLOSSIANS 3:2 NKJV

Andrea spent the morning cooking and baking, getting ready for a family get-together at her sister's house. She worked hard on each of her dishes, especially the pie, then loaded the food into the car and drove to her sister's. Delicious food covered the kitchen counter and Andrea added her contributions to the bounty. When it came time for dessert, Andrea sliced into the pie she had spent time carefully putting together. To her dismay, the filling had not set like it should have. Disappointment clouded her day. In spite of the good time she had visiting with everyone, she felt her time and money had been wasted on the pie.

Sometimes we worry about little things and forget to look at the big picture. If all we see are the things that go wrong or the trouble around us, we have missed what's important. Instead of focusing on spending time with her family, Andrea fretted about how long it had taken her to fix the pie and how much she had spent on the ingredients.

As Christians, we can focus on our problems and the little things that frustrate us or we can keep our minds on heavenly things and know we have hope beyond what troubles us here. Christ is bigger than anything we may have to endure here on earth.

*Lord, help us to keep our minds fixed on You so that the
problems we face are seen through Your grace in our lives.*

DAY 124
Under Vine and Fig Tree

" 'And I will remove the iniquity of that land in one day.
In that day,' says the LORD of hosts, 'everyone will invite
his neighbor under his vine and under his fig tree.' "
ZECHARIAH 3:9–10 NKJV

The context of today's scripture is the prophet Zechariah's vision in which he saw Satan accusing Joshua, the high priest of Israel. Joshua was clothed in filthy garments, which represented his sin and thus revealed his inadequacy in serving as the spiritual leader of God's people. However, God rejected Satan's accusations and commanded that new clothes be given to Joshua. God took away his sins and gave him another chance to be the high priest. He promised to soon send His servant the Branch, at which time the sins of the people would be removed in a single day and there would be rejoicing.

About five hundred years later, Jesus came as the promised Branch of the family tree of King David. Through His sacrifice, our sins were removed and we were washed clean. In Hebrew the names Joshua and Jesus are the same: Yeshua, meaning "God who saves." Where earthly high priests, like Joshua of Zechariah's time, failed to bring redemption for people, Jesus, as the true High Priest (see Hebrews 7) and as the God who saves, offered Himself and made a way back to God. Now it is time to invite our neighbors to celebrate under our "vine and fig tree."

God of angel armies, thank You that where spiritual leaders on earth fail,
You sent Jesus to remind us that You are the One who saves. Amen.

DAY 125
Everything You Need

And this same God who takes care of me will supply all your needs from his glorious riches, which have been given to us in Christ Jesus.
PHILIPPIANS 4:19 NLT

Have you ever gone through a period in your life when you were completely dependent on God to supply everything for you? Perhaps you lost your job or had an extended illness. It can be humbling to be unable to provide for yourself and your family.

The Israelites faced similar circumstances when God freed them from slavery in Egypt. As He led them through the desert toward the Promised Land, He provided water and food in miraculous ways. Every morning, one day's supply of manna would appear. Any attempt to save it until the next day was futile; the manna would rot. God wanted them to rely on Him daily for their provision. Yet the Israelites' response wasn't to be grateful but to complain they didn't have enough variety!

God often takes us through the desert before we get to the Promised Land. It's in the desert that we learn the lessons we will need to use in the Promised Land, most of which involve trusting Him. It's in the desert that we learn God is who He says He is. It's in the desert that we learn to obey Him, not because He says to, but because it's what will ultimately give us the life we were designed to live.

Lord, we don't always live our lives as if all of our provision comes from You. Remove our fear and help us to trust in You and take You at Your Word. Amen.

DAY 126
Trust and Lean

*Trust in the L*ORD *with all your heart and*
do not lean on your own understanding.
PROVERBS 3:5 NASB

This verse contains two commands—trust in the Lord and don't rely on your own understanding.

You can rely on God because He is truly trustworthy—He has the strength to sustain, help, and protect you and an incomprehensible love for you that cannot be broken or grow stale. You are not bringing your prayers before someone who is powerful but fickle, or one who is loving and good, but weak. You pray to a God who is all-powerful, but also good and loving. Therefore, you can be confident that your life is placed firmly in His hands and His control and that He considers it precious.

How often do you lean on your own understanding and strength instead of God's? You are remarkably less capable of controlling your life than God is. Instead of trusting yourself, someone who doesn't know the future and certainly can't control it, lean on the all-powerful God who knows each step you will take. Relinquish all your anxious thoughts over to His control. Trusting God with your future is far more productive than worrying about it. So lean on Him and trust Him with *everything* in your heart. He will sustain you.

Lord, forgive me for not trusting You as I should. Forgive
me for leaning on my own understanding instead of relying
on Your infinite wisdom and strength. Thank You that these
commands You give me are for my greatest benefit.

DAY 127
Refuse to Quit

And I will pray the Father, and he shall give you another Comforter,
that he may abide with you for ever; Even the Spirit of truth; whom
the world cannot receive, because it seeth him not, neither knoweth
him: but ye know him; for he dwelleth with you, and shall be in you.
JOHN 14:16–17 KJV

There are days when it seems that nothing goes right and you struggle just to put one foot in front of the other. The good news on a day like that is the truth that you are not alone. Whatever obstacle is in your way, you don't have to overcome it in your own power. God is with you. Jesus sent the Comforter. The Holy Spirit is your present help in any situation.

The Holy Spirit is the very Spirit of God Himself. He is with you always, ready to care for and guide you. By faith you can rest and rely on the Holy Spirit for strength, wisdom, and inspiration.

The next time you feel like giving up, refuse to quit. Ask the Holy Spirit to intervene, to provide you with the strength and wisdom to continue your journey.

Jesus, You have sent the Comforter to me. I believe He is with me always,
providing what I need today to refuse to quit. I take the next step in my
journey knowing He is with me. I can press on by faith today. Amen.

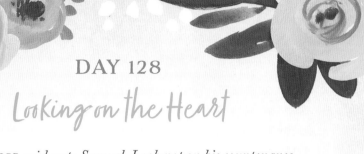

DAY 128

Looking on the Heart

But the LORD said unto Samuel, Look not on his countenance,
or on the height of his stature; because I have refused him:
for the LORD seeth not as man seeth; for man looketh on the
outward appearance, but the LORD looketh on the heart.

1 SAMUEL 16:7 KJV

Everywhere you look, there are beauty products, weight loss programs, and procedures to make you look younger. It seems we never tire of trying to improve our appearance. There's nothing wrong with trying to look our best, but if we're not careful, we can become obsessed with our appearance. Many women worry about how they look to the world around them and whether they live up to the world's standards of beauty.

When God sent Samuel to anoint a new king for Israel, Samuel asked Jesse, the Bethlehemite, to bring out his sons. The sons of Jesse were evidently good-looking men, because Samuel thought that surely the Lord's anointed stood before Him. God said, *"No, I don't look on the outward appearance; I look on the heart."*

In our pursuit of improving our appearance, it's best if we first make sure our hearts are clean. We might look good on the outside, but if our hearts aren't pure before God, then we aren't pleasing to Him. Before we jump on the bandwagon and spend a lot of money on cosmetics, maybe we should ask God about our hearts and make sure He approves. It's far more important to please Him than to please the world.

Lord, give me a pure heart. Help me to desire
Your approval over man's approval. Amen.

DAY 129

Consider Forgiveness

*Rejoice the soul of Your servant, for to You, O Lord, I lift
up my soul. For You, Lord, are good, and ready to forgive,
and abundant in mercy to all those who call upon You.*

PSALM 86:4–5 NKJV

The beginning of a new year is a good time to consider those to whom you
have yet to extend forgiveness. Yes, there are people in our lives who have
an amazing capacity to push our buttons. And, yes, there are people who
have maimed us by their words and actions. But because God is so willing
to forgive those who push His buttons and have harmed His good name,
we should be willing to wipe the slate clean of those who have frustrated
and offended us. So before you lift up Your soul to God, forgive and bless
those who have hurt and upset you. And while you're at it, forgive and
bless yourself. Then go to God, ready to have your missteps erased and to
be renewed by His amazing mercy and grace.

*Lord, I want to have a fresh start in this new year. So I am telling You now
that I have forgiven those who have hurt me in the past. Please bless their
lives this year. And now I lift up my soul to You, asking for Your forgiveness
and blessing. Fill me with Your mercy and grace. Make me a better and
more peaceful person because I have been in Your presence. Amen.*

DAY 130

God's Upside-Down Kingdom

"Then, Lord," Simon Peter replied, "not just
my feet but my hands and my head as well!"
JOHN 13:9 NIV

This is the well-known scene where Jesus is washing the disciples' feet before His death. Peter, the disciple known for his enthusiastic jump-first-then-look attitude, is having none of it. He is not letting Jesus wash his feet because he doesn't understand the purpose behind what Jesus is doing.

Jesus' reaction here is so different from what we might say. Instead of saying to Peter, "Stop telling me what to do! You have no idea what's going on here," He gently explains the lesson and purpose.

God loves our enthusiasm even if it's misdirected. Often we think we know what God is doing or would want done and so we jump ahead of Him. He calmly pulls us back and reminds us that our thoughts and plans are not His.

His plans can seem counterintuitive to us. They are opposite of the world's definition of success. Jesus was God, and He descended to earth to become man. And not a powerful man, but a poor man. And to His disciples, He became a servant. Our society tells us to push up, to rise to the top. But He descended, came down to save us by dying a criminal's death.

Dear Jesus, help us to emulate You and how You serve. Make us sensitive
to the gentle nudge You give us to sacrifice, give, downscale, or decrease
in some way to serve You and advance Your kingdom. Open our eyes to
the blessings You have given us in ways we weren't expecting. Amen.

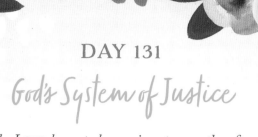

DAY 131

God's System of Justice

*Yet the LORD longs to be gracious to you; therefore he
will rise up to show you compassion. For the LORD
is a God of justice. Blessed are all who wait for him!*
ISAIAH 30:18 NIV

Do you yearn for more of God? This scripture tells us He longs to be gracious to us. If we believe that, our response should be a longing for more of Him, more of His grace, unless pride makes us pull away and try to earn His favor.

That famous line, quoted as though it is scripture, says "God helps those who help themselves." The truth is, when we can't do anything for ourselves, we're in the perfect place for God to pour out His grace.

The world's justice tells us we don't deserve God's graciousness—we've made too many mistakes—but God's justice is wrapped in love and mercy. Instead of pointing to our failures and telling us we're worthless, He forgives our sins and totally forgets them. They're as far from His thoughts as the east is from the west (see Psalm 103:12).

When we run into His arms of love and let His grace overwhelm us, we will long for more of Him. He's too magnificent to ignore. It's impossible to turn our backs on all He does for us. The natural response is to accept His compassion. He longs to give it, and waits patiently until we're ready to receive.

*Dear Lord, I long to receive Your gracious compassion. I yearn
for more of You! Help me set aside my own desires and fall
down before You, amazed by Your astonishing justice. Amen.*

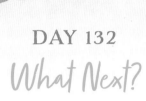

DAY 132
What Next?

If any of you lacks wisdom, you should ask God, who gives
generously to all without finding fault, and it will be given to you.
JAMES 1:5 NIV

Ever been lost in an unfamiliar place? Trees block street signs, and other streets aren't marked at all; construction causes confusing, squiggly detours. Embarrassment or even panic grows as the minutes pass.

In life, we hit unexpected detours that make us unsure where to turn next. They might be difficult decisions involving family, healthcare, jobs, or relationships at church. Maybe the weight is migrating from the tension in your shoulders to settle in your heart.

The good news is that our heavenly Father knows the way out of our confusion and will help us when we are at our most frantic. James tells us that God promises to give wisdom to those who ask for it in faith; He gives wisdom "generously" and "without fault." Sometimes it's intimidating to ask for advice from others, but God doesn't look down on us for admitting our weakness. He chooses to lavish His love and His gifts on error-prone people because they are a part of His family in Christ. We can entrust ourselves and our lives to our heavenly Father, knowing that through Christ, we have access to "all the treasures of wisdom and knowledge" that our Savior possesses (Colossians 2:3 NIV).

Dear heavenly Father, thank You that You have my days planned out for
me and I am safe in Your hands. Please grant me wisdom when I am at
a loss and help my spirit be sensitive to Your Spirit's leading. Amen.

DAY 133
Clear Vision

So shall the knowledge of wisdom be to your soul; if you have found it, there is a prospect, and your hope will not be cut off.
PROVERBS 24:14 NKJV

If you've ever worn glasses, you know what it's like to try to go without them. Talk about a fuzzy world! You take tentative steps, cautiously moving forward, knowing that, at any minute, you might trip over something or knock something down.

Clarity of vision is a wonderful gift. Once you put those glasses on, you can clearly see the road ahead and take bold, big steps. Confidence rises up inside you as you focus on the path set before you.

In this same way, God can bring clarity and vision to your path when you ask for His wisdom. Picture yourself in a rough situation. You don't know which way to go. You ask for the Lord's wisdom. He offers it, and the road ahead of you is suddenly clear. It's as if you've put on spiritual glasses! That's what His wisdom does—gives definition. Boldness. Confidence. Makes clear the path.

What are you waiting for? No need for a fuzzy road ahead. Put on those glasses, girl, then take a bold step forward!

Father, I'm so excited that I don't have to walk around confused and blinded. No fuzzy roads for me, Lord! Today I pause to ask for Your wisdom so that the road ahead will be clear. Thank You for great vision and the confidence to move forward.

DAY 134
Hunger for God's Word

When your words came, I ate them; they were my joy and my
heart's delight, for I bear your name, LORD God Almighty.
JEREMIAH 15:16 NIV

Why does God tell people to read His Word? He commands this because it is His primary means of communication with His children. Believers are inexorably bound to Him, and because of this great bond only the will of the Father gives the greatest comfort. Jeremiah's words may seem extreme, but God wants to give a startling picture of what it means to hunger for His words.

Jesus, while on earth, knew the Old Testament scriptures by heart; Paul as a Pharisee may have spent years poring over the books of the law (the first five books of the Bible written by Moses). The disciples too, although mostly poor, came to a deep and saving knowledge of God's words as they listened to Jesus.

If people are God's children then they also should find delight in reading His Word. They should wrestle with it, analyze it, let it convict and change them; it should be their sustenance just as food and water. Just like earthly hunger cannot be satisfied by eating once a day, His children also continually desire more spiritual growth until they are finally united with Jesus in heaven.

Great Provider, let Your words be sweet as honey to Your daughters.
Give us diligence to read—to eat—from the Scriptures daily,
even when we are tired or our spirit rebels. Thank You for the
peace You fill us up with when we spend time with You.

DAY 135

Do You Want to Be Healed?

When Jesus saw him lying there and learned that he had been in this
condition for a long time, he asked him, "Do you want to get well?"
JOHN 5:6 NIV

The pool of Bethesda was where disabled people would go, waiting for an angel to stir the waters. The legend went that if someone made it into the water when the angel troubled the waters, that person would be healed. So Jesus' question doesn't seem to make sense. *Of course* the man wants to be healed. He's at a place where people go when they want to be healed.

When Jesus asks a question, it's not because He doesn't know the answer. He asks because He's all-knowing. He's asking it for our benefit.

The man's response to Jesus' question is also interesting. Instead of saying, "Yes, of course! Heal me!" he makes excuses as to why he hasn't been healed.

Isn't that like us? We want to be healed, but we make excuses why we aren't. Jesus is right there waiting to heal us of our wounds, our addictions, our bitterness—anything that keeps us from the best life He has for us. But He doesn't force Himself on us. He asks us, "Do you want to be healed?" We must reach out to Him. We must exercise our faith in Him.

Lord Jesus, thank You for Your great love for us. Give us the
courage to reach out to You for our healing. Help us move past
our excuses and reach for that best life You have for us. Amen.

DAY 136

Say It Again—Rejoice!

Always be full of joy in the Lord. I say it again—rejoice!
PHILIPPIANS 4:4 NLT

Do you feel like life is a fifty-pound backpack? Life can get "heavy" if we aren't careful, with everyday worries wearing us down and making us exhausted. Even small decisions tend to grow in our minds to be more important than they really are. Big decisions can completely take us over so that even the most wonderful news becomes tainted.

Look away from the cares of this world! Rejoice in what the Lord has done! Instead of lending every thought to the troubles at hand, praise God for the ways He has provided in the past and doubtless will again in the future!

Begin to count your blessings, and feel the weight lifting off your shoulders. Feel the freedom you have to enjoy your life. Enjoy your home and the comfort it brings. Enjoy your family, pets, and things you have. Allow yourself to fully feel the joy that comes with the first snow, the first warm breeze of spring, or the first rays of sun in the morning. There are so many wonderful things to enjoy even as you read this!

Life is complicated, yes. But it should never be allowed to rob you of the joy the Lord provides. "I say it again—rejoice!"

Lord, You are so good! Teach me Your ways and show me
Your faithfulness, that I may be full of joy because of You.
You created this earth to be enjoyed, and enjoy it I shall!

DAY 137
Heart Check

Why are you in despair, my soul? And why are you restless within me? Wait for God, for I will again praise Him for the help of His presence, my God.
PSALM 42:11 NASB

A woman can be going through her day, minding her own business, and suddenly find herself frowning, discontent. At such times, she would do best to stop whatever she's doing and perform a heart check by asking her inner self, "What's up? What's the matter? Why so down?" She may come up with a specific instance when someone slighted her. Or maybe it's the anniversary of a tragedy in her life. Or maybe it's the holidays, and her mind is filled with voices of those no longer among the living. Or maybe she's just plain blue, for no reason at all.

Whatever the cause of her being down, the remedy is certain: She is to tell her inner woman to hope in God. To wait for Him. Because no matter how she feels today, or may feel tomorrow, she will in all certainty "yet praise Him"! There's no doubt about it. So, after allowing herself one quick moan, she can turn her "phaser" to "expectation of praise," and squeeze the trigger. Before she knows it, praises will be bubbling up from her heart and come streaming through her lips, turning her frown upside down.

Help me to remember to check my heart each day, Lord, making sure I'm tuned out of hopelessness and in to great expectations in You.

DAY 138
Sin No More

*Straightening up, Jesus said to her, "Woman, where are they?
Did no one condemn you?" She said, "No one, Lord." And Jesus said,
"I do not condemn you, either. Go. From now on do not sin any longer."*
JOHN 8:10–11 NASB

This beautiful passage illustrates Jesus' countercultural treatment of women and His treatment of sinners. The male leaders of the time forcefully brought this adulterous woman into court to degradingly use her as a tool to catch Jesus in a wrong statement. They then planned to brutally stone her. Imagine the fear this woman must have been experiencing, surrounded by a crowd of onlookers in front of a notable teacher of the law.

Instead of condemning her, Jesus poignantly pointed out the sin and hypocrisy of the supposedly pious people who had dragged her to Him. He put this woman, who was worthless in the eyes of the culture, on a level playing field with the leaders of the society. He didn't condone the sin, but rather condemned all sin and loved this broken, scared sinner. He then told her to go and sin no more. This woman, standing alone with Jesus, faced not her condemner, but her Savior.

Christ came not to condemn, but to save. As His daughter, confess your sin; then go and sin no more.

Lord, thank You that You came to save me and free me from sin.

DAY 139
No Fear

"When you pass through the waters, I will be with you; and when you pass through the rivers, they will not sweep over you. When you walk through the fire, you will not be burned; the flames will not set you ablaze."

ISAIAH 43:2 NIV

Can you imagine standing at the edge of the Mississippi River and having the waters part so you could walk across on a dry river bed? To call it a miracle would be an understatement.

Scripture tells us over and over again of God's mighty acts. He parted the Red Sea so thousands of Israelites could cross on dry land. Daniel spent the night in the company of hungry lions and emerged without a scratch. Three of his friends were unscathed after hours in a blazing furnace.

These are more than Sunday school stories. They are real miracles performed by your God. These miracles were not included in scripture merely for dramatic effect, because God's power wasn't just for the Israelites, Daniel, and Shadrach, Meshach, and Abednego. One of the reasons God recorded His mighty acts was so we would have the assurance His power is available to us as well. When you are facing what seems to be impossible odds, return to scripture. Recount His marvelous deeds. Then remember that this promise in Isaiah is yours.

Heavenly Father, when I am facing an impossible task, help me to remember all the miracles You have performed. Thank You for the promise that this same power is available to me whenever I need it.

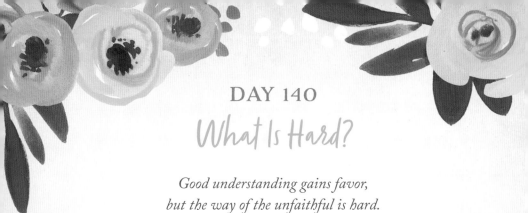

DAY 140
What Is Hard?

Good understanding gains favor,
but the way of the unfaithful is hard.
PROVERBS 13:15 NKJV

A heart open to understanding indeed gains favor; people will trust and seek her out for comfort and advice. Having an understanding heart is not easy. Why then does Solomon write that the way of the unfaithful is hard? It seems much easier to fall into unfaithfulness, to not bother with trying to understand the hurt or joy of others. On the outset it may seem like less work, but the outcome is bitter.

Faithful followers of God throughout the Bible reach a point where they see the wicked prosper while the faithful struggle. They question God's judgment, but they ultimately realize that the prosperity of the wicked is fleeting and that it often comes at the expense of others. While it is hard to remain faithful in this broken world—to read God's Word, to pray, to meet regularly with believers, and to love sacrificially—the path of the unfaithful offers no hope. It is hard: a brutal and self-inflicted separation from the one they were created to be with. We need spiritual eyes to see the consequences as deadly hard. For a growing spiritual awareness and for a heart good at understanding, we also need patience. "Patience, hard thing!" exclaims Gerard Manley Hopkins. But we have a patient Father, who in His "delicious kindness" gives us all we need.

Understanding One, let me choose the difficult life of faith now but
which allows me to be with You here and in the hereafter. Amen.

DAY 141
You've Got God's Attention

*I will bless the LORD who guides me; even at night my
heart instructs me. I know the LORD is always with me.
I will not be shaken, for he is right beside me.*
PSALM 16:7–8 NLT

Phone calls or text messages—they can all interrupt and completely end
a conversation with someone. Worse yet, once you've regrouped from
the distraction, you find that the person you were talking to wasn't even
listening in the first place.

Have you ever been in a crowd desperately trying to get someone's
attention? Maybe you were telling someone something very important,
while they looked over you to see who else was in the room. It can make
you feel worthless.

Your heavenly Father would never do that. He loves you and values
every moment you are willing to give to Him. You are His focus. His eyes
are constantly on you; His ears are tuned to your every word. He's seen
every tear you've cried and celebrated every joy of your heart with you.

Even when you feel most alone, you can trust that He is there. He is
your constant audience. The more time you spend with Him, the more you
will realize that He has a lot to share with you. If you return the favor by
giving Him your attention, He will lead you, guide you, and show you things
that you'd never discover on your own. He wants to share your life today.

*God, thank You for giving me Your undivided attention.
Show me the plans You have for me today. Amen.*

DAY 142

Wait Expectantly

Listen to my voice in the morning, LORD. Each morning
I bring my requests to you and wait expectantly.
PSALM 5:3 NLT

Why would the psalmist say he waits *expectantly* upon praying to the Lord each morning? Perhaps it is because he had seen God answer prayers time and time again! When we develop a habit of prayer, of seeking God and presenting Him with our deepest needs, we also learn to expect Him to answer. When we pray, God listens. He shows up. He never fails to hear His children.

Your heavenly Father is eager and ready to meet with you when you come before Him in prayer. The Bible tells us that His eyes are always roaming across the earth, searching for those who are after His own heart. When you lift your requests to the Sovereign God, rest assured that He is ready to answer. Wait expectantly!

Lord, thank You that You are a God who hears my prayers and answers.
Thank You in advance for all that You are doing in my life. Amen.

DAY 143

Answer Me!

*Answer me when I call to you, my righteous God. Give me relief
from my distress; have mercy on me and hear my prayer.*

PSALM 4:1 NIV

Have you ever felt like God wasn't listening? We've all felt that from time
to time. David felt it when he slept in a cold, hard cave night after night,
while being pursued by Saul's men. He felt it when his son Absalom turned
against him. Time and again in his life, David felt abandoned by God.
And yet, David was called a man after God's own heart.

No matter our maturity level, there will be times when we feel abandoned by God. There will be times when our faith wavers and our fortitude
wanes. That's okay. It's normal.

But David didn't give up. He kept crying out to God, kept falling to
his knees in worship, kept storming God's presence with his pleas. David
knew God wouldn't hide His face for long, for he knew what we might
sometimes forget: God is love. He loves us without condition and without
limit. And He is never far from those He loves.

No matter how distant God may seem, we need to keep talking to
Him. Keep praying. Keep pouring out our hearts. We can know, as David
knew, that God will answer in His time.

*Dear Father, thank You for always hearing my prayers.
Help me to trust You, even when You seem distant. Amen.*

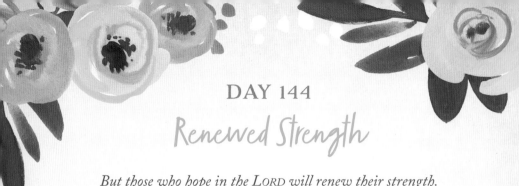

DAY 144
Renewed Strength

But those who hope in the LORD will renew their strength.
They will soar on wings like eagles; they will run and
not grow weary, they will walk and not be faint.
ISAIAH 40:31 NIV

Several times throughout scripture, the Lord had the writers use the eagle as a comparison to His people. Moses, speaking to the children of Israel just before his death, draws a beautiful picture of the eagle caring for her young. He then compares it to the Lord's leading in our lives. "He found him in a desert land and in the wasteland, a howling wilderness; He encircled him, He instructed him, He kept him as the apple of His eye. As an eagle stirs up its nest, hovers over its young, spreading out its wings, taking them up, carrying them on its wings, so the LORD alone led him, and there was no foreign god with him" (Deuteronomy 32:10–12 NKJV).

Isaiah carries that metaphor a bit further in Isaiah 40. Women seem to be most involved in nurturing their children, and as a result we tire easily. Starting in verse 27 in the Isaiah passage, Isaiah wonders how God's people can say that God is too busy or tired to care for His people. Instead he turns it around and says that even young men and children get tired. Only those who hope in the Lord will He carry on His wings, renewing their strength.

Father, thank You for these comparisons that show Your
loving heart in caring for Your children. I praise You for
enabling us to do the work You have called us to do.

DAY 145

Love's Current

The grace of our Lord was poured out on me abundantly,
along with the faith and love that are in Christ Jesus.
1 TIMOTHY 1:14 NIV

Giving a gift to a loved one often gives us great pleasure. We shop in anticipation of the recipient's excitement in our purchases. When we love that person, our joy can be even greater. So it is with God's love for us. He gave us His Son: a pure and perfect gift because He loves us in vast measure.

No matter what our attitude may be toward God, we can never forget His precious gift of Jesus Christ. Even if we reflect despair or anger, He loves us. Scripture states grace and love is given abundantly, which means bountifully, plenteously, generously. How can we miss God's love when He is so gracious?

The famous theologian Charles Spurgeon put it this way: "Our God never ceases to shine upon his children with beams of love. Like a river, his lovingkindness is always flowing, with a fullness inexhaustible as his own nature."

This day, rise with the expectation of God's great grace and love. Let your life reflect that love and feel His pleasure. Plunge into the river of His love and feel Him carry you on its current. Relax in His arms in the knowledge that He cares for you.

Lord, carry me along in the current of Your
love's stream. I love You extravagantly. Amen.

DAY 146
Most Satisfied

"Who has known the mind of the LORD? Or who has become His counselor?" "Or who has first given to Him and it shall be repaid to him?" For of Him and through Him and to Him are all things.
ROMANS 11:34–36 NKJV

We know that no one has lent God anything, nor has anyone given God advice. We were made in His image, but He is nothing like us and we are nothing like Him.

Everything, from the bright spring breeze to a newborn's laugh, was created by Him. God does not depend on anyone or anything. He is completely self-sufficient. It is because He doesn't rely on anyone that He can love perfectly. How often do we seek man's acceptance over God's acceptance? If we are honest with ourselves, we do this daily. How often are our motives tainted with manipulation because we want to please or be pleased?

God is impervious to manipulation; it is not in His character. He will never tweak His ways to get us to like or accept Him. His complete independency means we can trust His love. He withholds things for our good; He grants things for our good. But don't miss the pinnacle part of Paul's message, "to whom be glory forever." Everything you do as a child of God is for His glory, and everything God does is for His glory. We are most satisfied when God is most glorified.

Thank You for withholding and giving me things that are only for Your glory and my good. Help me to find peace in the trying times and know that You are faithful, even in the midst of the storm. Amen.

DAY 147

To Know Him Is to Trust Him

Those who know your name trust in you, for you,
O Lord, do not abandon those who search for you.
PSALM 9:10 NLT

Names often reveal the character of a person. This is true in biblical times, especially when it comes to the names of God. A study of His names often brings a deeper awareness of God and who He is. Isaiah, in predicting the birth of Christ, listed several of His names: "For a child is born to us, a son is given to us. The government will rest on his shoulders. And he will be called: Wonderful Counselor, Mighty God, Everlasting Father, Prince of Peace" (9:6 NLT).

In other places He is referred to as Lord Jehovah, Almighty God, Shepherd, Priest, King of kings, and Lord of lords. He is the God who Sees, the Righteous One, Master, Redeemer, the All-Sufficient One. Each name describes a little different attribute or includes the many sides of His character. All are perfectly true about Him.

A study of the names of God, Jesus, and the Holy Spirit not only gives us a deeper insight into the nuances of who He is, but it also strengthens our ability to trust Him implicitly with every detail of our lives. He has promised to reveal Himself to those who truly seek Him out, who truly desire to "know Him and the power of His resurrection and the fellowship of His sufferings, being conformed to His death" (Philippians 3:10 NASB).

Father, reveal Yourself to me through Your names, so I will trust You more.

DAY 148

Get Up and Try Again

But may the God of all grace, who called us to His
eternal glory by Christ Jesus, after you have suffered
a while, perfect, establish, strengthen, and settle you.
1 PETER 5:10 NKJV

Have you ever fallen down in your Christian walk? It doesn't mean you are no longer a Christian, but you stumbled over something in your path that caused you to lose your footing. Perhaps you didn't see the obstacle in time. It's painful to fall, and sometimes it's hard to get up and continue on. While you're lying on the ground spiritually, Satan uses this opportunity to taunt you and accuse you. "You're not really a Christian. If you were, you wouldn't have fallen. You wouldn't have made a mistake. God doesn't need people like you. He's tired of fooling with you. Why don't you just give up?"

Sound familiar? Not only does it sound familiar, but if you're not careful, you will begin to believe it. The shame and remorse you feel because of your shortcoming only add to the lie Satan has just whispered in your ear. Don't listen to any more of his lies. God is a God of grace. The key is to stand up from the place where you have fallen and allow God to restore you, strengthen you, and establish you. He is faithful to His people.

Lord, forgive my shortcomings and extend grace once more
to Your servant. Give me strength to continue the race.

DAY 149

Second Chances

"I, even I, am he who blots out your transgressions,
for my own sake, and remembers your sins no more."
ISAIAH 43:25 NIV

How many of us have hung our heads low, knowing we really messed up? Wishing we could redo that work assignment, take back the unkind words that leaped from our mouths without thinking, or even pull back that email message right after we clicked SEND. We've all done something we wished we could undo. Often, we think we have failed not only ourselves but also God.

In fact, the Bible is full of people that God used despite their errors. Moses had an anger problem. David was lustful. Jacob was deceptive. The wonderful thing about our faith is that we serve a God of second chances. Not only is He willing, He wants us to confess our sins so He can forgive us. Sing praises for the wonderful blessing of starting over!

Gracious and heavenly Father, we are grateful that we serve a God of second chances. In fact, You give us more than two chances, and You don't keep score. We are all prodigals, and we need to feel Your love and forgiveness. Thank You for loving me enough to not give up on me. You are still with me! Amen.

DAY 150
Staying Close

"Be strong and courageous. Do not be afraid; do not be discouraged,
*for the L*ORD *your God will be with you wherever you go."*
JOSHUA 1:9 NIV

It's easy to tell others not to worry. It's easy to remind our friends that God is with them and He's got everything under control. And it's easy to remind ourselves of that, when everything's going smoothly.

But when life sails us into rough waters, our natural instinct is to be afraid. We worry and fret. We cry out, not knowing how we will pay the bills or how we will face the cancer or how we will deal with whatever stormy waves crash around us. When life is scary, we get scared.

And believe it or not, that's a good thing. Because when we are afraid, when we are overwhelmed, when we realize that our circumstances are bigger than we are, that's when we're in the perfect place for God to pour out His comfort and assurance on us.

He never leaves us, but sometimes when life is good, we get distracted by other things and don't enjoy His presence as we should. When we feel afraid, we are drawn back to our heavenly Father's arms. And right in His arms is exactly where He wants us to be.

Dear Father, thank You for staying with me and giving me
courage. Help me to stay close to You, in good times and bad. Amen.

DAY 151

Tempted without Sin

*Then Jesus was led up by the Spirit into the
wilderness to be tempted by the devil.*
MATTHEW 4:1 NKJV

Christ, being fully God and fully man, could (1) as a man be tempted
and (2) as God resist all temptation. But Christ didn't merely refuse to
act on Satan's terms and lures; He had no inward desire or inclination to
sin, since these in themselves are sin (see Matthew 5:22, 28). We follow
a Shepherd who went His entire life without sin. Just because He was
fully God does not mean He did not struggle with hunger, pain, or
sorrow. We serve a Lord who entered into our humanity and can empa-
thize with us. When we wish to discuss a certain matter—health issues,
parenting, relocating our lives—we don't seek sympathy; we wish to hear
wisdom and encouragement from someone who has been there. We seek
empathy. Our Savior has tread this earth, defeated death and sin. We don't
serve an oblivious lord. Our Lord knows the intricacies of our hearts.

*Lord, thank You for knowing temptation and not succumbing. Thank You
that You know what is occurring; not only do You know, but You have
planned this time. Help me to trust in Your promises and great name. Amen.*

DAY 152

The Comparison Trap

But let each one examine his own work, and then he will have rejoicing in himself alone, and not in another. For each one shall bear his own load.
GALATIANS 6:4–5 NKJV

In John 21, the apostle John records a conversation Jesus had with Peter shortly after His resurrection. Jesus prepared a breakfast for His disciples after a night of fishing. Then Jesus invited Peter to go for a walk. Just days before, Peter had denied knowing Jesus. Now, three times Jesus asked Peter if the fisherman-turned-disciple loved Him. By asking this question, Jesus not only let Peter know that he was forgiven for his lapse of faith, but also He let Peter know that God still had a purpose and plan for Peter. He also spoke of how Peter would eventually die for His Gospel.

Peter, maybe a little embarrassed by all the attention he was getting, looked over his shoulder and saw John following them. Peter asked the Lord, "What about him? How will he die?" Peter fell into the comparison trap.

Jesus answered, "What does it matter to you what I have planned for another? Live your life according to My plan. That's all you need to be concerned about."

And that's all Jesus still requires of His followers. God has a unique plan and purpose for each one, equipping them as they keep their eyes on Him and follow Him daily.

Father, show me Your plan for today and help me not to compare my path with others. Amen.

DAY 153
Get Above It All

*Set your mind and keep focused habitually on the things
above [the heavenly things], not on things that are
on the earth [which have only temporal value].*
COLOSSIANS 3:2 AMP

If you've ever taken a trip by airplane, you know with one glimpse from the window at thirty thousand feet how the world seems small. With your feet on the ground, you may feel small in a big world; and it's easy for the challenges of life and the circumstances from day to day to press in on you. But looking down from above the clouds, things can become clear as you have the opportunity to get above it all.

Sometimes the most difficult challenges you face play out in your head—where a struggle to control the outcome and work out the details of life can consume you. Once removed—far away from the details—you can see things from a higher perspective. Close your eyes and push out the thoughts that try to grab you and keep you tied to the things of the world.

Reach out to God and let your spirit soar. Give your concerns to Him and let Him work out the details. Rest in Him and He'll carry you above it all, every step of the way.

*God, You are far above any detail of life that concerns me. Help me
to trust You today for answers to those things that seem to bring me
down. I purposefully set my heart and mind on You today. Amen.*

DAY 154
The Spirit of Truth

"If you love me, keep my commands. And I will ask the Father, and he will give you another advocate to help you and be with you forever—the Spirit of truth. The world cannot accept him, because it neither sees him nor knows him. But you know him, for he lives with you and will be in you."
JOHN 14:15–17 NIV

Turn the other cheek. Love your enemies. Do good to those who hurt you. Give generously, Don't be anxious. Store up treasures in heaven. In the Sermon on the Mount (Matthew 5–6), Jesus presents a perspective on living that must have confused many of His listeners.

For those who don't know or recognize the Holy Spirit, Jesus' teachings don't make any sense. They are countercultural and go against the grain of natural instinct. When Christians are able to forgive those who have hurt them, give generously, or refuse to follow the latest trends and fashions, the world gets confused. To those who don't have the Holy Spirit, these seemingly extraordinary actions must seem unreal, impossible even. Knowing the Holy Spirit makes all the difference. When the Holy Spirit lives in us, we can finally see truth. We have the advocacy and the help we need to follow Jesus' commands—and they make all the sense in the world.

Jesus, thank You for the gift of the Holy Spirit. My life would be so meaningless and confusing without this precious Comforter, Advocate, and Friend. Help me to follow Your commands and shine Your light to a watching world. Amen.

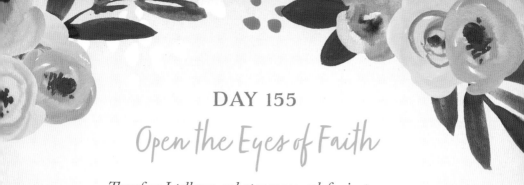

DAY 155

Open the Eyes of Faith

Therefore I tell you, whatever you ask for in prayer,
believe that you have received it, and it will be yours.

MARK 11:24 NIV

At the conclusion of World War II and the end of the Holocaust, these words were found scratched on the wall of an abandoned farmhouse: "I believe in the sun even when it does not shine. I believe in love, even when it is not shown. I believe in God, even when He is silent." Sketched alongside the time-worn prose was the Star of David.

Have you ever prayed for something or someone, and God seemed to turn a deaf ear? One woman prayed for her son's salvation for seven years. Each day she knelt at the foot of her tear-stained bed, pleading for her child. But God seemed silent. Yet, what she failed to understand was that the Lord had been working all along to reach her son in ways unknown to her. And finally her son embraced the Gospel through a series of life-changing circumstances.

The world says, "I'll believe it when I see it," while God's Word promises, "Believe then see."

Someone once said, "The way to see by faith is to shut the eye of reason." When we pray, rather than ask God why our prayers remain unanswered, perhaps we should ask the Lord to close our eyes so that we might see.

Lord, I believe, even when my prayers go unanswered.
Instead, I know You are at work on my behalf. Amen.

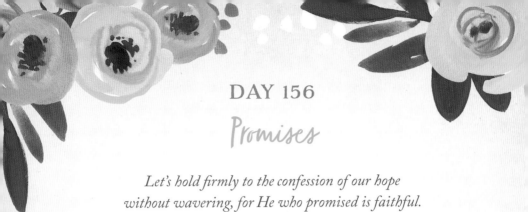

DAY 156

Promises

*Let's hold firmly to the confession of our hope
without wavering, for He who promised is faithful.*
HEBREWS 10:23 NASB

In this life, you can have endurance and hope because your God is faithful to keep His promises. The Christian life would be hopeless if God were not faithful and trustworthy. But He will absolutely keep His promises. You can (and do) bet your life on that.

God has promised to complete and perfect the good work He has started in you (Philippians 1:6). He will never leave you or forsake you (Hebrews 13:5). He has promised that He will wipe away every tear from your eyes and that in heaven there will no longer be any mourning or crying or pain (Revelation 21:4). He will never allow you to be separated from His love (Romans 8:38–39). He promises that He will come again and that you will be with Him forever (1 Thessalonians 4:16–17). He assures you that no one can take you from His hand (John 10:29).

These are just some of the promises God has made. These aren't just nice sentiments. These are things that God will, without question, bring to pass. He does not break His promises—He will do what He has said He will do. You can put your hope in these promises, knowing that you won't be disappointed.

*Lord, in a world where promises are so often broken, thank You
that I can trust that You will keep Yours. What beautiful promises
You have made. I put my hope firmly in their fulfillment.*

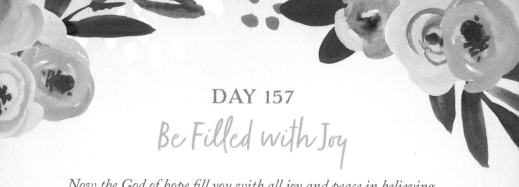

DAY 157
Be Filled with Joy

Now the God of hope fill you with all joy and peace in believing,
that ye may abound in hope, through the power of the Holy Ghost.
ROMANS 15:13 KJV

Are you fighting a battle that seems futile? Have you lost hope of seeing a resolution? Take heart, you're not alone. Paul, the writer of today's verse, knew about battles, persecution, and rejection. He spent a lot of time writing his messages of hope while in jail. You may not be in a physical jail, but Satan may have you bound in a spiritual prison. It's time to break out of jail and be the victorious Christian you want to be. "How can I do that?" you ask. Look at what Paul wrote:

1. We serve a God of hope. Trust Him to supply you with hope to make it during dark days.

2. God is your source. Rely on Him to fill you with joy and give you peace in the time of trouble.

3. Believe that God is who He says He is, that He has made a way for you through His Son, Jesus.

4. Allow the Holy Ghost to empower you to abound in hope. We are often powerless to conquer our problems, but God's Spirit can arise within us to make us overcomers.

Push the darkness away. God is on your side. Allow Him to work for you.

Father, empower me by Your Spirit to abound in hope as You
fill me with Your joy and peace through the Holy Ghost. Amen.

DAY 158
Expect the Unexpected

*Then, leaving her water jar, the woman went back to the
town and said to the people, "Come, see a man who told
me everything I ever did. Could this be the Messiah?"*
JOHN 4:28–29 NIV

In this story of the woman at the well, Jesus did the unthinkable by talking to a woman, which was not something men did in that time if they were not related to the woman. And He wasn't talking to just any woman but to a woman of ill repute—a fact the woman herself pointed out.

When she took up her jar to get water at the town well, timed to avoid the respectable women who drew water earlier, she had no idea how one conversation would change her life. It is easy to get comfortable in our routines and not look for the unexpected in our walk with Jesus. Like the woman at the well, we come to Him for one thing and get so much more.

Just as Jesus told the woman to leave her past behind and move forward, He wants us to move into the future He has for us, to move beyond just asking for one thing, and to change our thinking into serving Him and telling others about Him.

*Lord Jesus, open our eyes to see Your hand working in unexpected
ways. Give us courage to step out into the plans You have for us,
to see how You would have us serve, and to tell others about
the amazing things You have done for us. Amen.*

DAY 159

The Gift of Prayer

First of all, then, I urge that requests, prayers, intercession, and thanksgiving be made in behalf of all people…This is good and acceptable in the sight of God our Savior.
1 TIMOTHY 2:1, 3 NASB

There is such joy in giving gifts. Seeing the delight on someone's face to receive something unexpected is exciting. Perhaps the absolute greatest gift one person can give to another doesn't come in a box. It can't be wrapped or presented formally, but instead it is the words spoken to God for someone—the gift of prayer.

When we pray for others, we ask God to intervene and to make Himself known to them. We can pray for God's plan and purpose in their lives. We can ask God to bless them or protect them. You can share with them that you are praying for them or do it privately without their knowledge. Who would God have you give the gift of prayer to today?

Lord, thank You for bringing people to my heart and mind who need prayer. Help me to pray the things that they need from You in their lives. Show me how to give the gift of prayer to those You would have me pray for. Amen.

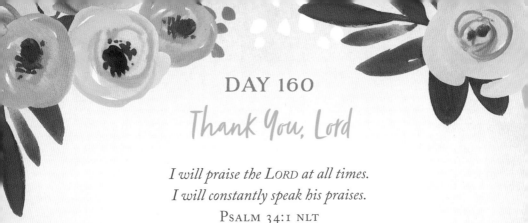

DAY 160

Thank You, Lord

I will praise the LORD at all times.
I will constantly speak his praises.
PSALM 34:1 NLT

While imprisoned, the apostle Paul gave thanks to God, even singing His praises, and it resulted in the salvation of the jailers. What a great lesson for every Christian—when you feel least like giving thanks, that's precisely when you should!

What is your response when you find yourself trapped in traffic, late for a meeting, frustrated in your plans, sick in bed, hurting emotionally, overwhelmed with work, lonely, tired, or confused? Our human nature teaches us we should gripe and fret. Yet scripture says we should give thanks. Only when we surrender our lives to Him and His control is this possible.

Learn to thank Him. Thank Him for being your help in times of trouble. Thank Him for His great wisdom and power. And thank Him for causing every situation in your life to work together for your good.

Giving thanks may not change your circumstances significantly, but it will change you. You'll feel yourself focusing on God—His goodness, kindness, and grace—rather than your own anger, pride, sickness, or inconvenience. Maybe that's why it's such fertile soil for miracles. The biblical commentator Matthew Henry stated it well: "Thanksgiving is good, but thanks-living is better."

Lord, I choose to give You thanks today for whatever comes my way.
I love You, Lord, and I am grateful for Your goodness. Amen.

DAY 161
Love Leads the Way

*You yourselves have seen what I did to the Egyptians, and how I
carried you on eagles' wings and brought you to Myself.*
EXODUS 19:4 NASB

When Moses led the children of Israel out of Egypt toward the Promised
Land, he did not take them on the shortest route. God directed him to
go the long way lest the people turn back quickly when things became
difficult. God led them by day with a pillar of clouds and by night with
a pillar of fire. How clearly He showed Himself. The people placed their
hope in an almighty God and followed His lead. When they thirsted, God
gave water. When they hungered, He sent manna. No need was unmet.

The amount of food and water required for the group is unimaginable.
Moses depended upon God. He believed God would care for them. Because
he knew of God's great love and trusted in the Creator.

If God can do this for so many, do you not think He will care for
you? He knows your needs before you even ask. Place your hope and trust
in Him. He is able. He's proven himself over and over. By reading the
scriptures and praying to the One who loves you, you can feel His care is
infinite. His word is final. God loves you.

*Lord, help me see You gave Your life for me.
Teach me to trust in You. Amen.*

DAY 162

Forgiveness

*But Esau ran to meet Jacob and embraced him; he threw his
arms around his neck and kissed him. And they wept.*
GENESIS 33:4 NIV

Jacob cheated Esau out of his birthright and the father's blessing reserved for the eldest son. Jacob's act changed both their lives forever. Esau hated Jacob for his deception and betrayal. His anger ran so deep that he planned to kill Jacob, and would have had Jacob not fled for his life. Jacob stayed away for twenty years and then started for home even though he feared Esau. What a surprise when Esau ran to meet him and threw his arms around Jacob. He had forgiven Jacob even though his betrayal had been a cruel one.

Forgiveness isn't always easy. Sometimes the hurt is deep and the pain lingers for a long time. The other person seems to get on with her life while you suffer. Esau could have hung on to his anger and killed Jacob when he saw him coming. Instead, he took the first step and ran to meet Jacob, forgiving him. We too can take the first step toward forgiveness. In doing so, we let go of the pain we've been carrying. We find freedom for ourselves and offer the same to the one who hurt us. Is there someone you need to forgive today? Take the first step toward reconciliation. God will give you the strength to go the full distance.

*Lord, give me courage to take the first step toward
forgiveness even if it's the other person's fault. Amen.*

DAY 163

Draw Near with Confidence

Therefore let's approach the throne of grace with confidence, so that
we may receive mercy and find grace for help at the time of our need.
HEBREWS 4:16 NASB

In this verse you are told that you can approach God's throne with confidence. Why do you approach the throne? So that you can receive mercy and find grace to help in time of need. Why would you need to receive mercy? Those who need mercy are those who have done something wrong, those who are not in right standing with whomever they are asking mercy from. Inevitably you come before the throne of God with the baggage of your sin. And yet you are told to come with confidence before the throne of a holy God who hates sin. You don't need to be perfect or have your act together to come before God with confidence. You only need to be covered in Christ's blood. This confidence with which you approach God's throne is not a self-confidence, but a God-confidence. It's a confidence that assures you that God is for you, that He loves you, and that He sees Christ in you. Your standing before God depends completely on His view of you and not on your own merit. And He sees you as His beloved child. So go boldly to the foot of His throne, knowing that you will receive mercy and grace.

Lord, thank You that I don't need to be perfect before I
can come before You. I come before You now with my
confidence placed in You, not in my own merit.

DAY 164

G.R.A.C.E.

And of His fullness we have all received, and grace for grace.
JOHN 1:16 NKJV

Perhaps you've seen the acronym for G.R.A.C.E. (God's Riches at Christ's Expense). What does that mean to us, His daughters? We face all sorts of challenges and sometimes feel depleted. Dry. In those moments, all of God's riches (peace, joy, longsuffering, favor, help) are ours. What did we do to deserve them? Nothing. That's the point of grace: someone else paid the price so that we could receive God's gifts for free.

Take a good look at today's scripture. God promises to give not only grace and truth, but one gift after another. Picture yourself as a little girl at your daddy's knee. Now picture him giving you not one gift. . .not two . . .but one on top of the other, on top of the other. He overwhelms you with his beautifully wrapped gifts, topped off with ribbons and bows. Talk about knocking your socks off!

God does the same thing when He "gifts" us with things we don't deserve: forgiveness, comfort, satisfaction, provision. What a generous God we serve!

Father, I know that I haven't done anything to deserve Your grace. . .Your gifts. And yet, You continue to pour these things out on my life anyway. Thank You for Your grace, Lord. You give, and give, and then give some more.

DAY 165
A Touch of Faith

Jesus, turning and seeing her, said, "Daughter, take courage; your
faith has made you well." And at once the woman was made well.
MATTHEW 9:22 NASB

There once was a woman who'd been hemorrhaging for twelve years. She sought help from a myriad of physicians and spent all that she had, but her issue of blood was worse than ever before. Then one day she heard a healer named Jesus was coming to town. Although she was considered the lowest of the low, someone who shouldn't even be out in public, she decided to make her way through the crowd and reach out to this Man. Risking all she had left, she came up behind Him and touched His garment, for she kept saying to herself, "If I can just touch his robe, I will be healed" (Mark 5:28 NLT). Instantly her bleeding stopped. But the story doesn't end there. Jesus immediately felt power flowing out of Him and demanded, "Who touched me?" (Mark 5:31 NLT). Shaking with fear, the woman confessed it had been her. Jesus responded with tenderness and encouragement, "Daughter, your faith has made you well. Go in peace. Your suffering is over" (Mark 5:34 NLT).

What issue have you needed Jesus' help with? What desperately bold exchange between your soul and Jesus have you kept secret? What story can you share with others to remind them of His power and tenderness, to give them a touch of faith?

Give me the courage, Jesus, to not just come to You with all my
issues but to share my story with others, to touch them with
my faith in You and Your faithfulness to me. Amen.

DAY 166

Grace Accepted

But because of his great love for us, God, who is rich in mercy,
made us alive with Christ even when we were dead in
transgressions—it is by grace you have been saved.
EPHESIANS 2:4–5 NIV

Have you ever been wrongly accused of something or completely misunderstood? Have the words of your accusers struck your heart, making you feel like you have to make it right somehow, but no amount of reasoning with them seems to help?

If anyone understands this situation it's Christ Himself. Wrongly accused. Misunderstood. Yet He offered unfathomable grace at all times and still offers it today.

This reminds us that we are to aim to offer this same grace to our accusers and those who misunderstand us. We will be misunderstood when we try to obey and follow God in a culture that runs quite contrary in many ways. Our job is to first accept God's grace and then offer it up to others as lovingly as we can. Like Christ.

God, help us to continually accept Your grace through Christ
and reflect You by offering that same grace to others. Amen.

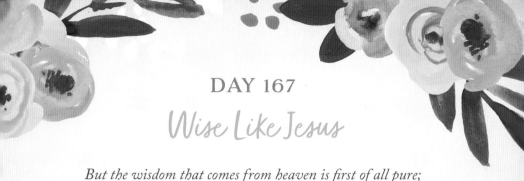

DAY 167
Wise Like Jesus

*But the wisdom that comes from heaven is first of all pure;
then peace-loving, considerate, submissive, full of
mercy and good fruit, impartial and sincere.*
JAMES 3:17 NIV

Who has wisdom? Look at the fruit of her life. From this verse, we know a wise woman chooses to pursue peace in her community—she forgives someone who hurt her instead of writing him off. She is considerate; she sees others with God's eyes—worthy of her love because they are loved by their Creator, no matter what they have done or left undone. She submits her hurts to her Father, learning from Him how to show mercy as He does. Sincerity blossoms throughout her words and deeds.

If this description of a wise woman leaves you thinking *That's not me!*, don't worry, you certainly aren't alone. Wisdom is a gift from God, born from a desire to follow His Word out of love for Him. Our own efforts can only conjure up an imperfect wisdom and love for others because our natural state is selfish. Humanity lost its capacity to love purely when Adam and Eve disobeyed God in the Garden.

Thankfully, Jesus changes our hearts when we trust in Him so we can be wise as He is wise. With the Holy Spirit's help, we can grow more like Jesus each day. May His wisdom and love deepen in us and spill over to others!

Father God, thank You for Your promise of wisdom. Grant me a deeper knowledge of Your Son so that I may grow wise in Your ways. Amen.

DAY 168

Encouragement during Difficult Assignments

Then they answered Joshua, "Whatever you have commanded us we will do, and wherever you send us we will go. Just as we fully obeyed Moses, so we will obey you. Only may the LORD your God be with you as he was with Moses. Whoever rebels against your word and does not obey it, whatever you may command them, will be put to death. Only be strong and courageous!"

JOSHUA 1:16–18 NIV

God gives us difficult assignments just as He did with Joshua. We *know* God will bless us if we're faithful, but we don't always *feel* it. Often the job seems bigger than our capabilities, and we get discouraged. But God wants us to *know* and *feel* He is responsible for the outcome. We just need to be faithful to act.

As with Joshua, God brings people into our lives to encourage us. The men in today's verses encourage Joshua in four ways: they assure him of their allegiance and willingness to help, they pray for him, they take their own responsibilities seriously, and they offer Joshua words of encouragement he has heard before.

Our assignment is for our benefit and to benefit those around us. While we need to be obedient to do the next right step, we also need to encourage others around us. How can you use one of those four ways to encourage someone else?

Heavenly Father, thank You for loving us enough to include us in Your work. Bring people into our lives to encourage us on the journey, and open our eyes to see others who need encouragement. Amen.

DAY 169
The Reward of Faith

"So on that day Moses swore to me, 'The land on which your feet have walked will be your inheritance and that of your children forever, because you have followed the LORD my God wholeheartedly.'"
JOSHUA 14:9 NIV

If we look back on the story of Caleb in Numbers 13 and 14, we see that his heart overflowed with confidence in God. If God said Israel was supposed to get the land, then it didn't matter who was living there; the Israelites would defeat them. Caleb believed that God would do what He said He would do. He was enthusiastically optimistic.

The Anakites, the giants Caleb and Joshua originally spied over forty years earlier, still controlled the land Caleb was to inherit. And he was eighty-five years old. But he was not ready for retirement. He had followed God wholeheartedly, the key to his effectiveness. He was filled with the presence and the power of God. He had pursued God, like a hunter closing the gap on his prey. Caleb still welcomed a challenge. Caleb believed God still had work for him to do and would give him the strength to remove the giants from his land.

Ultimately, this is God's story, not Caleb's. Caleb just applied the principle of sowing and reaping, and God showed up like He said He would. Like Caleb, we can rely on God's strength and power to work through us even if we have physical and mental limitations.

Heavenly Father, thank You for always showing up, bigger and better than we expect. Show us where we need to trust You. Amen.

DAY 170
A Day Like That

When you were dead in your sins and in the uncircumcision of your flesh,
God made you alive with Christ. He forgave us all our sins, having
canceled the charge of our legal indebtedness, which stood against us
and condemned us; he has taken it away, nailing it to the cross.
COLOSSIANS 2:13–14 NIV

Have you ever had a day that felt doomed for dismal right out of the gate? No, forget the gate; you didn't make it that far. It was right out of the warm blankets that you didn't want to leave.

The demands of the day were firmly in place, and they beckoned you out into a much colder space, sometimes quite literally. You took no time to pause with God. "Took time?" you say. There was no time. Your attitude suffered miserably in the trenches of your duties. Yes, now you are in the trenches.

There (in the trenches), other people are quite miserable as well, and you all say and do miserable things. You offend people. They offend you. You forgot for a while what God did for you—redeeming you on the cross.

Now you come to God asking again for His forgiveness, and you forgive the other people from that miserable day.

Have you ever had a day like that?

Lord, thank You for placing our sins on the cross and
redeeming us. Thank You for Your forgiveness and love. Amen.

DAY 171
Music to His Ears

Speaking to one another with psalms, hymns, and songs from the Spirit. Sing and make music from your heart to the Lord.
EPHESIANS 5:19 NIV

One of the most powerful moments in the Christian life may turn out to be at a supper table with fellow believers or conversations around a fire. Uplifting and encouraging one another can also happen when we sing. Today many churches resound with praise music which fills the congregation with enthusiasm. These songs should not be directed to those around us but in our hearts to the Lord. Spiritual fullness comes to expression in joyful fellowship, in song and thanksgiving.

King David crawled in caves and crevasses hiding from his enemies, yet he found time to pen many praise songs to the King of kings. Despite his circumstances, he knew God was in control. Paul sang in the dank darkness of a dungeon cell, praising his Creator even though life looked bleak. God's grace was extended to these men as they praised in their suffering.

How much more should we make a melody to the Lord when we are free to move about, to worship, to sing. God wants to hear music from our hearts, not arias with perfect notes. So we will lift up our voices and join in the praise to our Creator and Lord. Harmonious, harsh, or hoarse, He's filtering our melodies with His love.

Dear heavenly Father, I worship You. I adore You.
Thank You for Your goodness and mercy. Amen.

DAY 172

Love and Assurance

Little children, let's not love with word or with tongue, but in deed and truth. We will know by this that we are of the truth, and will set our heart at ease before Him, that if our heart condemns us, that God is greater than our heart, and He knows all things.

1 JOHN 3:18–20 NASB

These verses start out with an admonition—you ought to show your love in what you do. Love is not well expressed by superficial, noncommittal statements. Rather, a true, earnest love will drive you to action. Think about those around you to whom you can express love, not just by telling them, but by showing your love to them in your deeds. Don't allow laziness or excuses to keep you from reaching out to those who need love.

These verses end with a wonderful assurance for those of us who struggle with guilt and fear. When you are in Christ, be encouraged that nothing can take away your salvation. Your heart may condemn you when you fall into the same pattern of sin again or when you fail to do what you promised yourself and God you would do. But be encouraged—you are not in charge of your standing before God. God is. He is greater than any guilt-ridden and self-abasing heart. Once you are one of His children, you will always have that status. He knows all things, including the fact that your name is written, irrevocably, in the book of life.

Lord, help me to show love not only in what I say, but even more so in what I do. Thank You that You are greater than the fears of my heart.

DAY 173

Perfect Love

And there were shepherds living out in the fields nearby, keeping watch over their flocks at night. An angel of the Lord appeared to them, and the glory of the Lord shone around them, and they were terrified. But the angel said to them, "Do not be afraid. I bring you good news that will cause great joy for all the people. Today in the town of David a Savior has been born to you; he is the Messiah, the Lord. This will be a sign to you: You will find a baby wrapped in cloths and lying in a manger."
LUKE 2:8–12 NIV

The holidays can be a time when fear creeps up on us unexpectedly. We can fear for our country, fear the family conflicts that may surface over holiday dinners, fear the state of our finances and relationships. . .the fear list can be long.

What the angel said to the shepherds applies to us now and always. "Do not be afraid. I bring you good news that will cause great joy for all the people." Today, let your focus be on that joyful news. Jesus' birth gives us hope. We don't have to fear.

1 John 4:18 tells us that perfect love casts out fear. Perfect love was born on Christmas Day. Let that perfect love fill your heart with joy, hope, and peace. Then there will be no room in your heart for fear.

Dear Jesus, fill my heart with Your unfailing love for now and always. Thank You that I never have to be afraid. Amen.

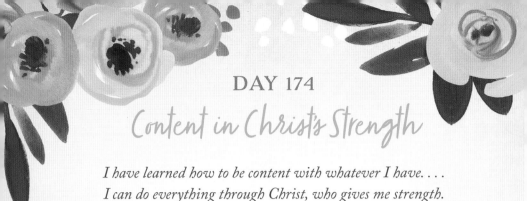

DAY 174
Content in Christ's Strength

I have learned how to be content with whatever I have. . . .
I can do everything through Christ, who gives me strength.
PHILIPPIANS 4:11, 13 NLT

Sometimes Paul seems like a giant of a man, way above everyone else on the spiritual scale. Granted, it is a manmade scale, certainly not one God uses.

Paul wrote his letter to the Philippian church from a prison in Rome. Prisons in the ancient world were nothing compared with those in our country today. In chapter one, we learn that Paul was guarded day and night by the emperor's own elite guards—the praetorians. Because Paul never backed down from sharing the Gospel with whoever crossed his path, many among the guards believed in Christ and then carried the Gospel into Nero's palace. Because of this unique opportunity to spread the Gospel, Paul rejoiced.

In the latter part of the letter he declared that the gift the Philippians sent him was welcomed with rejoicing. But even without it he could rejoice because he had learned to be content in whatever situation and condition he found himself. So how was Paul able to do this when so many of God's people today never learn his secret? Before Paul ended the paragraph, he told us: "I can do everything through Christ who gives me strength." Paul couldn't generate contentment in all situations, but Christ in him could. The same "secret" enables God's people to do the same nearly two thousand years later.

Father, thank You for enabling us to live
joyful, contented lives through Jesus Christ.

DAY 175

God's Love

*For I am convinced that neither death, nor life, nor angels,
nor principalities, nor things present, nor things to come, nor powers,
nor height, nor depth, nor any other created thing, will be able to
separate us from the love of God, which is in Christ Jesus our Lord.*
ROMANS 8:38–39 NASB

In this life we often feel we need to work for love. Love can grow stale or be lost altogether or given to another. The promise of love can be used as a weapon against us. But in this verse, an eternal, genuine love is promised you. This promise can be trusted because the love of God has been secured through the sacrifice and death of Christ. This is no promise made on a whim or as a manipulation but one made in blood by the perfect Lamb.

No natural or supernatural power can separate you from God's love. Nothing that is currently happening in your life will separate you from God's love. No matter how scary or uncertain the future seems, it will not separate you from God's love. No height of success or depth of depression and despair will separate you from God's love. Nothing that this life and those in it can throw at you and nothing that you do will separate you from God's love. Not even death, which separates us from everything else we know, will separate you from God's love.

Therefore, go forward in peace and boldness, knowing that you are eternally secure and eternally loved.

*Lord, I can't comprehend this kind of everlasting love, but I thank
You that I can rest in the promise that You will always love me.*

DAY 176

His Love Never Quits

Oh, give thanks to the LORD, for He is good! For His mercy endures forever. And say, "Save us, O God of our salvation; gather us together, and deliver us from the Gentiles, to give thanks to Your holy name, to triumph in Your praise." Blessed be the LORD God of Israel from everlasting to everlasting!

1 CHRONICLES 16:34–36 NKJV

God's Word tells us in Psalm 139 that we can never escape the presence of God. He is with us always, no matter where we go or what we do. His love never quits on us. First John 4:10 (NIV) says, "This is love: not that we loved God, but that he loved us and sent his Son as an atoning sacrifice for our sins." God doesn't love us because we did a lot of good things for Him. He doesn't love us because of our last names or because of the jobs we do. He can't love us any more or any less than He already does. He loves us simply because He is our Father and our Creator. In fact, He gave up His very life to show you how much.

You may have had a parent, friend, or spouse abandon you at some point in your life. God won't do that. You may feel alone and fearful. God won't leave you. You may feel sad and crushed. God says He is close to the brokenhearted and saves those who are crushed in Spirit (see Psalm 34:18).

God, please remove me from godless places of darkness and loneliness and fear. I trust that You love me and that You will be with me always. Amen.

DAY 177
Like Glue

Surely your goodness and love will follow me all the days of my life.
PSALM 23:6 NIV

Sometimes it's scary to look out into the great unknown. As we stand on the threshold of a new year, we don't know what to expect. Will good things be in store, or do terrible things await?

We don't have the ability to see the future. But we do know one thing for certain. As long as we remain close to our Father, His goodness and love will stay close to us. No matter where we go, no matter where our circumstances may force us, His love and goodness will follow us.

Even when we wander away from His perfect plan for us, He is only a breath away. He promised in Romans 8 that nothing will ever separate us from that love. When life is good, He is there. When life is hard, His love and goodness are right there. Nothing—no sickness or disease, no foul circumstance, no financial difficulty will remove His love from us. It sticks like glue.

The challenge lies in finding His presence in tough situations. Sometimes we may have to look a little closer or search some odd places. But these things will never change: He is there. He loves us. He is good. And He will never leave us.

Dear Father, thank You for sticking with me, no matter what. That knowledge gives me confidence to move into whatever the future holds. Amen.

DAY 178

God's Promises

*"God is not human, that he should lie, not a human being,
that he should change his mind. Does he speak and
then not act? Does he promise and not fulfill?"*

NUMBERS 23:19 NIV

Our opinions of God are often shaped by our experiences with people. When we've been hurt, we see God as hurtful. When people lie to us, we subconsciously think of God as a liar. After all, if humans are created in His image, it only stands to reason that God would be like the people in our lives. Right?

Well, no. Yes, we were created in God's image. But we humans are a fallen, broken race. We're sinful. God is without sin.

Humans lie. God doesn't.

Humans go back on their word. God doesn't.

Humans can be mean and hurtful. God is love, and He only acts in love.

God promised good things to those who love Him, those who live and act according to His will. That doesn't mean others won't hurt us or that we won't experience the effects of living in a sin-infested world. But where there's pain, we have a Healer. Where there's brokenness, we have a Comforter. And where we feel alone, we know we have a Friend.

And one day we'll experience the perfect fulfillment of all His promises without the burdens of this world to weigh us down.

Now that's something to look forward to.

*Dear Father, thank You for Your promises. When I feel
discouraged, help me to remember those promises. Amen.*

DAY 179

Knowing God

Whoever does not love does not know God, because God is love.
1 JOHN 4:8 NIV

At first glance, this is one of those sweet, easy verses. God is love. And we like to think about love. It's soft and cushy, like velvet.

Yet, if we want full access to that great love of God, we must love others the way He loves us.

Ouch.

If love is patient, then we must show patience to others, or we don't really know God. If love is kind, we too must be kind, or we can't claim a close relationship with God. If love always hopes, always protects, always endures. . .we must do all those things for others, or we can't know God intimately.

We can't be jealous of others, for love is never jealous.

We can't be easily angered, or brag, or dishonor others, or gossip, or seek to elevate ourselves above those around us, because none of those things are characteristic of God's kind of love.

If we want to know God intimately, if we want to experience the rewards of His great love for us, we must allow Him to live out that love in our lives. When we do, we experience a closeness with God that brings our spirits to that soft, velvety place that can only be found in His love.

Dear Father, I want to know You. I want to love like You love,
so that others can experience Your great love. Amen.

DAY 180

Fear Not: He Is Peace

*"You will keep him in perfect peace, whose mind
is stayed on You, because he trusts in You."*
ISAIAH 26:3 NKJV

What are you afraid of? Spiders, darkness, cancer, being alone? All the above?

Every human being has fears. Most of us are smarter than to deny that we have any. Bravery has been defined not as a lack of fear but as action in spite of fear. Anyone who has worn a uniform that put her on the front lines of battle whether in the jungle, desert, or city streets understands this principle.

But Jesus promised us more help than simply bluffing our way through the things that frighten us. He gave us the promise of peace. In John 14:27 (KJV), He said, "My peace I give unto you." This heavenly peace keeps our hearts and minds and gives us the strength to do things we never thought we could.

As we leave childhood behind and enter the multifaceted world of adulthood, our fears increase in proportion to our understanding of the world and the things that can go wrong. But the peace that He gives also multiplies to more than fit whatever need we have. And Satan has no fiery dart that can penetrate it.

*Lord, thank You for Your peace. Keep my heart
and mind through Christ Jesus. Amen.*

DAY 181

Boldly We Come

God's free gift leads to our being made right with God,
even though we are guilty of many sins.
ROMANS 5:16 NLT

Why do you think it is that as a general population of people, we often assume that God is out to get us? We tend to jump immediately to the notion that God is angry with us and ready to bring down the hammer. We become afraid to go to church or read the Bible—thinking that as soon as we enter the building or crack the cover, we will drown in waves of guilt and condemnation.

We even become too afraid to pray.

This must be one of the devil's most effective schemes—to convince us to fear talking with God—when talking with God is what will ultimately transform us from the inside out. Indeed, prayer is what we were created for. We were created for a relationship with Him—the entire Bible is the story of our being restored to that relationship.

The next time you are afraid to pray, refuse the fear. Know in confidence that, unlike the devil, you are covered by the blood of the Lamb and can enter freely into His presence. You can enter freely because He chose to open the way to you.

I will enter into Your presence and sit and talk with You.
I can feel You restore my soul, because this is what I
was made for. This is what I've been missing.

DAY 182
He Is More Than Able

*Now all glory to God, who is able, through his mighty power
at work within us, to accomplish infinitely more than we
might ask or think. Glory to him in the church and in Christ
Jesus through all generations forever and ever! Amen.*

EPHESIANS 3:20–21 NLT

Did you ever hear the saying, "The more you know, the more it is you know you don't know"? It's true. Whether it's bees or poetry or chemistry or space, the more we learn about a subject, the more we discover how much more there is to know. But while there is ultimately an end to man's knowledge of earthly things, it's impossible to even begin to grasp how big God is. We don't know even a fraction of His power. Our minds are just not capable of fully comprehending His ability, His character, and His love for us.

When we think of God, we tend to think about His abilities relative to our own. We don't even consider doing great things for Him, because we can't fathom how it could happen. Could you be unknowingly limiting God? Whether or not we recognize it, His mighty power, the Holy Spirit, is at work within us, doing more than we can imagine. Avail yourself of this power—let Him do through you things that you can't even begin to comprehend.

*Father, You are too big for me. I cannot even begin to comprehend
Your majesty. Thank You for the Holy Spirit, working in and
through me, to accomplish Your purposes through Christ and the
church. Help me to cooperate with Your Spirit's work. Amen.*

DAY 183
Pray Without Ceasing

Pray without ceasing. In every thing give thanks:
for this is the will of God in Christ Jesus concerning you.
1 Thessalonians 5:17–18 kjv

Pray without ceasing. Pray continually. Never stop praying. Pray all the time.
Regardless which translation of the Bible you choose, the command is the
same. It seems impossible! How can one pray all the time? Consider this.
You are young and in love. You must go to school and work. You may be
separated by a great distance from your beloved. And yet, every moment
of every day, that person is on your mind. You talk on the phone and text
constantly. His name is always on your lips. So much so that some of your
friends find it annoying! Is your relationship with Jesus like the one described
here? He wants to be the name on your mind when you are daydreaming.
He wants to be the first one you chat with each morning and the last one
you confide in each night. He wants you to be so utterly absorbed in Him
that it begins to annoy some of your friends! Pray without ceasing. Love
Jesus with all your heart. He is crazy about you.

Jesus, thank You that even in my sin, You died for me. May my
walk with You be the most important thing in my life. Amen.

DAY 184
Running the Race

*Wherefore seeing we also are compassed about with so great a cloud
of witnesses, let us lay aside every weight, and the sin which doth
so easily beset us, and let us run with patience the race that is set
before us, looking unto Jesus the author and finisher of our faith.*
HEBREWS 12:1–2 KJV

The Christian life is a race. It must be run with endurance. It requires
training and discipline. It is about putting one foot in front of the other,
sometimes quickly, sometimes slowly, but always, always moving forward.
When a runner stumbles in a 5K or marathon, what does he do? Does he
just sit down right then and there and call it quits? If the race is not run
with perfection, does he just throw in the towel? Of course not! Likewise,
as you are running the race, when you get sidetracked or distracted, when
you fall to temptation or take your eyes off the goal, ask Jesus to get you
back on track. An old hymn puts it like this: "Turn your eyes upon Jesus.
Look full in His wonderful face. And the things of earth will grow strangely
dim, in the light of His glory and grace!" Look to Christ, the author and
finisher of your faith. He will run right alongside you, encouraging you
every step of the way.

*Jesus, help me to keep my focus on You as I journey through this
life. It is not always easy, but You are always with me. Amen.*

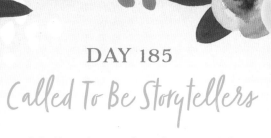

DAY 185
Called To Be Storytellers

*I will sing of the LORD's great love forever; with my mouth I
will make your faithfulness known through all generations.*

PSALM 89:1 NIV

In addition to being prayers and praise songs, some of the psalms also re-tell portions of Israel's history. The Israelites would sing them together to praise the past deeds of their Deliverer (e.g. Psalm 136). Today's worship songs don't list what He's done for us specifically like the Israelites' songs did, but we should definitely follow their example of remembrance.

Christians often use the word *testimony* to name the story of how they accepted Jesus as their Savior. Salvation is a great proof of God's love, but His work doesn't stop there. He daily fills our lives with His provision, nearness, and loving patience. When we recognize what He has done for us, we can be storytellers of His faithfulness, like the psalmist. We gather strength for the challenges ahead when we recall the victories He granted in the past, and our ongoing testimonies of His faithfulness display His love to those who don't know Him personally.

When you feel troubled, tell yourself *your* stories of His faithfulness. When did you feel His comfort when you called on Him for help? When has He provided for your needs beyond expectation? Just as He did then, your unchanging God will never stop caring for you.

*Father, thank You that You've never stopped working in my life.
When I am fearful, help me recall Your goodness and trust You
more. Give me opportunity to tell others what You have done
for me, so that they will come to trust You too! Amen.*

DAY 186
Simple yet Powerful Words

*Humble yourselves, therefore, under God's mighty
hand, that he may lift you up in due time.*
1 PETER 5:6 NIV

How can a person talk and talk and talk and yet when it comes time to speak words that have great importance, they are speechless? Two of those weighty words are "I'm sorry."

Without those words—and the sincerity of spirit backing them up—marriages fail, friendships break apart, family members suffer, working relationships become strained, and the church loses its ability to minister to people.

So why do we become tongue-tied on those simple words? Because it is easy to justify our position on any matter. Easy to take our own side in an argument. You name it, and we can find a way to point to someone else as the villain in any given circumstance. We must be the heroes, after all. We know our Bibles. We sit in the same pew every Sunday. We can spot sin in someone else's life faster than you can say, "Judgment Day!" But the truth is, sometimes even as Christians, we choose to play the villain in our life story. We forget kindness. We turn our head on justice. We forget the most important scriptures on love.

We need to take a deep look in the mirror, spiritually speaking, asking the Lord to show us if we are at fault and to give us the courage to make things right with others—to say the simple yet powerful words that can change a heart, a life.

Lord, please give me a humble heart so that I may always please You. Amen.

DAY 187

Be of Good Cheer

But the LORD said to Samuel, "Do not consider his appearance or his height,
for I have rejected him. The LORD does not look at the things people look at.
People look at the outward appearance, but the LORD looks at the heart."
1 SAMUEL 16:7 NIV

Many are waiting to hear from others that they are valuable. They go from group to group until they settle on the highest bidder. No matter how badly this group mistreats them they think, *This is what I am worth.* But that's not truth. Only God knows your potential. Only God knows the hidden talents He has placed within you. Only God knows His plan for you. Only God knows your heart. Other people will always sell you short!

God told the prophet Samuel to pick out the new king of Israel, for God had revealed he would come from that lineage. God looked over the ones who arrived and asked Jesse if he had another. God was after someone whose heart was turned toward Him. When the youngest, least likely boy arrived, the Lord said, "Rise and anoint him; this is the one" (1 Samuel 16:12 NIV).

David became the king of Israel because he listened to God and poured out his heart to Him. God chose David because God looked at David's heart. And He liked what He saw. Today, turn your heart toward God so He will be pleased.

Father, I choose You this day. Amen.

DAY 188
Don't Waste Your Talents

"His master replied, 'Well done, good and faithful servant!
You have been faithful with a few things; I will put you in
charge of many things. Come and share your master's happiness!' "
MATTHEW 25:23 NIV

Imagine inheriting a fortune and then burying the money in the backyard. You don't want to make a mistake in spending it, so you hide it. Most of us would agree this kind of thinking is ridiculous. We would spend the money, either putting it to good use or just for our pleasure.

The verse above is near the end of the parable of the talents. This servant used the talents the master had given him to create more talents. In biblical times a talent was a measure of weight used for precious metals. It was often used as money.

The spiritual gifts or "talents" God has given us are precious. Yet like a bar of gold sitting in a bank vault, they do no good unless they are used. Every believer receives spiritual gifts or "talents" after receiving Christ. The purpose of these gifts is to build up the Body of Christ.

When it comes to our spiritual gifts, many of us still have them buried in the backyard. We don't think we're good enough yet or we're afraid of making a mistake. But notice the servant didn't get judged on how well he did. Just on whether he used his talents.

Heavenly Father, give us the strength to step out
and use our talents without comparing ourselves with
others. Help us to glorify You in everything we do. Amen.

DAY 189

Kindness

"Here is my servant, whom I uphold,
my chosen one in whom I delight."
ISAIAH 42:1 NIV

Jackie and her daughters celebrated Advent in a unique way. They decided that every day they would perform little acts of kindness. They wrote their ideas down, and with much excitement they planned to surprise friends, family, and strangers with unexpected blessings. They paid parking meters that were about to expire, sang carols at nursing homes, gave hot chocolate to the mail carrier, babysat for free, and did many other things anonymously or expecting nothing in return. The result? They were blessed with smiles, thank-you's, and even a few happy tears; and they hoped that their acts of kindness would prompt others to do the same.

In 1 Peter 5:2, the Bible says, "Be shepherds of God's flock that is under your care, watching over them—not because you must, but because you are willing, as God wants you to be; not pursuing dishonest gain, but eager to serve. . ." (NIV).

God calls His people to serve, and service comes in many forms. Some work actively in the church as ministers and missionaries. Others volunteer in their communities through homeless shelters, fund-raising projects, food banks, and other causes. And every day, Christians like Jackie and her girls work silently in the background performing little acts of kindness. Can you encourage someone today through a little act of kindness?

Dear God, how can I serve You today? What can
I do to show kindness to others? Amen.

DAY 190

Let God Reign!

*Oh, how great are God's riches and wisdom and knowledge! How
impossible it is for us to understand his decisions and his ways! For
who can know the LORD's thoughts? Who knows enough to give
him advice? And who has given him so much that he needs to pay
it back? For everything comes from him and exists by his power
and is intended for his glory. All glory to him forever! Amen.*

ROMANS 11:33–36 NLT

It's easy for us to believe that we carry the world on our shoulders. We
tend to believe, though we may not admit it, that we alone make the world
turn. We convince ourselves that worry, finances, or power will put us in
control. But in truth God is the One who controls all.

What a blessed peace awaits us! As you go about your day, rest in the
assurance that God, not you, is in control. God understands every feeling you experience, and He can comfort you. God knows the best steps
for you to take in life, and He is willing to guide you. He is above all and
knows all, yet He is not out of reach.

Set your eyes firmly on the Lord, and He will care for you.

*Lord, please let this truth sink deep into my heart today so that I may
live in joy and peace. Please guide me by Your wisdom and provide
for me according to Your riches. I praise You because You are good!*

DAY 191

When You Give Your Life Away

Which of you, intending to build a tower, sitteth not down first,
and counteth the cost, whether he have sufficient to finish it?
LUKE 14:28 KJV

Henry David Thoreau once said, "The price of anything is the amount of life you exchange for it." Busy lives often dictate that there is no time for the important things. People say, "Oh, I don't have time for this or that," or, "I wish I had the time. . ." The truth is you make the time for what you value most.

Every person has the same amount of life each day. What matters is how you spend it. It's easy to waste your day doing insignificant things—what many call time wasters—leaving little time for God. The most important things in life are eternal endeavors. Spending time in prayer to God for others. Giving your life to building a relationship with God by reading His Word and growing in faith. Sharing Christ with others and giving them the opportunity to know Him. These are the things that will last.

What are you spending your life on? What are you getting out of what you give yourself to each day?

Heavenly Father, my life is full. I ask that You give me wisdom and instruction to give my life to the things that matter most. The time I have is precious and valuable. Help me to invest it wisely in eternal things. Amen.

DAY 192

Rejoicing!

Always be full of joy in the Lord. I say it again—rejoice!
<small>Philippians 4:4 nlt</small>

Have you ever watched a toddler laugh? It's amazing, isn't it? Those adorable giggles are contagious. Before long you can't help but join in, your laughter filling the room. After all, nothing compares to the sheer joy of an innocent child. It bubbles up from the deepest, God-given place, completely unhindered by concerns, worries, or distractions. How many times do we become so burdened by life's complexities that we forget to rejoice? What would it feel like to let those giggles rise to the surface, even on the worst days? What's that you say? You have nothing to feel joyful about? Look at those flowers blooming in the field! (Beauty!) Check out the food in your pantry. (Provision!) Glance into a grandchild's eyes or a coworker's heart. There's plenty of fodder for a joy-filled life. All we have to do is turn our focus from the pain to the glimpses of heaven right in front of us. Today, may your eyes be opened to many joy-filled moments.

I'm grateful for this reminder, Father, that I can be filled with joy, no matter the circumstances. They don't have to drive my emotions. Instead, my joy can drive my circumstances. Thank You for that reminder, Lord. Amen.

DAY 193
The Alabaster Box

*As she stood behind him at his feet weeping, she began to
wet his feet with her tears. Then she wiped them with
her hair, kissed them and poured perfume on them.*
LUKE 7:38 NIV

The story of Mary and her alabaster box of high-priced perfume is a familiar one. Historically, this kind of perfume was given to a woman by her parents as a dowry. It was to be used on her wedding night, to be poured out on her husband's feet in an act of submission. So when Mary poured out this costly substance onto Jesus' feet, it was a statement of her complete love, devotion, submission, and obedience. She offered Him all of herself.

Many who witnessed the outpouring of this expensive perfume were angered because it could have been sold for a lot of money and used to fund ministry. They missed the point of her extravagant love. She did not take cheap perfume but some of the most expensive ever made. And she didn't use just a few drops but emptied the container! Mary is a wonderful example for us—to love completely, being humbled at the feet of her Savior, and to offer her complete self. How beautiful and generous! May we be as well!

*Lord, I love You! May my love for You and Your people be like
a beautiful fragrance that leaves its essence everywhere I go.
I give myself wholly to You as You did for me. Amen.*

DAY 194

Giving Out of Need

"Give, and you will receive. Your gift will return to you in full—pressed down, shaken together to make room for more, running over, and poured into your lap. The amount you give will determine the amount you get back."

LUKE 6:38 NLT

As usual, Jesus saw things from a different perspective. He was in the temple, watching people bring their gifts. Instead of honoring the Pharisees, with all their pomp and circumstance, Jesus points out a poor widow. " 'Truly I tell you,' He said, 'this poor widow has put in more than all the others. All these people gave their gifts out of their wealth; but she out of her poverty put in all she had to live on' " (Luke 21:3–4 NIV).

While the rich gave out of their abundance, the widow gave out of her need. It's not difficult to give when we are sure all our needs are met. We just scrape a little off the top and leave it in the offering plate. Giving out of our poverty is a profound act of faith. When we lay our all on the altar, God promises to multiply it beyond our wildest imagination. What are you holding back from the Lord today? Give. God cannot wait to multiply your efforts.

Father, help me to be a giver. Teach me to give out of faith in You, not in my finances. Reveal to me where I may be holding back, waiting until my own needs for time or money are met. I long to trust You with the poor widow's faith. Amen.

DAY 195

True Beauty

Charm is deceptive, and beauty does not last; but a woman who fears the LORD will be greatly praised.
PROVERBS 31:30 NLT

Have you ever pondered the word *reflection*? When you stare at your reflection in the mirror, do you see your flaws or your beauty? Do you stare at your eyes or the wrinkles around them? Do you notice the intricacies of your mouth? Unless they're in putting-on-makeup mode, most women just take a quick glance in the looking glass before running out the door. Satisfied that the reflection meets expectation, a woman moves on. Oh, how God longs for His girls to see a different kind of beauty than the exterior. May your next glance in the mirror reveal a pure heart, generous hands, an uplifting mouth. When you fear/honor the Lord, your interior beauty will add all the sparkle and shine you need to an already lovely exterior.

Like most women, I focus too much on my looks, Lord. I see the good, the bad, and the ugly. Thank You for reminding me that true beauty isn't what I see in the mirror. It's what others see when they spend time with me. May I be a beautiful reflection of You. Amen.

DAY 196

Pride vs. Humility

A man's pride shall bring him low:
but honour shall uphold the humble in spirit.
PROVERBS 29:23 KJV

A great leader is known by his or her character. It is perhaps the things that one doesn't take part in that sets him or her apart. Great leaders are not prideful or boastful. They don't consider their accomplishments to be things they have done "in and of themselves," but they recognize the hand of God on their lives. Great leaders know that it takes a team to reach a goal. A great CEO treats the lowest man on the totem pole with as much dignity as he treats an equal. A great school principal knows that the teachers, assistants, bus drivers, and cafeteria workers make a huge impact on the students and the climate of the school. No one likes a bragger. It gets old hearing anyone go on and on about themselves. The Bible is filled with the teaching that the low shall be made higher and the proud will be brought to destruction. A paraphrase of this verse as found in *The Message* goes like this: "Pride lands you flat on your face; humility prepares you for honors." Take note of the areas of your own life where pride may sneak in and destroy. Replace pride with humility. Others will notice. You will not go unrewarded when you seek to be humble in spirit.

Father, root out any pride that You find in my heart
and replace it with humility, I ask. Amen.

DAY 197

Jonah's Prayer

*"When my life was ebbing away, I remembered you,
LORD, and my prayer rose to you, to your holy temple."*

JONAH 2:7 NIV

Jonah ran from God. He knew where God had directed him to go, but he refused. He thought he knew better than God. He trusted in his own ways over God's. Where did it get him? He ended up in the belly of a great fish for three days. This was not a punishment but rather a forced retreat! Jonah needed time to think and pray. He came to the end of himself and remembered his Sovereign God. He describes the depths to which he was cast. This was not just physical but emotional as well. Jonah had been in a deep struggle between God's call and his own will.

In verse 6 of his great prayer from the belly of the fish, we read these words: *"But you, Lord my God, brought my life up from the pit."* When Joseph reached a point of desperation, he realized that God was his only hope. Have you been there? Not in the belly of a great fish, but in a place where you are made keenly aware that it is time to turn back to God? God loves His children and always stands ready to receive us when we need a second chance.

Father, like Jonah I sometimes think my own ways are better than Yours. Help me to be mindful that Your ways are always good and right. Amen.

DAY 198

Choosing Faith

Be still in the presence of the Lord, and wait patiently for him to act. Don't worry about evil people who prosper or fret about their wicked schemes. Stop being angry! Turn from your rage! Do not lose your temper—it only leads to harm. For the wicked will be destroyed, but those who trust in the Lord will possess the land.

PSALM 37:7–9 NLT

Our faith is tested when life doesn't go the way we expect it to, when people who aren't following God prosper, and we seem to be an afterthought. At times we even go so far as to blame God for the things that are going wrong.

Even though it seems like the wicked are prospering and we are sitting on the sidelines, our daily grind is not in vain. Each day we are faithful is another seed planted. It may take time for it to grow, but grow it will. There will be a harvest.

Faith sees the facts but trusts God anyway. Faith is forcing yourself to worry no longer but to pray in earnest and leave the situation in His hands. Faith is choosing to trust and rest in His plan, rather than fret about what could happen. We must choose faith even when we don't feel it. It is through choosing faith that we please God. Choose faith, and see what He will do.

Lord, despite what logic or the world tells me, I choose now to let my worries go and have faith in You. I trust that You will take care of every need, and I lay down all my burdens at Your feet.

DAY 199
The Definition of Faith

Now faith is confidence in what we hope for and assurance about what we do not see. . . . And without faith it is impossible to please God, because anyone who comes to him must believe that he exists and that he rewards those who earnestly seek him.
HEBREWS 11:1, 6 NIV

Eyes of faith help us see the spiritual gifts God gives us. Faith allows us to see things normally unseen. Throughout the Old Testament, there are stories of people whose faith in God demonstrates what faith in action looks like: Abel sacrificed to God with a heart of worship, Enoch started following God in his later years, Elisha saw angel armies, and Noah built an ark in a land without rain.

In whom or what do you place your faith? God's character and His promises are faithful. Faith is the pathway to our relationship with God. We have faith to please God, to earnestly seek Him and believe in His reward, even when we can't see it with earthly eyes. We need to cultivate our eyes of faith, knowing that most of our reward for a faithful life will not be found in this life but in the next.

How do you grow your faith? Start with obedience. Worship, walk by faith, and share your journey with others. Faith will follow your obedience. Ask God to help you exercise your eyes of faith so you can see Him working. If you can't see Him, ask Him to reveal Himself to you.

Heavenly Father, thank You for making a relationship with You possible. Help us to see You working in our lives. Amen.

"In this world you will have trouble.
But take heart! I have overcome the world."
JOHN 16:33 NIV

During World War II, the Nazis imprisoned author Dr. Victor Frankl. As the Gestapo stripped him and cut away his wedding band, Frankl thought, *You can take away my wife, my children, and strip me of my clothes and freedom, but there is one thing you cannot take—my freedom to choose how I react to whatever happens to me.*

John 16:33 acknowledges that Jesus overcame the world on our behalf, so we are fully equipped to do the same.

It's difficult to trust God against all odds when problems slash us like a paper shredder. Yet it is during those times that God gives us a clear choice: choose faith or break under the harsh realities of life.

Dr. Frankl had learned somewhere in his life's journey to take the higher road. He knew that faith and how we react to people or problems is a choice, not a feeling. We can respond in the flesh or submit to the Holy Spirit whatever happens to us. Often that means asking for forgiveness though you've done nothing wrong, encouraging someone despite their negative attitude, or extending a hand and risking rejection.

Mature believers know that hardships are a part of life, but Jesus has paved the pathway to overcome. And although taking "the higher road" is less traveled, it's worth the trek.

Lord, whatever I face, may I act, not react,
with Your overcoming power. Amen.

DAY 201

Live in Unity

May God, who gives this patience and encouragement, help you live in complete harmony with each other, as is fitting for followers of Christ Jesus.
ROMANS 15:5 NLT

How does one live in unity with so many different types of people? One woman prefers vibrant, bold colors and has a personality to match. Another woman prefers muted tones, and her demur attitude fits accordingly. One church member might gravitate toward the classical, traditional hymns, while another prefers more contemporary music.

Christians disagree on a lot of issues, and conflicts often result—in and out of the Church. Yet we are to exercise the patience and encouragement God provides to help us live in harmony with one another.

One quotation says it well: "God prizes Christian unity above doctrinal exactitude." Our salvation is based on whom we worship, not where or how we worship. Quibbling over the cut, style, or color of our spiritual clothing causes us to succumb to our fleshly nature rather than God's will for us.

Personal preferences and heartfelt opinions are what make us individuals. Every believer has a gift to share within the Body of Christ. If we were all the same, how could we grow and learn? Jesus prayed for unity among the believers. God encourages us to do the same.

*Father, thank You that You give me the ability and power
to walk in unity with my brothers and sisters in Christ.
I pray for Christian unity. Let it begin with me. Amen.*

DAY 202

Use It or Lose It

"Therefore consider carefully how you listen."
LUKE 8:18 NIV

Doing God's Word, not merely hearing it, was one of Jesus' repeated themes. His parable of the sower illustrated four different responses we can have whenever the seed of the Word of God hits our thinking. With a hard heart, we will have no response and the truth will disappear as if *stolen*. A rocky heart *starves* the seed, not allowing it to take root. If our heart is cluttered with weeds of worldly cares, the seed gets *strangled*. But with a positive response to truth, we *sustain* it and let it change us, producing fruit in our lives.

Jesus concluded by saying that the more truth we learn and practice, the more God will reveal. But if we stop using what we learn, we will lose even what we thought we had (Matthew 13:12; Mark 4:24–25; Luke 8:18). If we do nothing with the seed, it can do nothing for us.

This principle reminds me to evaluate what I do with truth from God. When I read His Word or hear a sermon, do I respond to Him obediently? Does it correct my behavior, shape my worldview, and get all the way to my fingers and feet? Like panning for gold, the more I seek, the more I will discover. James 1:25 says that continuing in God's Word—not forgetting what we hear, but doing it—makes us blessed in what we do.

Perfect Father, every time I encounter Your Word, help me to respond positively and use it so that Your truth will grow and bear fruit in me.

DAY 203
True Friendship

Rejoice with those who rejoice; mourn with those who mourn.
ROMANS 12:15 NIV

True Christian friendship has this verse stamped all over it. Do you have a friend who truly finds joy in your successes? When you are on top of the world, this person is genuinely happy for you. When you are sad, you have seen tears come to her eyes. This is not a friendship found every day. It is rare and to be treasured.

As believers in Christ, we have this high call on our lives. Pray that you might truly celebrate with others, not secretly wishing you were the one receiving the blessing. On the other hand, know that at times sorrow and loss is so deep that a hug and an "I love you" will mean the world. Lots of words are not needed in such times. To mourn with the mourner is the greatest gift you can give. Just to show up, to extend help, to show love.

If you have such a friend, you no doubt cherish her. Make it your aim to live out Romans 12:15 in small ways this week. Stand and cheer when others are victorious. Stand close by and be ready to comfort them when they experience disappointment or loss.

Heavenly Father, help me to rejoice with those who rejoice
and to mourn with those who mourn. Give me a
sensitive heart that is focused on others. Amen.

DAY 204

A Friend Who Sticks Closer than a Brother

*Now it came about, when he had finished speaking
to Saul, that Jonathan committed himself to
David, and Jonathan loved him as himself.*

1 SAMUEL 18:1 NASB

The relationship between David and Jonathan was like that of brothers. Proverbs 18:24 (NIV) says it this way: "One who has unreliable friends soon comes to ruin, but there is a friend who sticks closer than a brother." Everyone hits a rough patch now and then. This world is not our home. As believers, we are aliens here. One day we will truly be at home in heaven with the Lord. Until then, it is important that we stand strong with one another through the ups and downs of life. Consider the depth of Jonathan's love for David:

Jonathan, the son of King Saul, protected David from death when Saul grew jealous of David. He created a secret way of getting the message to David that he indeed needed to flee the kingdom. The two hated to part, but it was their only option. In the end, the Bible tells us it was David who wept the hardest when he had to leave Jonathan. No doubt, David recognized the value of his true friend who stuck closer than a brother. Do you have a friend in need? Life gets busy. Don't ever be too busy to help your friends, to be there for them as Jonathan was for David.

*Father in heaven, may I be a friend who
truly sticks closer than a brother. Amen.*

DAY 205

A Joyful Noise

Sing aloud unto God our strength:
make a joyful noise unto the God of Jacob.
PSALM 81:1 KJV

Aren't you glad the Bible commands us to "make a joyful noise unto the Lord" instead of saying something like "Sing like an angel"? Many are born with amazing vocal abilities. They wow us with their choir productions and their amazing solo performances. But some of the rest of us are lucky to croak out a word or two in the right key.

God doesn't care about your vocal abilities. He longs to hear a song of praise rise up out of your heart, even if it's sung in three or four keys. Think about that for a moment. He's listening as millions of believers sing out—in every language, every key, every pitch. And it doesn't bother Him one bit because He's not listening to the technique, He's listening to the heart.

Still not convinced? Read the book of Psalms from start to finish. It will stir up a song in your heart, and before long your toes will be tapping and your heart bursting. Why? Because you were created to praise Him. So, don't worry about what others will think. Make a joyful noise!

Lord, my heart wants to sing happy songs today! I'm not going to worry anymore about my voice, whether I'm singing in church or in the car or in the shower. I was made to praise You, Father, so I choose to make a joyful noise!

DAY 206

A Creative God

In the beginning God created the heavens and the earth.
GENESIS 1:1 NIV

Did you realize that you are made (designed, created) in the image of a very creative God? It's true! He breathed life into you, after all. It stands to reason that some of His creativity would have spilled over into you, His daughter.

The same God who created the heavens and the earth—who decided a giraffe's neck should be several feet long and a penguin should waddle around in tuxedo-like attire—designed you, inside and out! And He gifted you with a variety of gifts and abilities, all of which can be used to His glory.

So, what creative gifts reside inside you? Have you given them a stir lately? Maybe it's time to ask God which gifts are most useable for this season of your life. He's creative enough to stir the ones that can be used to reach others. He will bring them to the surface and prepare you to use them—much like He did during Creation—to bring beauty out of dark places.

So, brace yourself! Your very creative God has big things planned for you!

Lord, thank You for creating me in Your image. I get so excited when I think about the fact that Your creativity lives inside me. Just as Your Spirit moved across creation in the book of Genesis, I ask You to move across the creative gifts in my life and stir them to life!

DAY 207
Unfailing Love

Let your unfailing love surround us,
LORD, for our hope is in you alone.
PSALM 33:22 NLT

We hope that our sports team will win the big game and that local coffee shop will bring back our favorite order. We also hope that our jobs will continue to fulfill us and pay our bills and that God will answer a heartfelt prayer with a long-awaited yes.

Whatever we're hoping for, it's easy to think that God doesn't care about the details of our lives. However, God longs to share every part of our day. Why not talk to Him about all our needs and desires?

As we sip our morning coffee, we can jot down thanks for morning blessings such as flavored creamers and hot water for our shower. While we do our jobs, we can regularly bring our concerns (and coworkers) before God's throne. We could keep scriptures scribbled on sticky notes in our cubicle—or on our desk—to remind us to think with God's thoughts throughout the day, instead of falling back on worldly patterns. When we lay our head on the pillow at night, we can voice the answered prayers which grace our lives, drifting off to sleep in gratitude at God's unfailing love.

Those small, simple actions add up to a day filled with hope and gratitude. . .and those days add up to a life well-lived.

Father God, thank You for Your unfailing love. Thinking
on that love, which I haven't earned and can't repay,
causes me to fall to my knees in hope, gratitude, and joy.

DAY 208
God Is in the Details

Give all your worries and cares to God, for he cares about you.
1 PETER 5:7 NLT

Do you ever wonder if God cares about the details of your life?

Take a look at nature. God is definitely a God of details. Notice the various patterns, shapes, and sizes of animals. Their life cycles. The noises they make. Their natural defenses. Details!

Have you wandered through the woods? Towering trees. Their scents. The cool refreshment their shade provides. The different types of leaves, and the tiny, life-bearing veins that run through them. How intricate!

What about the weather? It is filled with details from the hand of your God. The Creator sends raindrops—sometimes gentle and kind, other times harsh and pelting. He warms us with the sun, cools us with breezes, and yes—it is true—He fashions each snowflake, each unique, no two alike! The same way He designs His children!

Do you wonder if God cares about that struggle you are facing at work or the argument you had with a loved one? Is He aware of your desire to find that special someone or the difficulty you find in loving your spouse? He cares. Tell Him your concerns. He is not too busy to listen to the details. He wants to show Himself real and alive to you in such a way that you know it must be Him. The details of your life are not *little* to God. If they matter to you, they matter to God.

Thank You, Lord, for caring about the details of my life.
It means so much to know You care. Amen.

DAY 209

Just in Time

Therefore let's approach the throne of grace with confidence, so that we may receive mercy and find grace for help at the time of our need.
HEBREWS 4:16 NASB

As believers, our lives become exciting when we wait on God to direct our paths, because He knows what is best for us at any given moment. His plans and agenda are never wrong. We just need to practice living on His schedule and spending time in prayer. But that's easier said than done! Often we are chomping at the bit, and it's hard to wait.

Once we fully realize He knows best and turn our lives over to the Spirit for direction, we can allow God to be in charge of our calendar; His timing is what is paramount.

When chomping at the bit for a job offer or for a proposal, His timing might seem slow. "Hurry up, God!" we groan. But when we learn to patiently wait on His promises, we will see the plans He has for us are more than we dared hope—or dream. God promises to answer us; and it never fails to be just in time.

Lord, I want Your perfect will in my life.
Help me learn to wait upon You. Amen.

DAY 210
The Perfect Redeemer

"Who are you?" he asked. "I am your servant Ruth," she replied. "Spread the corner of your covering over me, for you are my family redeemer."
RUTH 3:9 NLT

Ruth was a woman of faith. After suffering the loss of her husband, she could have wallowed in grief and misery. Instead, she chose to follow her mother-in-law, Naomi, to a place where she knew no one, in order to honor her late husband (and, perhaps, the God he had introduced her to).

Ruth was also a woman of action. She worked hard to glean in the fields, toiling with intention and consistency. The owner of the fields, Boaz, noticed her work ethic and was impressed. Later, Ruth followed Naomi's advice and found Boaz at night while he was sleeping. Because he was a relative of hers and a man of integrity, he agreed to spread his covering over her as her "family redeemer." This meant he promised to marry and take care of Ruth (and Naomi).

Ruth's story has much to teach us. Just as Ruth moved on from grief to action, we can ask for God's help to move past our own losses and not get stuck in bitterness or anger. With His help, we can honor others and not wallow in self-pity or destructive habits. Also, as His strength and forgiveness covers our weaknesses and failures, we can find peace and joy. He is the perfect Redeemer who takes care of us so we don't have to worry about providing for ourselves.

My Rock and Redeemer, I praise and thank You for Your covering over me. You are a faithful provider.

DAY 211

I Am

God said to Moses, "I AM WHO I AM. This is what you are
to say to the Israelites: 'I AM has sent me to you.'"
EXODUS 3:14 NIV

The words "I am" ring out in the present tense. These words are used some seven hundred times in the Bible to describe God and Jesus. When Moses was on the mount and asked God who He was, a voice thundered, "I Am." In the New Testament, Jesus said of Himself, "I am the bread of life; I am the light of the world; I am the Good Shepherd; I am the way; I am the resurrection." Present tense. Words of hope and life. I Am.

Who is God to you today? Is He in the present tense? Living, loving, presiding over your life? Is the Lord of lords "I Was" or "I've Never Been" to you? Have you experienced the hope which comes from an everlasting "I Am" Father? One who walks by you daily and will never let go? "I Am with you always."

We are surprised when we struggle in the world, yet hesitate to turn to our very Creator. He has the answers, and He will fill you with hope. Reach for Him today. Don't be uncertain. Know Him. For He is, after all, I Am.

Father, we surrender our lives to You this day. We choose to
turn from our sins, reach for Your hand, and ask for Your
guidance. Thank You for Your loving-kindness. Amen.

DAY 212
God Is Good

Praise the LORD, for the LORD is good;
sing praises to His name, for it is pleasant.
PSALM 135:3 NKJV

We hear it in church. We say it to others. We want to believe it. God is good. All the time.

The Bible says it so we know it is true. Jesus lived it so we could see it in living color. But sometimes, when life yanks hard and pulls the rug out from under us, we begin to doubt. And that is probably a normal human temptation. Though we know that good parents discipline their children and sometimes allow them to learn "the hard way," we expect God, our heavenly Father, to do it differently.

So we need reminders. And He put them in our world everywhere we turn, at unexpected junctions and in the most ordinary places. Warm sunshine, brilliant flowers, rainbows after storms, newborn babies, friendships, families, food, air to breathe, pets, church dinners, sunrises, sunsets, beaches, forests, prairies, mountains, the moon and stars at night and puffy clouds in the day. All around us are hints that God is good and that His works are beautiful and life-giving.

When disease or tragedy or hardship enters our lives, we can rest assured that God is not the author of these destructive things and that someday He will cleanse this globe of its misery and set everything right. Until then, He has given us His strength, His hope, and His promise. That is enough to keep us going.

Father God, I praise You. You are good. Your works are
wonderful. I know You love me. Help me to trust Your
plan and purpose for me. In Jesus' name, amen.

DAY 213
Stand Still

And Moses said unto the people, Fear ye not, stand still, and see
the salvation of the LORD, which he will shew to you to day. . . .
The LORD shall fight for you, and ye shall hold your peace.
EXODUS 14:13–14 KJV

The Children of Israel enjoyed a triumphant exodus from Egypt, but danger soon overtook them. They had only journeyed a short time when they looked up to see Pharaoh and his army marching toward them. They were afraid and immediately started making accusations against Moses, claiming he had brought them to the wilderness to die. They said they would have been better off staying in Egypt. But Moses encouraged them not to be afraid. They were to stand still. The Lord, their God, would fight for them. They were to hold their peace.

Are you facing an enemy? Do you feel afraid of impending danger? Moses told the people to do four things: fear not, stand still, see the salvation of the Lord, and hold your peace. The Children of Israel experienced a great victory that day. God parted the waters of the Red Sea so they could cross over on dry ground, then He allowed that same water to drown the Egyptian army. Moses' advice is good for us also. We can put our trust in God without fear and wait for God to do battle for us. Whatever is coming toward you, God can handle it.

Lord, help me to stand still and wait
for You to work on my behalf. Amen.

DAY 214
Jesus' Perspective on Priorities

*But Martha was distracted with all her preparations; and she
came up to Him and said, "Lord, do You not care that my sister
has left me to do the serving by myself? Then tell her to help me."*
LUKE 10:40 NASB

We often wear busyness as a badge of honor because busyness can equal productivity and usefulness. It's important to ask ourselves, however, whether busyness takes away from—or adds to—our faith journey.

When Jesus dined in the home of Mary and Martha, Martha prepared the meal for her special guest, while Mary (in a highly unusual move for a woman during biblical times) sat at Jesus' feet, listening to His teaching. Martha understandably felt frustrated that Mary wasn't helping her, and she asked Jesus to rebuke her sister. However, Jesus told Martha that Mary had chosen the "better part." The Bible doesn't say what Martha replied, or how she felt. Perhaps she felt relieved.

Picture yourself receiving a text that an important person was coming to your house. You might scurry around, tidying the bathroom and plumping the couch cushions. If your guest said, "Sit down. Relax! I don't want you to make a fuss over me. I just want to be with you," you would feel grateful. . .peaceful. . .and treasured.

Today, as you plan your to-do list, prioritize time to sit and reflect on God's Word. Instead of rushing around to accomplish things you feel *should* be done, ask God what He wants you to do. You might be relieved.

*Jesus, give me Your perspective today as I plan my to-do's.
Show me what's important to You, and help me to follow through.*

DAY 215

Our True Enemies

*"I am not referring to all of you; I know those I have
chosen. But this is to fulfill this passage of Scripture:
'He who shared my bread has turned against me.'"*
JOHN 13:18 NIV

Jesus knows when He chooses His disciples that Judas would betray Him. That was the way God's plan of salvation would come about. And yet, until this point, Jesus never treats Judas in any way that would indicate He knew of Judas's impending betrayal. In fact, Jesus sharing His bread with Judas in this way shows honor. Jesus treats Judas with much more grace and love than we could imagine. For over three years, Jesus treats Judas like the other disciples.

But what Judas meant for evil was part of God's plan. Is it possible Christ loved Judas because He knew Judas was crucial to the redemption plan?

Ultimately, only God knows our true enemies. He reveals them to us when we need to know. Everything God does has a purpose, usually a far bigger one than we can see. Even when we are determined to do wrong, God loves us with an unfathomable love.

Is there something in your life you need to look at with new eyes, with the perspective that somehow God can use it for good and for His glory?

*Lord Jesus, thank You for Your amazing sacrifice and for Your
unfathomable love for us. Help us to view people and situations
with Your eyes and to remember Your love for them. Amen.*

DAY 216

Wise Woman

Then a wise woman cried out from the city, "Hear, hear! Please say to Joab, 'Come nearby, that I may speak with you'. . . . I am among the peaceable and faithful in Israel. You seek to destroy a city and a mother in Israel."

2 SAMUEL 20:16, 19 NKJV

In the midst of a siege on a city, the Lord sent an unlikely messenger to the commander of King David's army. A wise and courageous woman speaks into the chaos and preserves the city. She is Christ's calm in the storm, bringing reason into a tumultuous time.

We are called to be the calm in a storm. The only reason this woman could possibly speak with Joab amid the battle is through God's wisdom, power, and protection. She lays out the matter at hand before Joab and shows him his folly. She speaks the truth with grace and humility.

The same wisdom, power, and protection the Lord gave this wise woman He offers to you. In times of crisis, speaking and thinking rationally are difficult feats, but anchor your trust in the one and only unchanging God.

This woman did not demand; she did not provoke or diminish. She questioned Joab and asked for understanding. Our God is a God of understanding and wisdom, and though there are times He will not reveal the reason or purpose of an event, we must trust and rest in His unshakable character.

Lord, may I stop and consider Your wisdom and Your teachings when I face uncertainties. You are the only source of wisdom; all my thoughts outside of You fail. Forgive me for trusting in myself and not in You. Amen.

DAY 217

Move the Stone

"Roll the stone aside," Jesus told them. But Martha, the dead man's sister, protested, "Lord, he has been dead for four days. The smell will be terrible."
JOHN 11:39 NLT

Jesus had been a frequent visitor to Martha's home. Now He has come again to raise her brother from the dead. Though, if you asked Martha, if Jesus had come when they first asked Him to, her brother wouldn't be dead. And now He wants to open up the tomb. Martha doesn't understand any of it.

When Jesus asks for the tomb to be opened, Martha doesn't express amazement that Jesus intends to raise her brother from the dead. Instead, she's worried about the smell.

Aren't we often like that? God tells us to do something, to take a step of faith, to do our part so He can work. Instead of focusing on what God's going to do, we worry about how it's going to affect us.

It's also interesting that Jesus asked for the stone to be moved. If He was about to resurrect a dead body, moving a stone from in front of the tomb was a small thing. But He wanted their participation. He wanted them to put their faith in action. If they believed He was really going to raise a body that had been dead four days, then moving the stone from the tomb was the first step to show their faith.

Dear Lord, show us where we need to step out in faith and give us the courage to do it. Help us to trust You with everything. Amen.

DAY 218
Look Up!

"Your love, LORD, reaches to the heavens, your faithfulness to the skies."
PSALM 36:5 NIV

In Bible times, people often studied the sky. Looking up at the heavens reminded them of God and His mighty wonders. A rainbow was God's sign to Noah that a flood would never again destroy the earth. God used a myriad of stars to foretell Abraham's abundant family, and a single star heralded Christ's birth.

The theme of the heavens traverses the scriptures from beginning to end. The Bible's first words say: "In the beginning God created the heavens." The psalmist David shows God's greatness in comparison to them: "the heavens declare the glory of God." And in the New Testament, Jesus describes the end times saying, "There will be signs in the sun, moon and stars. . . At that time [people] will see the Son of Man coming in a cloud with power and great glory."

Some of God's greatest works have happened in the sky.

This immense space that we call "sky" is a reflection of God's infinite love and faithfulness. It reaches far beyond what one can see or imagine, all the way to heaven. Too often working, maintaining households, parenting, and doing other tasks keep us from looking up. So take time today. Look up at the heavens and thank God for His endless love.

Heavenly Father, remind me to stop and appreciate Your wonderful creations. And as I look upward, fill me with Your infinite love. Amen.

DAY 219

Cultivating Contentment

I wait for the LORD, my whole being waits, and in his word I put my hope. I wait for the Lord more than watchmen wait for the morning, more than watchmen wait for the morning.

PSALM 130:5–6 NIV

What are you waiting for—a job, a relationship, physical healing, financial provision? Whatever answer to prayer you are longing for, remember that often it's in the waiting that God performs His perfecting work on our character. Joseph waited for many years, serving in Pharaoh's house (even ending up in jail) before God promoted Him. Abraham waited until he was a century old to see the child God had promised to him and Sarah decades before. God was still at work in both men's lives, though His actions and plans were hidden.

Maybe you've waited for God to come through, and so far, He hasn't. The word advent means "arrival or coming, especially one which is awaited." Like the silence the people of Israel endured for 400 years between the last spoken prophetic word and the arrival of the Christ child, perhaps you've endured silence from God for so long that you think He's not there, not listening—or not inclined to come to your rescue.

No matter what you're going through, please know that God is for you, not against you. He aches with you. And He offers us a choice: be chained in fear or changed by grace.

Which will you choose today?

Father, forgive me for doubting Your love and mercy. Thank You that You are faithful and that You will provide for me. I believe. . .help my unbelief.

DAY 220

God Is Bigger Than the Wrong Done to You

"But if you do not forgive others their sins,
your Father will not forgive your sins."
MATTHEW 6:15 NIV

It can be tough to forgive. It presses us to the edge of ourselves where we are forced to acknowledge that God is greater than the wrong that has been done to us. When we choose to forgive, it keeps God's power in perspective.

Someone may stop loving you, insult you, steal from you, or abuse you, but that person will never be able to destroy the love that God has for you or His sovereign rule over all that concerns you. God's redeeming love is bigger than your enemies. This is what Joseph acknowledged after his brothers threw him in a pit and sold him into slavery: "You intended to harm me, but God intended it for good" (Genesis 50:20 NIV).

Think about something someone has done to you that has demanded forgiveness. Do you believe God is bigger than the wrong? Are you convinced His love and His rule are redemptive? If so, let the person who has wronged you off the hook. Stop thinking that he or she has ruined your life and that you will never recover—because God is a redeemer.

Lord, when someone wrongs me, I may want to lash out or hold
a grudge. Help me to remember that there is nothing that will
happen to me that You cannot redeem for my good and Your
glory. Help me to live in the freedom of this truth. Amen.

DAY 221
A True Heart

Jesus answered, "Isaiah was right when he spoke about you hypocrites. He wrote, 'These people show honor to me with words, but their hearts are far from me. Their worship of me is worthless. The things they teach are nothing but human rules.'"
MARK 7:6–7 NCV

Jesus considered the Pharisees hypocrites because they were pretending to honor the Lord so that others would think they were holy and hold them in high regard. But their hearts weren't in it.

God wants our hearts *and* our words. The Bible says in Luke 6:45 (NKJV) that "out of the abundance (overflow) of the heart his mouth speaks." What you think and feel inside is eventually what will come out. If your heart isn't really set on the Lord, people will see that your actions don't match up with what you're saying.

When you pray, always be honest with God and with yourself. When asked to pray in public, there is no need to use large, flowery words to impress others. God is the only One who matters.

A man was asked to pray a blessing before a big holiday dinner. He complied but spoke so softly that not many could hear him at all. When he said "amen," the family looked up to see if he was really finished.

"We couldn't hear you!" the family said.

"Well, I wasn't praying to you!" replied the man.

Dear Jesus, let my heart, my words, and my actions always be true to You. Amen.

DAY 222

No Condemnation

*Therefore there is now no condemnation
at all for those who are in Christ Jesus.*
ROMANS 8:1 NASB

There is no condemnation for you who are in Christ Jesus. This means there is no room for guilt or blame in your life. Even when you do things that make you feel like you have failed God, yourself, or others, your standing before God does not change. When you are in Christ, you are clothed in the clean, holy robes of God's Son. When God looks at you, He doesn't see the sins you've committed or the things you haven't done; He sees His holy, blameless Son.

How is this possible? It's possible because Christ died in your place. The sins that would have condemned you in God's holy court were placed on Christ's shoulders and buried with Him. They have no hold over you anymore. So let go of your guilt and regret. Acknowledge that Christ's work on the cross was enough to cleanse and purify you before a holy God. And live in the freedom of the knowledge that no one and nothing can condemn you. Christ has stood in your place so that you can come boldly before the Father in the clean robes that have been washed in the blood of the Lamb. Ask for His forgiveness and claim His forgiveness in your life.

Lord, thank You that I am not and cannot be condemned because I am in Christ. Help me to more fully understand what Christ did for me on the cross so that I can let go of the guilt and blame I so often carry.

DAY 223
Women of Faith

I call to remembrance the genuine faith that is in you,
which dwelt first in your grandmother Lois and your
mother Eunice, and I am persuaded is in you also.
2 TIMOTHY 1:5 NKJV

When the apostle Paul thought of young Timothy, one thing stood out. Timothy had true faith. He had been raised by his mother and grandmother to love and trust the Lord. Perhaps you come from a long line of Christian women, or maybe you are a first generation Christ-follower. Either way, these verses have a message for you. We all influence children. Perhaps you have your own children or nieces and nephews. Maybe you spend time with friends' children. Some of you may be grandmothers. Others may work with children either in your career or in a church ministry role. Whatever the situation, you have a great impact on children that look up to you.

It is important to note the trait that stood out was not perfection. It was faith. We cannot be perfect examples for our children. But we can teach them about faith! The way you respond to life's trials speaks the loudest. Children learn about faith when they see it lived out before them. Like Eunice and Lois were wonderful examples for Timothy, may you influence the next generation to place their faith in Christ Jesus.

God, help me to be a woman of faith, for I know that little ones
are watching and learning about You through me. Amen.

DAY 224
The Courage to See God at Work

So the king of Jericho sent this message to Rahab: "Bring
out the men who came to you and entered your house,
because they have come to spy out the whole land."
JOSHUA 2:3 NIV

God had rescued the Israelites from Egypt by dividing the Red Sea. He led the way through the desert as a pillar of cloud by day and a pillar of fire by night. He provided food and water. For forty years, their clothes did not wear out.

The king of Jericho had heard of this big God and His people, who were camped outside his city ready to attack. Rahab, a prostitute, had heard of this God. But her decision was different from the king's. She looked at the same evidence as the king and made a different decision.

She heard that God was a punishing God and a rescuing God. Jericho had been a wicked city and was going to be punished. She hid the spies that came in to scout out the city. She told them she believed in their God and wanted to be rescued, along with her family. Her actions flowed from her realization of who God is. Her faith not only gets her mentioned in James and Hebrews, but she also becomes part of the lineage of Christ.

What does your knowledge of who God is lead you to do? How can you step out in faith?

Dear God, thank You for rescuing us. Reveal Your character to us in a
new way, and show us how to act because of who You are. Amen.

DAY 225
Pass It On!

*After the usual readings from the books of Moses and the prophets,
those in charge of the service sent them this message: "Brothers, if you
have any word of encouragement for the people, come and give it."*
ACTS 13:15 NLT

Who doesn't need encouragement? After the reading in the temple, the rulers asked Paul and his companions if they had a word of encouragement to share. Paul immediately stood up and proclaimed how the fulfillment of God's promise came through Jesus; and whoever believed—whether Jew or Gentile—would receive forgiveness and salvation (Acts 13:16–41).

The scriptures state that as Paul and Barnabas left the synagogue, the people invited them to speak again the following Sabbath. And as a result of Paul's testimony, many devout Jews came to Christ. Not only that, on the next Sabbath, nearly the entire town—Jews and Gentiles alike—gathered to hear God's Word (Acts 13:42–44).

Encouragement brings hope. Have you ever received a word from someone that instantly lifted your spirit? Did you receive a bit of good news or something that diminished your negative outlook? Perhaps a particular conversation helped to bring your problems into perspective. Paul passed on encouragement and many benefited. So the next time you're encouraged, pass it on! You may never know how your words or actions benefited someone else.

*Lord, thank You for the wellspring of
encouragement through Your Holy Word. Amen.*

DAY 226

Loving Sisters

*But Ruth replied, "Don't urge me to leave you or to turn back
from you. Where you go I will go, and where you stay I will stay.
Your people will be my people and your God my God."*
RUTH 1:16 NIV

The story of Ruth and Naomi is inspiring on many levels. It talks of two women from different backgrounds, generations, ethnicity, and even religion. But rather than being obstacles to loving friendship, these differences became invisible. Both women realized that their commitment, friendship, and love for each other surpassed any of their differences. They were a blessing to each other.

Do you have girlfriends who would do almost anything for you? A true friendship is a gift from God. Those relationships provide us with love, companionship, encouragement, loyalty, honesty, understanding, and more! Lasting friendships are essential to living a balanced life.

Father God, thank You for giving us the gift of friendship. May I be the blessing to my girlfriends that they are to me. Please help me to always encourage and love them and to be a loving support for them in both their trials and their happiness. I praise You for my loving sisters! Amen.

DAY 227

A Loving Friend

A generous person will prosper;
whoever refreshes others will be refreshed.
PROVERBS 11:25 NIV

Are you convinced that you don't have enough friends—or perhaps your friends aren't meeting your needs? Consider what kind of friend you are. The timeworn axiom "To have a friend, be one" rings with truth.

Good friends listen deeply. We all need someone who can share our load and with whom we can be gut-level honest. This type of friend is invaluable when you feel you can't go one more step.

Good friends also mentor gently and lovingly. A friend pushes a friend to take care of herself and not forget her own needs in the midst of career, kids, and church activities. Maybe there is someone you could nudge into a healthier lifestyle or more active spiritual life.

Finally, good friends forgive freely. They don't judge too harshly or take things extremely personally. Instead, they give friends the benefit of the doubt, knowing that no woman is perfect and sometimes people make mistakes. They are thankful for grace-filled friends and try to forgive as God has forgiven them.

Heavenly Father, thank You for friends. Give us the ability to be forgiving, godly, listening friends—and provide us with relationships that will help us grow and mature. Most of all, thank You for the Friend we have in Jesus.

DAY 228

Be Known for Love

Dear friends, let us love one another, for love comes from God.
Everyone who loves has been born of God and knows God.
Whoever does not love does not know God, because God is love.
1 JOHN 4:7–8 NIV

"God is love." It is a verse many remember learning in Sunday school or Vacation Bible School. But what does it mean? God is, by His very nature, love. All that He does is out of a heart overflowing with unconditional love. God's unconditional love surpasses any other that we have ever received or given.

Christians are to be known by our love. Lyrics of a song written many years ago put it this way: "We are one in the Spirit. We are one in the Lord . . . . And they'll know we are Christians by our love." But do they? Do the people within your sphere of influence know that you are a Christian by your love? Or do you blend in with the crowd? Be a vessel of grace and peace. Let love be your trademark, a distinctive sign that you are a believer. You may never know the impact this will have for the kingdom.

What does love look like? It takes all shapes and forms. Some examples might be helping others, going the extra mile, offering words of encouragement, or putting your own ambitions aside in order to put others first.

Father, in my family and in my workplace,
please use me as a vessel of love. Amen.

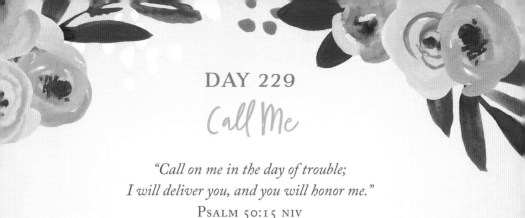

DAY 229
Call Me

"Call on me in the day of trouble;
I will deliver you, and you will honor me."
PSALM 50:15 NIV

"Call me and we'll do lunch."

"Call me and we'll talk more."

"Call if you need anything."

How many times have we said those words or heard them in return? Those two little words, *call me*, which hold such significance, have become so commonplace we barely think about them.

But when God says He wants us to call Him, He means it. He must lean closer, bending His ear, waiting, longing for the sound of His name coming from our lips. He stands ready to deliver us from our troubles or at least carry us through them safely.

David called on God in his troubles. Some of those troubles were of David's own making, while others were out of his control. It's a good thing God doesn't distinguish between the troubles we deserve and those we don't deserve. As far as He's concerned, we're His children. He loves us, and He wants to help us any way He can.

While He doesn't always choose to fix things with a snap of His fingers, we can be assured that He will see us through to the other side of our troubles by a smoother path than we'd travel without Him. He's waiting to help us. All we have to do is call.

Dear Father, I'm so glad I can call on You
anytime, with any kind of trouble. Amen.

DAY 230
Please God

*For God is pleased when, conscious of his will,
you patiently endure unust treatment.*
1 PETER 2:19 NLT

Few moms hear comments from their children or husband like, "Hey, thanks for washing my basketball uniform," or "I appreciate the way you remind me to do my homework," or "Wow, the toilet bowl is sparkling clean!" Face it. Women just don't receive that kind of encouragement; yet we do those things anyway, with no thought of receiving credit. It's simply what we do for our families.

The same is true as believers. It's always right to do right. Christians serve, give, pray, encourage, and bless others because it is the right thing to do. These actions are as natural to the true believer as escorting a five-year-old across the street is to a mother.

Are you discouraged when no one notices how well you conducted a Bible study or served a church dinner? Does it bother you if your good deeds go unnoticed? Then it's time for a motive-check. God, who knows the thoughts and intents of our hearts, is well pleased when we do what is right, whether or not anyone notices.

We serve without applause because we love God, not because we desire to please men. Besides, the only One we should strive to satisfy is our God, who sees what we do in secret and is well pleased.

*Dear Lord, thank You for the encouragement You give me daily.
Although I don't deserve it, I appreciate Your appreciation! Amen.*

DAY 231

God Loves You Individually

Nevertheless, each person should live as a believer in whatever situation the Lord has assigned to them, just as God has called them. This is the rule I lay down in all the churches.
1 CORINTHIANS 7:17 NIV

Sometimes we wonder why God puts particular information in the Bible—like the parts of the Old Testament with numbers and dates that don't seem relevant to our lives. What purpose does it serve for us? But its presence in God's inspired Word shows God is in the details and He loves us in a personal and intimate way. He has called us to the situations we are in, with the people who are around us, for a particular reason.

Other verses expand on this concept:

Matthew 10:29–31 tells us God has His eye on us individually. He's focused on our needs. He sees us.

Matthew 6:28–32 says God is well aware of our financial needs. He knows our specific needs and has plans beyond what we can see.

Romans 14:2–4 tells us God sees our individual weaknesses and struggles. He provides specific ways to help us grow our faith and provides people and situations to help us stand.

Romans 12:3–6 says we each have different gifts to serve, bless, and help others.

Think about a friend God brought into your life at a particular time when you needed that person, or when God provided for your needs in an unexpected way. Focus on how God loves you individually.

Dear Jesus, thank You for loving us in such a personal way and for having unique plans for each of us. Amen.

DAY 232

Trust in His Loving-Kindness

But I have trusted in Your faithfulness; my heart shall rejoice in Your
salvation. I will sing to the LORD, because He has looked after me.
PSALM 13:5–6 NASB

How do you trust in God's loving-kindness? First, you have to believe that He loves you, right now, as you are. Do you really believe that? Or are you still trying to earn God's love by attempting to do enough good things to merit His favor? Or maybe you're convinced that God is merely putting up with you and your daily failures to be perfect. Because you have received Christ, you must believe that God loves you fully, perfectly, and unconditionally, despite what you have or haven't done. Isn't this the kind of love we all long for? So accept it, be humbled by it, and be eternally grateful for it.

Because you know that God *loves* you and is *for* you, you can trust that He will take care of you and work out everything in your life for your good and His glory. It may be hard to comprehend how a certain circumstance could possibly be worked out for good. But the all-powerful, sovereign God is on your side. You can trust fully in His loving-kindness.

So praise God and rejoice in the love He has for you. He loves you and has set you aside as one of His own. There will not be one moment in this life, in death, or in eternity when He will not be with you. He has indeed dealt bountifully with you!

Lord, may I trust in Your loving-kindness more every day.

DAY 233

Different Kinds of Love

This is my commandment, that ye love one another, as I have loved you.
JOHN 15:12 KJV

Not all love is the same according to the Greek translation of God's Word. For instance, *philia* is defined as a loyalty and friendship for family members or friends. *Eros* is a passionate, sensual desire. *Storge* is a natural affection shown between parent and child.

The one most familiar comes from the word *agape*, meaning not only general affection but to hold someone in high regard. The New Testament applies agape love in the relationship between Jesus and His disciples. It is one of self-sacrifice and a giving spirit to all, both friend and foe.

Jesus commands us to love our neighbor as we love ourselves (Matthew 22:39). He doesn't say, "Love your neighbor as long as they keep their dogs from barking or if they maintain their yard and stay on their side of the fence." Rather, He commands us to love as He loves us.

That's God's agape love. It's unconditional and powerful. Agape love builds not destroys; it accepts others' imperfections and is tolerant of people who do things differently than we do.

What's your definition of love? Take some time today and exercise God's love in the same manner He loves you, and see what happens!

Lord, thank You for loving me unconditionally with all of my faults and flaws. Help me to love as I am loved. Amen.

DAY 234

He Is Good

"Will you discredit my justice and condemn me just to prove you are right? Are you as strong as God? Can you thunder with a voice like his?"

JOB 40:8–9 NLT

While God loves us unconditionally and wants to bless and love us, we must remember that He is first and foremost the one and only God. He is the last word—the final judge. Have you spent time reading through the Old Testament? There we see God display His power. We see Him destroy entire people groups. We see Him do some scary stuff that is hard to accept.

Seeing this side of God can strike fear in us—and it should. We should learn to fear God, because as the scripture says, His ways are higher than our ways, His thoughts higher than our thoughts. He will do things we don't understand.

But while He is huge and terrifying and sometimes confusing, we know we can trust Him. As you continue to read through the Bible, you'll also see that He protects, provides for, and unconditionally loves the people who trust Him. Not the people who are perfect, *the people who trust Him.*

"Then he isn't safe?" said Lucy.

"Safe?" said Mr. Beaver. "Don't you hear what Mrs. Beaver tells you? Who said anything about being safe? 'Course he isn't safe. But he's good."
—C. S. Lewis, *The Lion, the Witch and the Wardrobe*

Thank You that Your ways are higher than my own. Please give me a heart of understanding, that I may be open to all You do.

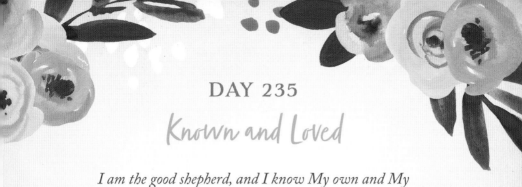

Known and Loved

*I am the good shepherd, and I know My own and My
own know Me, even as the Father knows Me and I
know the Father; and I lay down My life for the sheep.*
JOHN 10:14–15 NASB

Do you fear being known and rejected? Do you feel that if someone truly knew you they couldn't possibly love you? In these verses, Christ asserts that He knows you. But He doesn't just know you as a casual acquaintance or even an intimate friend. His knowledge runs deeper than that. He knows you in the same way that He knows the Father. In the Trinity, Christ and the Father are one. So He is saying that He knows you in the same way that He knows Himself. There could not be a deeper or more intimate knowledge. He knows all the things that you hide from everyone else—He knows the temptations, the frustrations, the lost hopes, the rejections, the insecurities, and the deep desires that you may hardly acknowledge to yourself.

Even though Christ knows the darkest and most secret parts of you, He still loves you. He doesn't love you because He can gain something from it. He doesn't love you on a surface, nonchalant level. He *laid down His life* for you. There is no greater love. He knows you better than anyone else does, and yet He loves you with a deeper, purer love than anyone else can give you. You are deeply known and deeply loved.

*Lord, I can't comprehend that You would love me in spite of all
my faults. Thank You for bestowing on me a love I don't deserve.*

DAY 236

Moving in God's Strength

*I am full of power by the Spirit of the LORD. . . . In God I have
put my trust; I will not be afraid. . . . I am for peace. . . . My help
comes from the LORD, who made heaven and earth. . . . . Because
You have been my help, therefore in the shadow of Your wings I
will rejoice. . . . Now therefore, O God, strengthen my hands.*
MICAH 3:8; PSALM 56:11; 120:7; 121:2; 63:7; NEHEMIAH 6:9 NKJV

At times, when a task lies before us, we begin to doubt our ability. Writers hesitate, their hands hovering above the keyboard. Mothers look at their to-do lists, the words blurring before them as overwhelmed feelings creep in. Businesswomen consider the meeting they will soon be leading, not sure of the words to say. Unfocused, unsure, untethered around the tasks before us, we flounder.

Let God take over. Tap into His power and claim it for yourself. Put all your trust in the God who vanquishes fear, who can help you do all He has called you to do. He's done so in the past, and He will definitely do so in the present. Rejoice in His presence, and allow Him to work through you as your hands begin moving in His strength.

*Lord, truly I am full of power by Your Spirit. Trusting You, I will not be
afraid but at peace because You are my help. As I rejoice in You, I feel Your
energy move through me, Your strength moving my hands. And I begin. . . .*

DAY 237
Secret Desires

Trust in the LORD, and do good; dwell in the land, and feed on His faithfulness. Delight yourself also in the LORD, and He shall give you the desires of your heart. Commit your way to the LORD, trust also in Him, and He shall bring it to pass.
PSALM 37:3–5 NKJV

Some of us never pursue our deepest desires out of fear of what people will think or fear of failure. But such fears can keep us from living the life we long for. So how do we slay the dream killers? We lean on God and become confident in Him. We do things His way. It is then we find ourselves dwelling in His territory and being fed on His promises. Such faithfulness sustains us in a way worldly fears cannot. And when we take joy in God's presence, allowing Him to be our guide and giving all our secret plans and dreams over to Him, He will give us the desires of our hearts. So put all your faith in God, the dream maker. Bring your desires before Him. Listen for every whisper, every leading He sends your way. Then simply trust as you commit your way to Him, not forcing the issue but confident that in His will, His way, His timing, He'll bring all your dreams into being.

Lord, I sometimes hesitate to tell You what my soul really craves. But I know that You alone can satisfy my longings, can make my dreams come true. So, as I delight in You, lead me in the way You would have me go. I am putting all my hope in You. Amen.

DAY 238

Perfect Peace

You will keep in perfect peace all who trust in you, all whose thoughts are fixed on you! Trust in the LORD always, for the LORD GOD is the eternal Rock.
ISAIAH 26:3–4 NLT

Our lives are a series of moments. And that's what our minds get caught up in, the day-to-day minutiae, the little niggling worries, the what-ifs, the how-comes, and the why-fors. But God wants us to have a different perspective, not an in-the-moment viewpoint but an eternal one. Because when we look at the big picture, our day-to-day worries—the ones that get our hearts beating out of control and our thoughts ricocheting around in our heads—are really nothing to be upset about. That takes trust in a power so much higher than ourselves. But when we have that trust, that confidence in the eternal Rock who can never be moved, we are blessed with a peace that blesses us within, keeping us healthy in mind, body, spirit, soul, and heart. Such a calm also blesses those around us, for it's contagious.

So fix your mind on the One who sees and knows so much more than you ever will. Put your confidence in the One who has your name written on the palm of His hand. Practice being in His presence during quiet hours. And then, the moment stress and chaos begin creeping in, call God to mind, and He will surround you with that big-picture, perfect peace.

*I need Your perfect peace, God. You are my eternal Rock.
Take me out of the present and into Your presence where
peace will reign and blessings abound. Amen.*

DAY 239
Even the Little Things

But be sure to fear the LORD and serve him faithfully with all
your heart; consider what great things he has done for you.
1 Samuel 12:24 niv

No one likes sweeping dust bunnies out from under the fridge, scrubbing grout, or filing taxes. Sometimes the boss will assign a grueling task, or worse, an extremely tedious one. It's tempting to expend the minimum effort required and get on with the better things in life. This can happen in relationships as well—we manage the minimum amount of closeness and small talk without any real depth or connection.

However, as God's children we are called to a higher standard. Not just to "get things over with," but to do all things to His glory. Practically, this means doing our best in whatever task or goal we pursue, knowing that He is the final inspector of our work, tasks both big and small.

So, should we scurry to scour the oven until the metal squeaks for mercy? No, we don't work out of fear or out of cold duty (though sometimes those are the motives that compel us), but because we desire to please God, knowing how much He loves us. The way we do the "little things" reveals for whom we labor—for us? For our employers, family, or friends? We may benefit from our efforts, but ultimately our work is for our Father.

Father God, You see all of my work. Please forgive me
for when I have complained, and help me do my
best in everything and do it out of joy in You.

DAY 240

Work as Unto God

Work willingly at whatever you do, as though you were
working for the Lord rather than for people.
COLOSSIANS 3:23 NLT

Whatever you do today, work as if you are working for the Lord rather than for man. What does that mean? For the employee, it means work as if God is your supervisor. He does see and hear everything you do. When you are tempted to slack off, remember that the Bible warns against idleness. When you are tempted to grumble about your boss, remember that God has put you under this person's authority—at least for this time. For the stay-at-home wife or mother, it means that even changing a diaper or washing dishes can be done for the glory of God. This verse has to do with attitude. Are you working in the right spirit? Work is not a bad thing. God created work. God Himself worked in order to create the earth in six days. And on the seventh, He looked at the work of His hands and He rested. Consider your work a blessing. If you are employed, remember today that many are without jobs. If you are able to stay at home with your children and keep your house, keep in mind that many are not able to do so for one reason or another. Whatever you do, work as if you are working for God.

Lord, help me to remember that I am working for You and
not for man. You are my eternal reward. I want to please
You in all that I set out to accomplish. Amen.

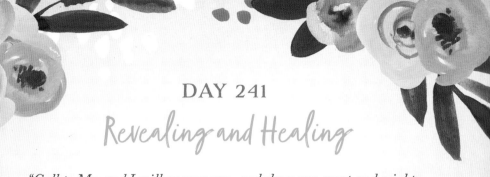

DAY 241
Revealing and Healing

"Call to Me, and I will answer you, and show you great and mighty things, which you do not know. . . . I will bring [them] health and healing; I will heal them and reveal to them the abundance of peace and truth."
JEREMIAH 33:3, 6 NKJV

God again beckons His people to put Him to the test. He wants His daughters to call to Him so that He can answer them. He longs to show them great and mighty things. One of these great and mighty things is healing—both physical and spiritual. Part of healing includes an abundant knowledge and experience of God's peace and truth.

In Jeremiah 33 God told the prophet His plans to restore Jerusalem, to bring the people back from captivity in Babylon and to forgive their rebelliousness. He promised mercy and the coming of a descendent of King David who would be called the Branch of Righteousness and who would rule in joy. Chapter 33 bursts with the beauty of God's grace as it points forward to the great plan of rescue, not just for the Jewish people captured by the Babylonian King Nebuchadnezzar during Jeremiah's time, but to the salvation of creation through Messiah Jesus. God accomplished in Jesus the mightiest of deeds, a plan for redemption which we could never imagine. Through Jesus, God revealed to us, daughters of Eve, peace and truth since He is the Prince of Peace and the Way of truth.

Lord of our righteousness, thank You for the beautiful picture of healing in Jeremiah 33 and for its fulfillment in Jesus. Keep healing! Amen.

DAY 242

Deep Roots

*"They will be like a tree planted by the water that sends out its roots by
the stream. It does not fear when heat comes; its leaves are always green.
It has no worries in a year of drought and never fails to bear fruit."*

JEREMIAH 17:8 NIV

Watering your garden doesn't seem difficult, but did you know you can
train a plant to grow incorrectly, just in the way you water it? By pouring
water from the hose for only a few moments at each plant, the root systems
become very shallow. They start to seek water from the top of the soil,
and the roots can easily be burned in the summer sun. By using a soaker
hose, the water slowly percolates into the ground, and the plants learn to
push their roots deeper into the soil to get water.

Jeremiah talked about a larger plant, a tree. A tree needs deep roots to
keep it anchored in the ground, providing stability. The roots synthesize
water and minerals for nourishment and then help to store those elements
for a later time. Our deep spiritual roots come from reading God's Word,
which provides stability, nourishment, and refreshment.

*Father, I do not want to wither in the sun. Help me to immerse
myself in Your Word. When I do, I strike my spiritual roots deeper
into life-giving soil and drink from Living Water. Help me to be
the fruitful follower of You that I am meant to be. Amen.*

DAY 243

Everyday Ways

The heavens tell of the glory of God; and their
expanse declares the work of His hands.
PSALM 19:1 NASB

Another day has come. You sit in your backyard and watch the sun rise. Glorious shades of pink meld with yellow and bright red, all artfully meshed at the edges with a now light-blue sky. It was unlike any sunrise you've ever seen. *God showing off again.*

If you think about it, no two sunrises are ever the same. The sun comes up in a slightly different location along the horizon each day at a slightly different time depending on the season. The color variations are never exactly the same, as if an artist had painted it.

But then, a great artist does paint it. Every day. Something new.

How deeply God must love you and each of His children to give us a fresh work of art in the skies every day of our lives. Many duties and burdens may fill our days, and He loves us in the midst of all of it, enough to provide beauty and wonder all along the way.

Father, thank You for Your everyday ways. Let the wonder of Your creation
continue to deepen our understanding of Your great love for us. Amen.

DAY 244
A Forever Love

But I trust in your unfailing love;
my heart rejoices in your salvation.
PSALM 13:5 NIV

The Bible tells us that God's love for us is unfailing. The dictionary defines unfailing as "completely dependable, inexhaustible, endless." Our hearts can truly rejoice knowing that we can never exhaust God's love. It won't run out. We can completely depend on God and His love for us at all times and in all situations.

Many people—even Christians—go through life believing that God is just a grumpy old man at the edge of heaven looking down on us with disappointment and disgust. That couldn't be further from the truth! Through Jesus Christ and His power at work within us, God sees us as *holy* and *dearly loved* (Colossians 3:12 NIV) children. His love is unfailing, and that can never change! Check out the following verses:

In your unfailing love you will lead the people you have redeemed. In your strength you will guide them to your holy dwelling. (Exodus 15:13 NIV)

Many are the woes of the wicked, but the LORD's unfailing love surrounds the man who trusts in him. (Psalm 32:10 NIV)

How priceless is your unfailing love, O God! People take refuge in the shadow of your wings. (Psalm 36:7 NIV)

The next time you start to think that God is upset with you, remember His unfailing and unchanging love.

Father in heaven, Your unfailing love surrounds me as I
trust in You. Thank You for Your amazing promise! Amen.

DAY 245
The Gift of Encouragement

We have different gifts. . . If it is to encourage, then give encouragement.
ROMANS 12:6–8 NIV

As a Christian, what is the inward desire of your heart? To witness? To serve? To teach? In the book of Romans, Paul lists the different gifts God gives His children according to His grace. These gifts of grace are inward desires and abilities used to further the kingdom of God. Encouragement is one of those gifts.

Have you ever met someone who seems to have the right thing to say at just the right time? Intuitively, she notices when someone is troubled and proceeds to listen and speak words to uplift and encourage.

Paul spoke of encouraging as a God-given desire to proclaim God's Word in such a way that it touches hearts to move them to receive the Gospel. Encouragement is a vital part to witnessing because encouragement is doused with God's love. For the believer, it stimulates our faith to produce a deeper commitment to Christ. It brings hope to the disheartened or defeated soul. It restores hope.

Perhaps you are wondering what "gift" you possess. The Bible promises us that every true believer is endowed with at least one or more spiritual gifts (1 Corinthians 12). How will you know your gift? Ask God, and then follow the desires He places on your heart.

Father, help me tune in to the needs of those around me so that I might encourage them for the Gospel's sake for Your glory and their good. Amen.

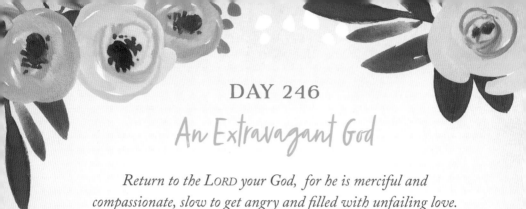

DAY 246
An Extravagant God

*Return to the LORD your God, for he is merciful and
compassionate, slow to get angry and filled with unfailing love.*
JOEL 2:13 NLT

There are often times when we are exhausted and discouraged and we
allow our minds to roam to dark places. Despair and disappointment set
in. A woe-is-me attitude prevails within us. How is it possible to rise from
the doldrums? How do we continue? We turn our faces toward the Lord
God and know He is in control.

Scripture tells of God's mercy and loving-kindness. It speaks out and
urges us to come back to God. This doesn't necessarily mean a change of
circumstances, but a change of heart. This change is a choice we intentionally make. It's not necessary to be in a church building or a revival
when we make this choice. While many changes happen there, ours can
be in our closet, our car, or our office. We reach inwardly to the Highest
and ask for His mercy. And scripture says He is merciful and full of grace.
He hears our prayers.

Focusing on the negative, choosing despair, doesn't bring life. Volun-
tarily focusing on Jesus will. Praise Him for all your blessings: they are
there, look for them. Some might be tiny, others magnificent. But they're
all because of our Lord Jesus Christ. He is a most patient God and extravagant in His love.

*O heavenly Father, I praise Your name. You are extravagant
in Your love, and I am grateful for all You've done. Amen.*

DAY 247
Never Quit

*Let us not become weary in doing good, for at the proper
time we will reap a harvest if we do not give up.*
GALATIANS 6:9 NIV

"They've broken my spirit," the elderly woman said as she assessed her damaged garden. Slashed cucumber vines and mutilated vegetables littered the once fruitful plot of land across the street from her home, alongside abandoned railroad tracks. Night vandals had ruined Mrs. Conner's labor of love.

For years she planted, cultivated, and watered her garden, laboriously hauling buckets of water across the street to provide vegetables for needy families. Although well into her eighties, she took pride and pleasure in her work.

As she cleared her vandalized garden of debris, she muttered, "I spent over one hundred dollars on the garden this year, and for what?" Then God spoke, "Don't quit. If you quit, they've won."

Are unexpected circumstances breaking your heart and spirit? Are vandals destroying your life's garden? The Bible teaches us to persevere at the exact time the voice within screams, "Give up!"

Difficulties can destroy and sabotage the fruits of our labor, but they cannot rob us of our faith and the power of prayer. Pray for the ones who hurt you; pray for strength and courage, and God will restore your garden in due course.

Mrs. Conner did, and she's still gardening today.

*Jesus, it's hard to keep going when times are hard. Help me
persevere in prayer when I'm tempted to quit. Amen.*

DAY 248

Only through God

For by thee I have run through a troop:
by my God have I leaped over a wall.
2 SAMUEL 22:30 KJV

We've all heard stories about people performing seemingly impossible acts of heroism in the face of danger—lifting a car off someone, carrying an injured person for several miles to reach help. Other stories tell how people survive being stranded in a blizzard or walk away from a terrible accident uninjured. How did they do this? Common sense often plays a big part in survival, but today's scripture tells us where our strength comes from. God enabled the writer of this verse to survive the obstacles he faced.

We may never face the tragedies we read about or see on the news, but we deal with adversity every day. A job loss, a bad medical diagnosis, or a child being bullied at school are only a few of the problems faced by people like us every day. How do we handle it? We can deal with the trouble that comes our way through God and His powerful strength. We may not face a troop or have to jump over a wall, but by our God, we can face a financial crisis, divorce, or disease. Take courage today in knowing that God is here for you and you can leap over that wall of adversity.

Father, give me the strength to face life's trouble
and run the race until the finish. Amen.

DAY 249

Hannah's Prayer

The eyes of the Lord search the whole earth in order to
strengthen those whose hearts are fully committed to him.
2 Chronicles 16:9 nlt

There are many great prayers in the Bible. There are prayers for wisdom and for unity, prayers of repentance and negotiation with God. Hannah's was an anguished prayer for a child.

Hannah was barren. She prayed before God with a broken heart and promised God that if He gave her a child, she would commit him to the Lord all the days of his life. God heard and answered her prayer. Does God always answer the prayer for a child in this way? No, He doesn't. There are women whom God loves deeply and unconditionally who will not bear a child in this life. But in this case, God granted Hannah a male child whom she named Samuel. She only had Samuel for a short time before she took him to Eli, the priest. Samuel was not an ordinary child. He heard the voice of God at a very young age. He grew up to become a judge and prophet that could not be matched in all of Israel's history.

God is looking for ordinary men and women whose prayers reflect hearts completely committed to Him. He found such commitment in Hannah, and He answered her prayer.

Father, may my prayers reflect a deep commitment to You, and may all
that I ask for be for Your kingdom and not for my own glory. Amen.

DAY 250

Forgiveness

*"For if you forgive other people when they sin against you,
your heavenly Father will also forgive you. But if you do not
forgive others their sins, your Father will not forgive your sins."*
MATTHEW 6:14–15 NIV

While checking your email, an invitation from a friend pops up in your inbox. Instead of excitement, a horrible, careless remark she once said about you leaps to mind. Your stomach clenches—the comment hurts as much as it did the moment you first heard it. You've tried to forgive her, but anger still needles your heart.

Forgiveness is much more costly than simply saying the words "I forgive you." Forgiveness means letting go of the right to hold a person's wrongs against them. Instead, you absorb the debt the offender owes you. We can give up our right to demand retribution because we are whole in Christ—forgiveness doesn't diminish us. It is out of His grace that we can offer grace to those who've hurt us. As Jesus' followers, we show our gratitude for His forgiveness toward us when we model His actions.

Often, forgiveness looks more like a process than an event. It's okay if forgiving someone takes a long time. Prayer will help that process; asking sincerely for God to bless those you want to forgive will keep your heart soft and free of bitterness. When hurt comes back to haunt you, throw your pain on Christ—He will help you let go.

*Father God, I need Your forgiveness every day. Help me to
forgive those who have hurt me, however long it takes,
and give my pain to You in the meantime. Amen.*

DAY 251
Blessed Redeemer

For God so loved the world that he gave his one and only Son,
that whoever believes in him shall not perish but have eternal life.
JOHN 3:16 NIV

Compassion is "sympathetic consciousness of others' distress together with a desire to alleviate it" *(Merriam-Webster)*. Oh, how our God loved us and showed His compassion. He knew we were a sinful people, and we were in peril. Our eternal lives were at stake. And He had a plan. He provided a way for redemption.

Despite the fact we did not deserve His unmerited favor, grace, He gave it to us anyway. He looked down on humankind and desired to bridge the separation between us. He sent His Son, Jesus, to die on the cross for our sins, so we might live the resurrected life. Once we've accepted this free gift, we can rejoice!

We were in distress, and God came to the rescue. What a mighty God we serve! And how He loves us. The rescuing Shepherd came for His flock. He bore what we deserved because He had such compassion. True love, which our Father gives, is eternal. He loved us before we loved Him. What an amazing concept He desires us to grasp! Know today your heavenly Father loves you.

Dear Lord, how gracious and loving You are to me.
Thank You, Father, for Your arms about me this day. Amen.

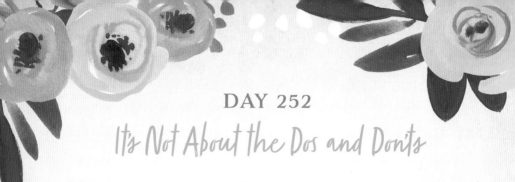

DAY 252
It's Not About the Dos and Don'ts

Who hath saved us, and called us with an holy calling, not according to
our works, but according to his own purpose and grace, which was given
us in Christ Jesus before the world began, but is now made manifest by
the appearing of our Saviour Jesus Christ, who hath abolished death,
and hath brought life and immortality to light through the gospel.
2 TIMOTHY 1:9–10 KJV

More than 600 Jewish laws are derived from the Ten Commandments
that God gave Moses. Before Jesus the Messiah came, they had to follow
a list of rules in order to live a life that pleased God and assured them of
His continued blessing in their lives.

Jesus came to the earth; gave His life; and defeated death, hell, and
the grave, so you could choose eternal life. You are not saved because of a
list of dos and don'ts you follow. Instead, it's all about surrendering your
heart to God. You are His child by His grace. Once forgiven, He doesn't
remember your sins.

Our world is moved by conditional love: I will love you if you do this
or that. Thankfully that has no place in your relationship with God. His
love is unconditional. You don't have to work from a list for God to accept
you. His grace has already made you lovable and acceptable to Him. There
is nothing you can do to make God love you any more or any less.

Lord Jesus, I surrender my heart to You.
Thank You for the gift of eternal life. Amen.

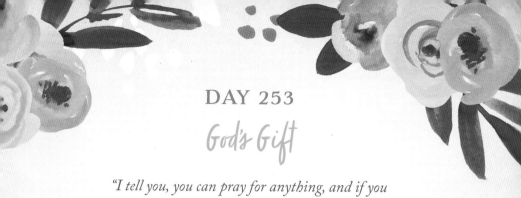

DAY 253

God's Gift

"I tell you, you can pray for anything, and if you
believe that you've received it, it will be yours."
MARK 11:24 NLT

Notice the words in this verse. It says we're to believe we have received what we pray for. That's past tense. It doesn't take faith to believe our prayers will be answered after what we asked for is in plain sight. Trusting Him for answers before we see them is what the Lord wants.

The Bible tells us that without faith it is impossible to please God (see Hebrews 11:6). That may sound harsh, but scripture also promises that He gives each of us a measure of faith (see Romans 12:3).

If you gave your daughter a present and she left it on a shelf, unopened, you'd be disappointed. It may have been something she really wanted, so you found the perfect gift and wrapped it beautifully, but it is useless just sitting there. It's the same with God's gift of faith. We don't have to struggle with positive thinking or work up enough faith. All we have to do is accept what He has already provided and exercise the faith He gives.

Some people misuse this scripture and pray for foolish things that aren't according to His will. But when we stay close to Him, our desires will line up with His, and we can have complete confidence that we will receive our request.

Dear Father, thank You for the faith You generously give me. I want
my desires to perfectly align with Your desires for me so I can ask with
true faith, knowing You have already provided the answer. Amen.

DAY 254
Trials and Wisdom

Consider it pure joy, my brothers and sisters, whenever you face trials of many kinds, because you know that the testing of your faith produces perseverance. Let perseverance finish its work so that you may be mature and complete, not lacking anything. If any of you lacks wisdom, you should ask God, who gives generously to all without finding fault, and it will be given to you.
JAMES 1:2–5 NIV

Trials and troubles are an everyday part of living here in a fallen world. Pastor and author Max Lucado says, "Lower your expectations of earth. This isn't heaven, so don't expect it to be."

Things won't be easy and simple until we get to heaven. So how can we lift our chins and head into tomorrow without succumbing to discouragement? We remember that God is good. We trust His faithfulness. We ask for His presence and peace during each moment. We pray for wisdom and believe that the God who holds the universe in His hands is working every single trial and triumph together for our good and for His glory.

This verse in James tells us that when we lack wisdom we should simply ask God for it! We don't have to face our problems alone. We don't have to worry that God will hold our past mistakes against us. Be encouraged that the Lord will give you wisdom generously without finding fault!

Lord Jesus, please give me wisdom. So many troubles are weighing me down. Help me give You all my burdens and increase my faith and trust in You. Amen.

DAY 255

The Next Step

Your word is a lamp for my feet, a light on my path.
PSALM 119:105 NIV

Change is unsettling. It doesn't matter who we are—old or young, rich or poor, married or single. Change can be exciting, but it also brings with it the unknown. And that can be a little unnerving.

When we face changes, the path ahead often looks dark and twisted. We squint and strain to see down the road, but we just can't see clearly. But we don't always need to see into the distance. We only need to see the step ahead of us. Then another step. Then another step.

When the path ahead is obscure, we can go to God's Word for guidance. His Word will light our way. Oh, it may not tell us exactly what's coming a year from now, or even a month from now. But if we depend on Him and follow the guidance He's given us, His Word will act as a road map for the step ahead. It will light the pathway at our feet, so we know we're not stepping off a cliff.

When we rely on His Word and follow it consistently, we can trust His goodness. Even when the future is unclear, we can move ahead with confidence, knowing He will lead us to the best place for us, and His goodness and love will stay with us every step of the journey.

My Guide, I will continue to spend time in Your Word and follow Your leading in my life. Even when I am unsure where this path will lead, I know I can trust You. Amen.

DAY 256
A Wonderful Cord-ship

*A person standing alone can be attacked and defeated, but
two can stand back-to-back and conquer. Three are even
better, for a triple-braided cord is not easily broken.*
ECCLESIASTES 4:12 NLT

Alone a woman may be beaten down spiritually, emotionally, or physically. But when one woman teams up with another, the two have a better chance of standing firm together! Like Ruth who refused to leave Naomi, a woman who pledges herself to a female friend not only pulls up and strengthens herself, but her friend as well. Their fates forged together, they seek to help each other in every manner of ways—building each other up, sharing life experiences, bearing each other's burdens, sharing each other's sorrows, celebrating each other's successes, seeking wisdom in the quest to understand the opposite sex, discussing methods of child rearing, exploring new employment avenues, challenging and comforting one another, and keeping each other firmly footed on the spiritual path.

When two women who are bound in such a friendship add love and fellowship with God to their "cord-ship," they become even stronger. With Christ in the mix, this now "triple-braided cord" will not easily fray.

May all women on this National Women's Friendship Day find a special way to honor their girlfriends, their God, and their special cord-ship.

*Thank You, Lord, for my girlfriend and for Your presence between us.
Help me to be as good a friend to her as You are and have been to me.*

DAY 257
Building Friendships

A friend loves at all times, and a brother is born for a time of adversity.
PROVERBS 17:17 NIV

Today's world isn't designed for friendship. It's too fast paced, with too many demands and too much stress. Oh, we're connected to everyone, all the time, through text messaging and cell phones and Facebook. But as fun as Facebook may seem, it robs us of face-to-face time. We're so distracted with everything at once, we find it hard to focus on one thing, one person at a time.

But friendship demands one-on-one, face-to-face time. And although most of us don't feel we have a lot of time to give, we must! We simply must make friendship, and building real flesh-and-blood relationships, a priority.

God created us for relationships. And although a well-timed email or text message may lift us up at times, there's simply no replacement for a real, live hug. There's no substitute for a friend sitting beside you in the hospital, holding your hand. And we won't have those things unless we're willing to put aside our high-tech gadgets and invest time in the people around us.

Today, let's make it a point to turn off our cell phones. Let's step away from our computers for a while and have a real conversation with someone. That person may just turn out to be a true friend.

Dear Father, teach me to be a true friend. Help me to make friendship a priority and invest in the people around me. Amen.

DAY 258
Without Love

*If I speak in the tongues of men or of angels, but do not have
love, I am only a resounding gong or a clanging cymbal.*

1 CORINTHIANS 13:1 NIV

Without love, all the good deeds in the world are just a bunch of noise!
Like resounding gongs or clanging cymbals, the Pharisees of Jesus' day
went about their good works. Over and over, they repeated them. They
were duties, not desires of the heart. They based everything on ritual rather
than relationship. Are there Pharisees among us today? Certainly! Our job
as Christ-followers is to show the world the love of God. We do this with
open hearts and open arms. We do it in the workplace, in the marketplace,
and in our homes. We do it as we come and go; with our children and with
other people's children; with our spouses, neighbors, and coworkers. The
world desperately needs to see extravagant love in us, love that cannot be
explained by any means other than the fact that we walk with the Author
and Creator of love. Don't go about your good deeds out of guilt or so
that someone will notice how nice you are. Do good deeds so that others
will notice Jesus in you and glorify your Father who is in heaven. Do good
deeds out of love. It will always come back to you tenfold.

*Lord Jesus, give me opportunities to love this
world so that others might see You in me. Amen.*

DAY 259
Three Strings

*Two people are better than one, because they get more done by
working together. If one falls down, the other can help him up. But
it is bad for the person who is alone and falls, because no one is there
to help. . . .a rope that is woven of three strings is hard to break.*
ECCLESIASTES 4:9–10, 12 NCV

God uses His people to encourage and strengthen one another. As iron sharpens iron, so a friend sharpens a friend (Proverbs 27:17). We get more accomplished in our own lives—and in the grand scheme of things—when we are open to the help and encouragement of others.

If you see a friend in need of physical, emotional, or spiritual help—ask the Lord to give you the wisdom and understanding to be used in helpful ways. And when a friend offers similar help to you, don't be too proud to accept it.

Ask the Lord to guide you in finding a "three-string" accountability partner. Look for a Christian woman with a strong faith in the Lord who is willing to pray with you, encourage you in your faith, and be honest about your strengths and weaknesses. Meet together several times a month and ask each other the hard questions: Were you faithful to the Lord this week? Did you gossip? Is there anything you're struggling with right now? How can I pray for you?

With God, you, and a trusted Christian friend working together, you become a rope of three strings that is hard to break!

*Father, thank You for using Your people to encourage and sharpen
me. Guide me as I seek an accountability partner that will
help me grow in my relationship with You. Amen.*

DAY 260
The-God-Who-Sees

Now the Angel of the LORD found her. . . . [and] said to her, "Return to your mistress, and submit yourself under her hand". . . . Then she called the name of the LORD who spoke to her, You-Are-the-God-Who-Sees.
GENESIS 16:7, 9, 13 NKJV

Hagar ran away from her circumstances: Sarai, an abusive mistress. Part of Hagar's trouble had been caused by her own actions. For having become pregnant by Abram, she had begun disrespecting the childless Sarai.

We too sometimes think we can run from our troubles. But when we come to the end of ourselves, God is there, ready to give us the wisdom we need but may not want. He may ask us to go back, telling us how to "be" in our circumstances: submissive, obedient, loving. He had a vision for Hagar that she would be the mother of a son and have many descendants.

Even today, this God-Who-Sees sees you and your situation. He is ready to reveal Himself to you and share His wisdom. He may not remove you from your circumstances, but He will give you the word you need to get through them. Afterward, you'll see your situation in a new light, with a new hope for your future, step by step.

Lord, You constantly reveal Yourself, manifest Yourself to me. In fact, You see me before I even come to You. So be with me now. Show me where You want me to submit. Remind me that You have a plan and vision for my life—and that it is all meant for my good. Amen.

DAY 261
With All Your Strength

Whatever your hand finds to do, do it with all your might.
ECCLESIASTES 9:10 NIV

"Now we have one day more," said Oxford chaplain Joseph Alleine in 1664. "Let us live well, work hard for souls, lay up much treasure in heaven this day, for we have but a few to live." Little did he know that only four years later, at age thirty-four, his time on earth would end.

Every single moment of life is a gift. We dare not waste one. "To live is Christ," said the apostle Paul (Philippians 1:21 KJV). Our lives were made to reflect God's glory, not just on Sundays or mission trips or during women's Bible study class, but in respecting our husbands and modeling decency and kindness for others. It's in the things we say, do, and think when no one is there to give credit. It's in the times we choose to do the right thing, even when it hurts.

Every moment has a purpose for God's kingdom. It's time to be zealous for righteousness in the course of everyday life, and God has promised a treasure trove awaiting us in heaven. The irony is that earthly life will also be filled with treasures—happy marriages, strong children, peace of mind, and joy unspeakable and full of glory.

God, I pray that my passion for You shows through my daily life.
Put a fire in my soul that burns so bright others can see it. Amen.

DAY 262

What's Your "But God" Story?

But God demonstrates his own love for us in this:
While we were still sinners, Christ died for us.

ROMANS 5:8 NIV

Some people believe God set the world in motion, then stepped back just to watch it spin without intervening in the lives of men. A simple search for the phrase "but God" in scripture shows otherwise. According to Khouse.org, the exact phrase "but God" is used 64 times from the Old Testament through the New.

In Genesis 20:3, Abraham gave his wife, Sarai, to Abimelek, but God intervened and came to Abimelek in a dream telling him that he was as good as a dead man since Sarai was married.

In Genesis 41:16, Joseph couldn't give Pharaoh the interpretations for his dreams, but God could (and did).

In Genesis 45:5, there was a famine, but God sent Joseph ahead of his family through a nasty betrayal to save the lives of many people, including his brothers who had betrayed him.

In Jonah 1:17, Jonah ran from God, but God provided a great fish to swallow Jonah.

In Acts 2:24, Jesus was put to death, but God raised him from the dead.

How awesome! But God! God was involved in the lives of men and He is still involved now, intervening, guiding, and ruling. What's your "but God" story?

Lord, thank You that You are always at work in my life. Help me to notice all the ways You intervene to guide me, lead me, and provide for me. Amen.

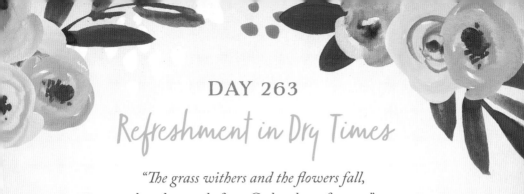

DAY 263

Refreshment in Dry Times

"The grass withers and the flowers fall,
but the word of our God endures forever."
Isaiah 40:8 niv

The grass was lifeless, crunchy, and brown. The trees had already started to lose their leaves, and it was only August. Flowers wilted, and the ground was nothing but dry dirt. The previous winter was unseasonably warm with very little snow. Spring had been practically nonexistent, and summer was day after day of relentless, scorching heat with very little rain. It was a drought with no change in sight.

Sometimes our lives feel just like the grass—dry and listless. Maybe we're in a season where things seem to stand still, and we've tried everything to change our circumstances for the better to no avail. It is during those times that we need to remember the faithfulness of God and the permanence of His Word. His promises to us are many and true! God will never leave us or forsake us; and He will provide for, love, and protect us. And, just like the drought, eventually our personal dry times will give way to a time of growth, refreshment, and beauty.

Dear Lord, help me to remember Your love during difficult times
of dryness. Even though it's sometimes hard to hear Your voice or
be patient during hard times, please remind me of Your many
promises, and remind me to stand firmly on them. You are
everything I need and the refreshment I seek. Amen.

DAY 264

This Is My God

"The Lord is my strength and my song; he has given me victory. This is
my God, and I will praise him—my father's God, and I will exalt him!"
Exodus 15:2 nlt

In Acts 17, Paul was preaching to the people of Athens who were worshipping a host of gods. He even found an idol they had built to an "unknown god." Paul called out their ignorance and told them the truth about the Living God:

The God who made the world and everything in it is the Lord of heaven and earth and does not live in temples built by human hands. And he is not served by human hands, as if he needed anything. Rather, he himself gives everyone life and breath and everything else. From one man he made all the nations, that they should inhabit the whole earth; and he marked out their appointed times in history and the boundaries of their lands. God did this so that they would seek him and perhaps reach out for him and find him, though he is not far from any one of us. "For in him we live and move and have our being." (v. 24–28 niv)

This is our God, and He is worthy of all our praise! He is our strength and our song. He gives us victory through Christ. We are exactly where He has placed us, and He has a great purpose for doing so.

Lord of heaven and earth, I know that You are the only
true and living God! I praise You that You are not far
from me. You are my life and my very breath. Amen.

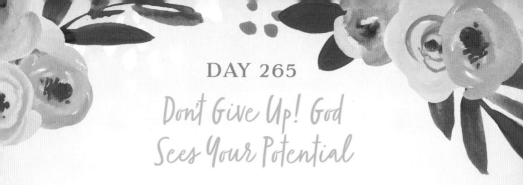

DAY 265
Don't Give Up! God Sees Your Potential

*"The LORD does not look at the things people look at. People look
at the outward appearance, but the LORD looks at the heart."*
1 SAMUEL 16:7 NIV

"I'm sorry, miss," the metro newspaper editor began as he addressed one of his journalism students. He couldn't remember her name. "You're just not cut out for the writing life. I can't pass you. Find another field of study."

The college student's eyes misted. "But I was tops in journalism at my junior college."

"You've got straight F's because you're a poor proofreader. That's where good writing starts. Change fields of study."

Miss J.'s heart was on the ground. She graduated in another field. Years later, she enrolled in a noncredit class: magazine writing. Her first story was purchased by a popular slick magazine. Over the decades, hundreds of articles followed, as well as anthologies and an award-winning book.

Miss J. smiled the day she was asked to be a writing workshop leader—in the city where she washed out in journalism. God had seen all along what she could be.

Our Creator sees more of our hearts and potential than anyone on earth. Just as He saw a king in David—while his siblings might have thought of him as only a pesky little brother—God sees the best of what we can be. He believes in us.

When it comes to believing what others believe we can and can't accomplish—trust in God instead and soar without limits!

Heavenly Father, thanks for my skills and the way You lead me in using them.

DAY 266
Thunder Roars

But everyone who calls on the name of the LORD will be saved.
JOEL 2:32 NLT

Do you ever tremble with fear? Whether it be from dangers without or emotional distress within, fear can paralyze people. It is as though a hand grips us by the throat and we are pinned in place with nowhere to go. Yet the Lord our God has said do not be afraid, He will save us.

The book of psalms reveals a man who quivers and hides in caves to escape his enemies. Time and again David calls out to the Lord, because he has been taught God will calm his fears. The circumstances do not always change, the thunder may still roar, but just like David we can know our lives are secure in the hand of the Almighty Creator of the Universe. He *will* save us. It's a promise.

Today make a list of those things which cause you to quake in your boots. Read the list out loud to the Lord and ask Him to provide the necessary bravery to overcome each one. Ask Him to see you through the deep waters and to hold you tightly over the mountaintops. For when you call on His Name, He hears and answers. Listen closely and remember He saves.

Father, I'm scared. Please hold me close and calm my anxious heart.
Tune my ears to hear Your Word and know what to do. Amen.

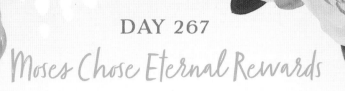

DAY 267
Moses Chose Eternal Rewards

Choosing rather to suffer affliction with the people of God than to enjoy the passing pleasures of sin, esteeming the reproach of Christ greater riches than the treasures in Egypt; for he looked to the reward.
HEBREWS 11:25–26 NKJV

How could affliction and reproach be a greater goal than ruling a country and owning fabulous wealth? Human thinking would see Moses as accomplishing great things for God by becoming Pharaoh and freeing the Hebrew slaves. But then Moses would get the credit, and no one would witness the power of the one true God. Even though Moses experienced failure, exile, and a forty-year-long wait, God could only use a humble servant. Moses chose to lay up treasure in heaven, even if it meant giving up the fortune he deserved on earth.

This eternal perspective kept Moses from enjoying sin's temporary pleasures. Instead of looking at the benefits of being the son of Pharaoh's daughter (Hebrews 11:24), he focused on spiritual things, choosing "the reproach of Christ" and enduring "as seeing Him who is invisible" (11:26–27 NKJV). Moses lived for eternal, not earthly, rewards.

As Christians, we get to choose our focus and the goals we devote our lives to. While eternal life is a free gift, not a reward, to everyone who believes in Christ, the Bible also teaches that believers will receive rewards in heaven for being "good and faithful servants."

Lord, I want to remember that my life here is a temporary one so that my choices will glorify You. Make me willing to give up human pleasures in exchange for future joys at Your right hand forever.

DAY 268

Seeking Advice

The LORD says, "I will guide you along the best pathway for your
life. I will advise you and watch over you. Do not be like a senseless
horse or mule that needs a bit and bridle to keep it under control."
PSALM 32:8–9 NLT

There is a key word in this passage: "advise." The Lord says He will advise us and watch over us. But what if we don't take the time to ask for His guidance? How many times have we been sidetracked, lost, and confused simply because we never asked for the Lord's advice?

In the hurried lives we live, it's easy to fall into a routine and switch over to autopilot. Our calendars are teeming with activities and deadlines, and all too often we simply enter "survival mode." You could say that we become similar to the mule in this scripture—putting hardly any thought into our days and simply being guided by chaos and distraction.

God has more for us. If we take the time to seek out His counsel, He will advise us. He will guide us along the best pathway for our lives and watch over us. He will give us purpose, and our lives will be filled with adventure and divine encounters.

Lord, thank You for opening my eyes to the reality that You desire to
guide my life. Forgive me for being so busy, and help me to slow down
and seek Your counsel. I want to walk this journey of life with You.

DAY 269

Call unto Me

Look to the LORD and his strength; seek his face always.
PSALM 105:4 NIV

A young woman received distressing news from her boss. In a panic, she phoned her mother to ask for guidance; she called her best friend for an opinion; she discussed the matter at lunch with coworkers. But not once did she seek the Lord's face.

Scripture encourages us to pray about everything—to send our cares and petitions heavenward. Why do we persist in running to others instead of Him? David, the psalmist, had no choice but to rely on the Lord as he fled his enemies. The lyrics of the Psalms remind us he was no stranger to loss and fear. Yet he cried unto the Lord. His words in Psalm 105 encourage us to remember what He has done before. Paul sat in the pits, literally, and sang songs of praise. While we might not be in dire straits like those men, we certainly have problems and can read scripture to see how the Lord has worked and have confidence He is near.

Let us work to seek His face always. Know the Lord cares about each detail of your life, and nothing is a secret or a surprise to Him. Reach for the best and expect results. It might require a time of waiting, but His answers are always unsurpassed.

Almighty Father, thank You for loving me so well. In times when I fear, help me fall into Your embrace. Amen.

DAY 270

Creative Image-Bearer

So God created man in His own image; in the image of
God He created him; male and female He created them.
GENESIS 1:27 NKJV

As children we learned we are different from animals because we reason, but much more than that sets humans apart. We are made in God's image. We can reason, because God reasons. But what else do we do that bears His likeness?

Is bearing God's image limited to demonstrating character qualities like love, forgiveness, hope, or honesty? Is it doing good deeds and acts of kindness? Does it mean every conversation should be peppered with spiritual language? Or is there a larger sense in which we bear God's image?

In the context of Genesis 1, when we imagine, create, and bring order to our world, we are bearing God's image. To bake a beautiful cake or design a quilt is to reflect God's creativity. To put a budget together in a systematic fashion, write a report, or bring organization to a pile of dirty laundry is to show God's ability to make order and beauty out of chaos.

As we work on projects and do our jobs, we reveal the Creator God to a world that doesn't recognize Him. When we get stuck, when no idea will come to mind, we can ask the One whose imprint we bear. The Creator who made us and loves us puts every good, true, and lovely thought in our minds.

Father, may we bear Your likeness better today than yesterday.
Cause us to remember that You are the source of creativity,
imagination, and organization. Help us do Your will.

DAY 271
Right People —Right Place —Right Time

And so find favor and high esteem in the sight of God and man.
PROVERBS 3:4 NKJV

When God laid out the blueprint for building your life, He scheduled the right people in the right places at precisely the right times for every phase of your life. He provided favor, lined up doors of opportunity, and arranged for perfect connections to help you construct a great life. God's blessings have already been ordered and are placed precisely throughout your journey called life.

But now it's up to you to recognize the opportunities and meet each appointment God has for you. You must walk by faith, listening to His direction and instruction so you can be quick to experience every good and perfect gift He has for you. God wants you to experience every favor and rich blessing He's prepared. By faith, expect blessing to meet you at every turn.

Imagine what your future holds when you become determined to step out to greet it according to God's design. Remain alert and attentive to what God wants to add to your life. Expect the goodness He has planned for you—doors of opportunities are opening for you today!

Lord, thank You for setting favor and blessing in my path and help me to expect it wherever I go and in whatever I do. Amen.

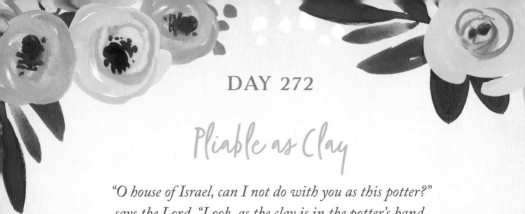

DAY 272

Pliable as Clay

"O house of Israel, can I not do with you as this potter?"
says the Lord. "Look, as the clay is in the potter's hand,
so are you in My hand, O house of Israel!"
JEREMIAH 18:6 NKJV

God has great plans for your life. He is the expert craftsman. He has drawn the blueprints and created the clay—that is, you. He has a design in mind that specifically uses your talents, gifts, interests, strengths, and experiences. His design for your life takes all of these factors into account to form one master plan for a valuable piece.

But He won't shape you by force. You must surrender your clay to be shaped by the Master. You will need to ask yourself what it means to be "like clay in the hand of the potter." What does it look like?

To surrender yourself, you must give up any selfish claims on fashioning your own design. The clay cannot tell the potter what it intends to be.

Begin by discovering your talents, interests, and strengths. What are the activities you especially enjoy? What skills come naturally to you? Once you discover your unique qualities, turn to observation. Where do you see needs in your home? In your school? At work? At church? In your community? How are you especially gifted to meet those needs?

Open yourself to the possibility of being molded into the best version of yourself. God wants to fashion your character, your heart, your life. Let Him.

Lord, forgive me for selfishly holding back my talents and gifts. Amen.

DAY 273

Breathing Room for Our Souls

He's solid rock under my feet, breathing room for
my soul, an impregnable castle: I'm set for life.
PSALM 62:2 MSG

In a materialistic, ambitious society like ours, the idea of taking time to rest and play isn't always our highest priority. After all, we're told that to get ahead you have to work longer and harder than everyone else.

But God, in His infinite wisdom and love, formed us with a need for downtime. He who created us longs for us to recreate—to enjoy recreation—regularly. So don't let a fear of falling behind rob you of the joy and necessity of recreation. Our bodies and souls need fun in order to thrive.

Find some way to blow off steam, whether it's gardening, painting, or scrapbooking. What did you like to do as a child? Answering that question can guide you to a hobby that relaxes you and gives you deep, abiding joy. Maybe you would enjoy watching movies, running races, or playing Bunco with your girlfriends.

And as believers, we can—and should—invite God into our recreation times. He wants to be a part of every area of our daily lives, whether we're working, resting, or blowing off steam.

After all, He is the place where our souls find their ultimate rest and peace.

Father, I praise You for the way You made me—with a need to
work, rest, and play. I invite You to join me while I recreate.

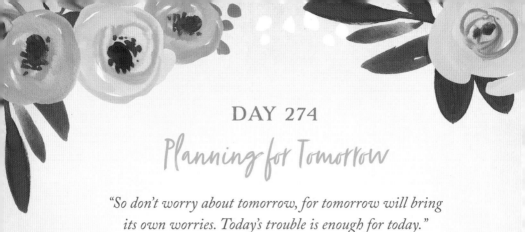

DAY 274

Planning for Tomorrow

*"So don't worry about tomorrow, for tomorrow will bring
its own worries. Today's trouble is enough for today."*
MATTHEW 6:34 NLT

The feeling of being at a crossroads comes to many of us in the years following high school and college and during the initial stages of a career. Hitting the "real world" for the first time, it's easy to lose sight of the present and focus on the future. Setting goals can easily turn into constant concern over what is to come.

Where to move, what career path to take, what job to apply for, and even whether to attend more schooling are just a few of the constant questions that can lead to a daily sense of worry and stress.

But God reminds us that those worries are to be left for tomorrow.

Thinking about the future has its place and setting goals is important, but these things should not become our all-consuming focus in life. Jesus said, "Tomorrow will have its own worries," so we need to learn to be content with today and remind ourselves that God will take care of our needs. If we trust in Him each day, a path will be made known. And those worries for tomorrow will fade.

*Dear Lord, remind me that You are in control yesterday,
today, and tomorrow. Help me not to worry about
the future, but actively seek You each day. Amen.*

DAY 275
Reflecting the Goodness of God

For if you listen to the word and don't obey, it is like
glancing at your face in a mirror. You see yourself,
walk away, and forget what you look like.
JAMES 1:23–24 NLT

Are you real? There are many reasons people wear masks and refuse to become completely transparent even with those they consider their closest friends.

It's so wonderful to find people who can be real with us. We are drawn to them because they are genuine and true—never pretending. Such boldness and confidence comes with knowing who we are in Christ. As we trust Him to help us, we examine our lives and then learn to shape them to reflect the goodness of God.

It is a process. We begin by looking into the mirror to see what we need to remove of the old person we used to be, so that we can take on the character and nature of God.

Too often, we miss the value of sharing our failings. We don't want to be vulnerable, so we hold back. In doing so, we deprive others of who God created each of us to be. When you share from your own experience—especially your failures—you increase empathy, you're more approachable, and you increase your "relatability" to others. Let your guard down and be all you were created to be.

Lord, help me to be real with those You have put around me. I pray
that they see You through me and it draws them closer to You. Amen.

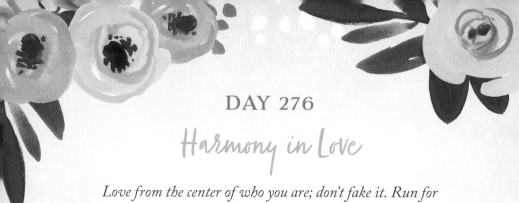

DAY 276

Harmony in Love

*Love from the center of who you are; don't fake it. Run for
dear life from evil; hold on for dear life to good. Be good
friends who love deeply; practice playing second fiddle.*
ROMANS 12:9–10 MSG

The call to love in Romans 12:9–10 is extremely difficult to put into practice. Sure, it's easy to love friends and family, but how easy is it to love that person at school or at work when you just cannot relate to her on any level? Being polite is one thing, but truly loving that person is much harder.

Paul tells us that we should not fake love. God says we sin against Him when we *pretend* to love others but dislike them. Instead we are called to *genuine* love. We must be good friends to everyone—the kind of friends who love deeply, from the center of our beings.

The Message uses the metaphor, "practice playing second fiddle," to help us understand how we are to honor one another. In a musical ensemble, the first fiddle typically plays the melody and all the fancy runs. The second fiddle performs the supporting role, harmonizing with the first fiddle, and acting as the musical anchor. We should always take the second part, putting others before ourselves, and encouraging them with all our love and devotion. When we love without hypocrisy and honor others above ourselves, we will live in beautiful harmony with one another.

*Dear Lord, please help me to love with a genuine heart
and to take second place to those around me. Amen.*

DAY 277

Rejoice! Rejoice!

Rejoice in the Lord always. I will say it again: Rejoice!
PHILIPPIANS 4:4 NIV

Paul must have really wanted the Philippians to know he was serious about this idea of rejoicing. He says it not once, but twice. Perhaps Paul wanted to emphasize the double impact of what the Lord has done for them—and us. We have new life because Jesus died on the cross for our sins!

Paul was also aware that our actions as Christians cannot be self-absorbed. We must be constantly focused on our brothers and sisters and on those outside the faith.

Paul's command to rejoice affects others as well as ourselves. Smiles are contagious, and true joy spreads easily. When we rejoice, we encourage others and remind them of our blessings in Christ. Those who do not know the peace of Christ see our great joy and want to know what is different about us. By constantly rejoicing in the Lord, we are able to spread the Word of God and tell others about the love of Christ.

Dear Lord, thank You for Your love. Teach me to continually rejoice, and may my joy spread to those around me. Amen.

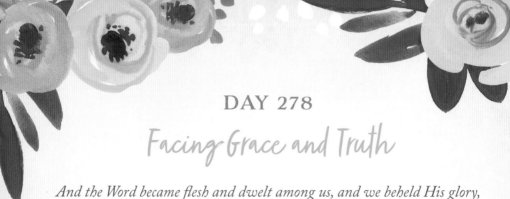

DAY 278

Facing Grace and Truth

And the Word became flesh and dwelt among us, and we beheld His glory,
the glory as of the only begotten of the Father, full of grace and truth.
JOHN 1:14 NKJV

In the life of Jesus, we behold the glory of the Father. The Word became flesh so that we could know God intimately. We see in Jesus what the Father is like. The Incarnation shows us that God is full of grace and truth.

When we belong to Christ and are in Him, we are surrounded by grace and truth. Grace is unmerited favor and approval. Truth is an absolute standard, a definitive answer, or a measuring rule. Grace is the cleansing, rushing water of a river. Truth, the banks holding fast, gives the water its power and force.

What does that mean for us in our daily lives? Truth tests thoughts, ideas, and things we hear and see. It helps us evaluate our culture, face our past, and acknowledge and confess our sins. Facing the truth is necessary for repentance.

We must stop denying and rationalizing, and admit our problem before we can truly turn in a new direction. Having faced the truth, we turn in repentance, and what we find before us is grace. Grace forgives us, saves us, loves us, and accepts us unconditionally. Experiencing this grace frees us to forgive, love, accept, and choose others regardless of their performance.

Father, thank You for giving us the Son, full of Your grace and truth.

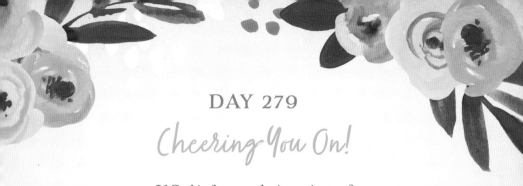

DAY 279
Cheering You On!

If God is for us, who is against us?
ROMANS 8:31 NASB

When others believe in you, they encourage and promote you. You know they're going to lift you up, and it helps you to reach higher for your goals and stand stronger against your opposition. It helps to know that they are supporting you—cheering you on.

Think about a little boy on a baseball team. It's his first year and he's just learning the game, but his coach lets him know he's nothing special. The boy knows his coach doesn't believe in him, and he doesn't have one, single good game all year.

The next year he has a new coach who sees potential in all his players. The coach treats the boy like a star. With encouragement from him, the boy performs like the winner his coach sees him to be.

Consider your own support network. Who do you rely on to help you up when you're down or to inspire you to new heights? The Lord is your number one fan. He sees you at your fullest potential, and He's always ready to hold you up. The Bible is a great place to find His encouraging words and instruction. No matter what you're facing, He's cheering you on right now.

Lord, help me to see myself as You see me. I know that You believe in me, and that brings courage to my heart. I am determined to reach higher and stand stronger knowing You are on my side. Amen.

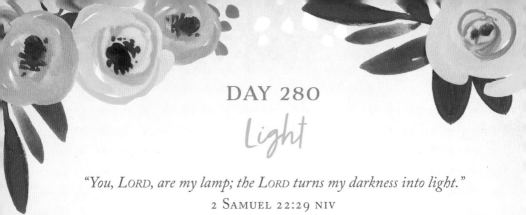

DAY 280

Light

"You, LORD, are my lamp; the LORD turns my darkness into light."
2 SAMUEL 22:29 NIV

The Bible begins with light. Genesis 1:3 (NIV) says, "And God said, 'Let there be light,' and there was light." It also ends with light. Revelation 22:5 (NIV) says, "There will be no more night. They will not need the light of a lamp or the light of the sun, for the Lord God will give them light."

Unfortunately, there's a lot of darkness in between. War. Murder. Pain. Loss.

Scripture certainly doesn't candy-coat the difficulties of life, but even in the midst of the darkness there are glorious glimpses of His marvelous light. David's sin is forgiven, and he becomes a man after God's own heart. Paul is transformed from a murderer of Christians to a passionate evangelist. Peter denies Christ, but later defends Christ to the death. God has the amazing ability to turn even our darkest situations into personal and spiritual victories.

Perhaps you are facing a dark situation right now. Maybe you've suffered loss, a moral failure, or missed a chance to defend your faith. If so, you're not alone—you have a lot of company. When it seems that you're surrounded by darkness, remember that light is both your foundation and your future. Release the situation to His marvelous light and know that He is able to transform it into something more than you could ever dream.

God, You are Light. In You there is no darkness at all.
Thank You that Your light illumines even my blackest night.

DAY 281

Commands and Reminders

Make allowance for each other's faults, and forgive anyone who offends you. Remember, the Lord forgave you, so you must forgive others.
COLOSSIANS 3:13 NLT

Paul gives the Colossians a pretty difficult command: Forgive others and bear with each other's faults. Why do we have such a hard time forgiving people? When other people offend or hurt us, it is hard for us not to want to get even or to hurt them back. We want them to suffer as we have suffered and to feel the consequences of their hurtfulness.

Paul wisely includes more than the command to forgive and make allowances, though. He also offers a reminder. The command to forgive would probably be rather ineffective by itself. It's such a difficult one to follow that we might be tempted to give it up as impossible. But Paul's reminder, "the Lord forgave you," is enough to stop us in our tracks. Time after time we hurt God with our flagrant sins. We have caused Him pain with our indifference or downright disobedience—yet He still forgives us our sins. Surely we can forgive others for their offenses when God has forgiven us so much more.

Dear Lord, please teach me to forgive, and give me the strength to love others. Thank You for Your forgiveness for my sins. Amen.

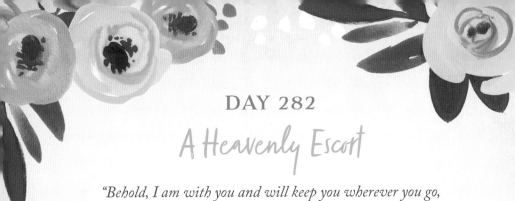

DAY 282

A Heavenly Escort

*"Behold, I am with you and will keep you wherever you go,
and will bring you back to this land; for I will not leave
you until I have done what I have spoken to you."*

GENESIS 28:15 NKJV

The journey into adulthood is marked with milestones: the beginning of a career, the beginning of a family, the beginning of a future. It can be scary to face so many decisions and so many unknowns. It's difficult to put one foot in front of the other on such a winding path, with no way to see what lies at the end.

A young woman once moved across the country to follow a career opportunity. Steeped in fear, she stared out the window of the plane as it began its descent. Silently she begged God for an answer to her most pressing question, "Will I feel Your presence here?" Over the next few years that were full of successes, failures, joys, and disappointments, she realized that He was there, in that foreign land, because she was there.

On our journey, there are two things that we, as children of God, can claim for ourselves: God's presence and His perfect preservation. He will be with us no matter where life takes us, and He will keep us securely in the palm of His hand.

Heavenly Father, please escort me on my journey. Guide my path and reveal Your will to me every step of the way. I claim the promises of Your presence and Your preservation in my life. Amen.

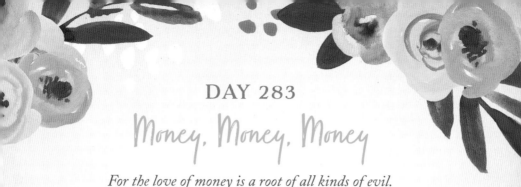

DAY 283

Money, Money, Money

*For the love of money is a root of all kinds of evil.
Some people, eager for money, have wandered from
the faith and pierced themselves with many griefs.*

1 TIMOTHY 6:10 NIV

Wealth management. Asset allocation. Financial planning. What is God's perspective on money? Many heroes of the faith were financially independent. Abraham was a wealthy landowner. Joseph was Pharaoh's right-hand man. David lived in an elegant palace. Why, then, did Jesus say it was easier for a camel to go through the eye of a needle than for a rich man to enter the kingdom of God?

Money is not the issue. It's our attitude toward money that Jesus warns about. When we love money, it becomes an idol that dominates our thoughts and actions. We are driven to accumulate more. Compromises are made. Corners are cut. People are trampled. Greed tempts us to make poor business decisions. Hoping to hit that financial home run, we may make foolish risks and lose it all. Loving money also prevents generosity. We become miserly when we cling tightly to our assets, unwilling to let go.

Perhaps these heroes of the faith were blessed financially because they had the ability to put money in its proper perspective. They loved the Lord above anything else. Money never hindered their relationship with Him. Let's strive to follow their example.

*Dear Lord, may I have Your perspective regarding
money and may I love You foremost. Amen.*

DAY 284
Behind the Scenes

Now faith is confidence in what we hope
for and assurance about what we do not see.
HEBREWS 11:1 NIV

Movies, theater, or sports productions all require people working behind the scenes. The audience very seldom sees what it takes to bring the final product together. Hours of preparation, planning, and technical assimilation come together before an audience sees a single performance—the outcome of the production company's hard work.

In the same way, your faith works behind the scenes of your life to produce a God-inspired outcome to situations you face. What you see is *not* what you get when you walk by faith.

Be encouraged today that no matter what takes place in the natural—what you see with your eyes—it doesn't have to be the final outcome of your situation. If you've asked God for something, then you can trust that He is working out all the details behind the scenes.

What you see right now, how you feel, is not a picture of what your faith is producing. Your faith is active, and God is busy working to make all things come together and benefit you.

Heavenly Father, what I see today is not what I'm going to get. Thank You for working behind the scenes to bring about the very best for my life. Amen.

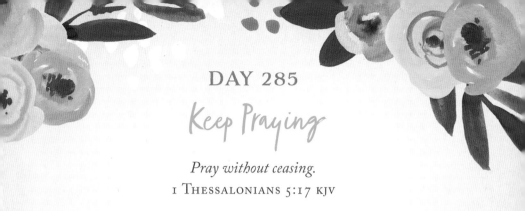

DAY 285

Keep Praying

Pray without ceasing.
1 Thessalonians 5:17 KJV

"Talking to men for God is a great thing, but talking to God for men is greater still" (E. M. Bounds). Did you realize that we can witness all day to someone and never reach that person for Christ until prayer energizes our words?

Perhaps you have a wayward son or daughter, or an unsaved husband. You're heartbroken and have tried to share the message of salvation repeatedly to no avail. You've prayed, but nothing changes. Hoping to open their eyes, you continue to "preach," but soon your preaching becomes nagging and they resist your words all the more. So what should you do? Stop sharing the truth that you know will set them free? Keep silent and hope for the best?

Jesus said, "No one can come to Me unless the Father who sent Me draws him [giving him the desire to come to Me]. . ." John 6:44 (AMP). Prayer is a prerequisite to salvation. Consistent and passionate prayer for others moves God to draw them through the power of the Holy Spirit. Our prayers soften hardened hearts and prepare the heart's soil to receive God's Word.

It's our job to pray specifically for the needs of a person, and it's God's job to change that person's heart to receive the Gospel message.

So don't despair. Just keep praying.

Lord, when I get frustrated and fail to see the results of my prayers, encourage me to keep praying. Amen.

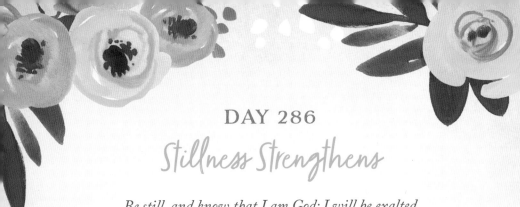

DAY 286

Stillness Strengthens

Be still, and know that I am God: I will be exalted
among the heathen, I will be exalted in the earth.
PSALM 46:10 KJV

The radio plays in the car. The TV blares in the house. Phones ring in both places. The computer delivers email and instant messages. Text messages beep on a handheld device. Our modern world rarely thrusts quiet upon us. Our society rushes from one thing to the next. For many people stillness and quiet don't happen until they fall asleep.

Yet God says He is known in stillness. In Isaiah 30:15 (KJV) we read, "For thus saith the Lord GOD, the Holy One of Israel; in returning and rest shall ye be saved; in quietness and in confidence shall be your strength: and ye would not." God says stillness is good for us. It is how we come to know Him and gain our strength from Him.

He is the Creator of the universe. He makes each twenty-four-hour day. He rules the sun and the moon, the day and the night. He knows every sparrow that falls to the ground. He never slumbers nor sleeps. We can trust Him with the moments of our lives. We can make time for solitude and trust Him to order our day. We can trust Him to meet us in the pause. He is God, so we can be still.

Father, help me today to be still before You.
Enable me to trust You with the cares of my life.

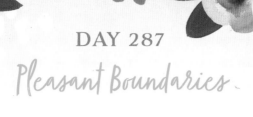

DAY 287
Pleasant Boundaries

*Lord, you alone are my portion and my cup; you make
my lot secure. The boundary lines have fallen for me in
pleasant places; surely I have a delightful inheritance.*
PSALM 16:5–6 NIV

Granted, they didn't have much notice, but when the angel of God told
Lot and his family to leave Sodom, he wasn't kidding. There was no time
to spare. The instructions were clear: Pack up, leave, don't look back. But
Lot's wife couldn't do it. The temptation to look back on all she had left
behind was too great. She paid for her disobedience with her life.

Obeying God's commands is difficult when we focus on what we're
giving up. His guidelines for living a holy life can seem restrictive and
unfair when we think about all we're leaving behind. However, if we look
back, we miss what's ahead.

God's boundaries may seem restrictive at times, but the truth is, He put
them into place because He has our best interests in mind. For example,
sex creates intense emotional attachments. God knows that emotional
attachment without commitment equals heartache, so He has reserved
sex for marriage.

When we only look at what we're missing out on, it's difficult to see
what lies ahead. But you can trust your heavenly Father. His boundaries
provide security and protection, and your future holds great promise and
reward.

*Father, thank You for the boundaries You have placed around
my life. Help me to focus on what I'm gaining rather than
what I'm leaving behind when I choose to obey You.*

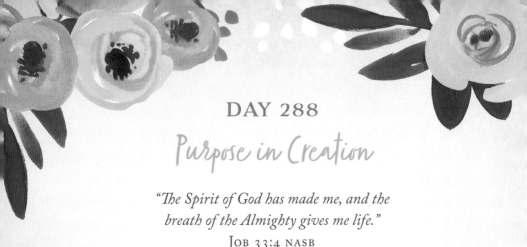

DAY 288

Purpose in Creation

*"The Spirit of God has made me, and the
breath of the Almighty gives me life."*
JOB 33:4 NASB

Life can often be difficult to understand. When we're hurting or when we've experienced loss, we find it easy to question our existence and purpose.

Job easily might have questioned his reason for living; he experienced a number of hardships in a short span of time. By the thirty-third chapter of the book of Job, he has lost his livestock, his farmhands, his shepherds, his servants, his sons and daughters, and he is suffering from terrible boils all over his body. His three friends and his wife have suggested that he curse God and die, but Job refuses to do so. Instead, he remembers with praise the God who created him.

When we question our existence on this earth, we question God's most treasured creation. Trials and tribulations are certain to come our way—Jesus has promised us that. But we are also promised faithfulness, and we know that even amid our greatest challenges, God will strengthen us.

When life becomes difficult and we wonder what we are doing, let's remember that God created us and that He breathed life into us. We were made on purpose, *with* a purpose, and no matter how challenging our life becomes, God is there to comfort and sustain us.

*Dear Lord, You have given me life. Let me use this gift to
praise Your name and further Your kingdom. Amen.*

DAY 289

God's Light for Our Path

*So the cloud of the LORD was over the tabernacle by day,
and fire was in the cloud by night, in the sight of
all the Israelites during all their travels.*
EXODUS 40:38 NIV

Have you ever been forced to choose between "good" and "best"? When life presents us with more than one great opportunity, it can be hard to decide what to do. The path we should take depends on many different factors, and the road may not be clear at first.

How do we determine God's will? It's an age-old question, and to be sure, discovering God's choice for us is not easy. But it *is* simple. First, we must pray for God's guidance. He promises to give us wisdom when we ask for it. Second, we need to search His Word and make sure our potential decision lines up with scripture. Third, we should ask for counsel from godly advisors. And fourth, we must search our hearts to see if the opportunity fits well with the personality, talents, and priorities God has given us.

Rest assured, God *will* shine His light on the right path, just as He led the Israelites with a cloud by day and a fire by night. And when it comes, His guidance will be accompanied with peace, joy, and a certainty that we have followed One who has our (and His) best interests at heart.

*Faithful Father, I praise You for Your compassion and concern for
me. Guide me with Your holy light as I seek Your will for my life.*

DAY 290

Lover of My Soul

Aware of this, Jesus said to them, "Why are you bothering this woman? She has done a beautiful thing to me. . . . When she poured this perfume on my body, she did it to prepare me for burial."
MATTHEW 26:10, 12 NIV

She understood who Jesus was and what was about to happen. Even these men who walked with Him didn't get it. To her, no gift was too lavish. No words were adequate to express her gratitude for what He was about to relinquish—His life!

The beauty of it all? Jesus knew her very soul! He knew her heart longed to give more. He knew her message, beyond any words, was a pale reflection of her gratitude. He knew her soul so wholly, so intimately, so deeply. What a connectedness they shared. That is why He said, "What she has done will always be remembered."

This intimate, loving Lord is the same Lord today. He hasn't changed. He knows the depths of our hearts. He knows what we try to express but fall short. He sees our intentions. Take comfort in His level of understanding and in the intimate relationship He wants with us. Its depth is beyond any friendship, parental devotion, or even earthly marital union. It is a spiritual melding of souls, an amazing truth of a perfect loving Bridegroom becoming one with His bride by laying down His life for her.

Oh, Lover of my soul, You know my every thought. As my soul thirsts for You, so You desire realness and oneness with me. Remove all that hinders that intimacy. May my heart be solely Yours. Amen.

DAY 291

Introducing Jesus

He first found his own brother Simon, and said to him, "We have found the Messiah" (which is translated, the Christ).
JOHN 1:41 NKJV

"We have found. . ." These are loaded words. The speaker implies that he has been looking for something. Andrew's words indicate a prior sense of expectation, longing, and watchfulness. There is triumph in his voice, and the first person he tells his good news to is his own brother, Simon. The Bible does not tell us Andrew worried about Simon's reaction. He simply talks about whom he has found. He introduces his brother to Jesus. Beyond that point, Christ takes the initiative. He immediately calls Simon to Himself and changes his name to Peter.

We often make evangelism much more complicated than it has to be. Witnessing is as simple as what Andrew said to Simon Peter, "We have found. . ." How often do we lose sight of what we have found while focusing on another's problem? Jesus is not merely one part of our lives. He is the Messiah, the Christ, and our Savior. We simply need to say "I found Him"—the simplest way to introduce Him to others. And like He did with Simon Peter, Jesus will take over from there.

Lord Jesus, help me remember the thrill of meeting You and convey that to others. Show me the things that have lured me away. Draw me back to the joy of my salvation, and use that to draw others to You.

DAY 292

A Perfect Fit

You were bought at a price.
1 Corinthians 6:20 niv

Sometimes life can feel like a huge puzzle, and we're constantly trying to figure out how our piece of life fits into the big picture. We all have a desire to belong to something special—someone important. Surprisingly, we can overlook the most important connection we have: We belong to God.

No matter where you've been or what you've done, God has accepted you. He is all about your future, and that includes spending eternity with Him. He shaped you to the perfect size to fit into His purpose and plan. And no matter what road you take, He has made a place for you. He purchased you with the price of His own Son's life. And He gave you everything you need to be accepted as a joint heir with Jesus.

When it seems others do not want you on their team or you find you're having a hard time fitting in, remember you are part of God's family—born of the household of faith. He created you and formed you to be a perfect fit.

Heavenly Father, thank You for paying the ultimate price for me to be a part of Your family. When I'm tempted to feel rejected or unwanted, remind me that I don't have to look far to find my perfect place in You. Amen.

DAY 293

Working Together

For we are labourers together with God:
ye are God's husbandry, ye are God's building.
1 CORINTHIANS 3:9 KJV

Isn't it amazing that God allows us to work with Him to accomplish great things for His kingdom? In reality God could have called on His angels to do the jobs He assigns to us. He could have chosen a method to fulfill His work that would have required less dealing with stubbornness and excuses; but God chose to use us—His human creation. What a wonderful privilege we have!

Not only does God choose to use us in His work, He also continues to work in our lives to mold us into the masterpieces He has planned. The more we allow Him to do *in* us, the more He will be able to do *through* us.

It is important to realize that God wants to work in and through us all our lives. We are not complete until we reach heaven, when we will see Christ as He is. If we become satisfied with who we are while yet on earth, it is pride—the beginning of our downfall. The more content we are with our spiritual maturity, the less God can use us. We must strive daily to be more like Christ if we desire to be useful to God.

O great God, it is an honor to serve You. I ask You to
work in my life that I might be useful to Your work.

DAY 294

Working 9 to 5

For we hear that some among you are leading an undisciplined life,
doing no work at all, but acting like busybodies.
2 Thessalonians 3:11 nasb

The job you have now may not be exactly the glamorous career you had in mind. You may struggle with what to do between 9:00 a.m. and 5:00 p.m. Should you actually do all the mundane things your boss wants you to accomplish, or should you spend a more pleasant day chatting on the phone, reading magazines, and texting your friends?

It may be difficult to stay on task at a job that's less than rewarding, but God's Word tells us about the importance of living a disciplined life and working hard. Even if you hate your job, ask God to change your attitude about work in general. Instead of considering your work torture, see it as an opportunity to serve the Lord. Work hard and let your actions serve as an example for others. Be cheerful in adversity.

Most of all, try to see your office as a mission field. Instead of chatting on the phone, show the love of Christ to someone at work who needs Him. The most difficult office situation can be turned into an opportunity with a little prayer and dedication.

Father, it's not always easy to stay focused at my job. Help me to remember
that what I'm doing at work is all part of my service to You. Amen.

DAY 295
Juggling It All

God will make you fit for what he's called you to be, pray that he'll fill your good ideas and acts of faith with his own energy so that it all amounts to something.
2 THESSALONIANS 1:11–12 MSG

Do you feel like your life is a nonstop juggling routine? Maybe some days feel more like a juggling act on an ever-swaying, sometimes-lunging cruise ship. Now that takes a special set of skills!

Most of the time our busy schedules aren't as enjoyable as a juggling routine: maintaining a well-ordered home, endless laundry, career, school, kids, grocery shopping, and don't forget small-group Bible study for fellowship and church to feed the soul. To top it all off, maybe there's a nagging sense of failure you feel that each area is done with less than your best effort.

Know that God will make you fit for each task He's called you to do, giving you the energy you need. What doesn't get done lies in His hands. He'll provide the creativity and resources you need through the times of ever-swaying circumstances.

God, anchor of my soul, steady me through these unpredictable times. Help me to balance all You want me to do. I trust You with the rest. Amen.

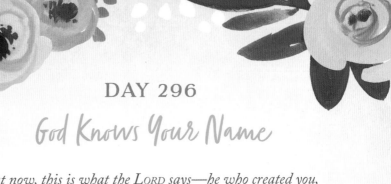

DAY 296

God Knows Your Name

But now, this is what the LORD says—he who created you,
Jacob, he who formed you, Israel: "Do not fear, for I have redeemed
you; I have summoned you by name; you are mine."
ISAIAH 43:1 NIV

Do you remember the first day of school? The teacher called the roll, and you waited for your name to be announced. When it was, you knew that you were a part of that class—you belonged there.

We wait for our names to be called a lot in life: when captains pick teams, while sitting in a doctor's waiting room, or to be called in for a job interview. There is comfort in hearing our own names, in being recognized.

God knows your name. He created you and redeemed you from sin through His Son, Jesus, if you have accepted Him as your personal Savior. He knows you. He put together your personality and topped off His masterpiece by giving you all sorts of likes and dislikes, dreams and desires, passions and preferences. You are His unique design, His daughter, His beloved one.

No matter if you feel you don't belong, *you belong to God*. He takes great joy in you. You are His treasure. He sent Jesus to die on the cross to give you an abundant life. He wants to spend eternity with you! He calls you by name, and your name is music to your Father's ears.

Lord, I thank You for knowing my name
and loving me unconditionally. Amen.

I Think I Can

"Do not be afraid; only believe."
MARK 5:36 NKJV

A children's story from the 1930s, *The Little Engine That Could,* tells of a small switch engine that is asked to pull a long train up over a high mountain after many larger engines refused the job. Someone had to do it, and the optimistic little engine succeeds by repeating to himself, "I think I can! I think I can!"

Our society is filled with people who tell us we can't do this or that. Maybe you were told not to get your hopes up, yet those who defy the odds become heroes as we see their amazing stories on the news. They refused to be stopped by something that only looked impossible.

Take a trip through the Bible and you'll see that those God asked to do the impossible were ordinary people of their day, yet they demonstrated that they believed God saw something in them that they didn't see. He took ordinary men and women and used them to do extraordinary things.

When you believe you can do something, your faith goes to work. You rise to the challenge, which enables you to go further than before, to do more than you thought possible. Consider trying something new—if you think you can, you can!

God, I want to have high expectations. I want to do more than most think I can do. Help me to reach higher and do more as You lead me. Amen.

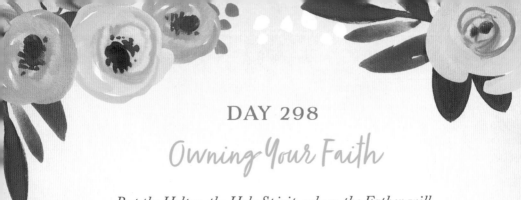

DAY 298

Owning Your Faith

*But the Helper, the Holy Spirit, whom the Father will
send in My name, He will teach you all things, and bring
to your remembrance all things that I said to you.*
JOHN 14:26 NKJV

Is your faith deeper and stronger than when you first accepted Jesus? Or are you stuck back in the early, childish days of your faith?

We each must make our own personal choice to continue to build our faith. Rather than just taking things at face value, we need to wrestle with issues so that we can own God's truths and share them with others. No longer a simple, "Because the Bible says so," it now becomes a matter of, "Where does the Bible say it and why?" Instead of expecting others to lead us, we each need to nurture a personal desire for deepening our relationship with God.

While we are responsible for choosing to grow in faith, we don't do it on our own. Jesus promises that the Holy Spirit will teach and guide us if we allow Him to. He will help us remember the spiritual truths we've learned over the years. Fellowship with other Christians also helps us to mature as we share our passions and are encouraged.

God wants you to own your faith. Make it real with words and actions.

*Jesus, I want to know You intimately. Help me to mature in my walk
with You daily. Guide my steps as I seek You through Your Word. Amen.*

DAY 299

Ask for Joy

Rejoice the soul of Your servant, for to You, O Lord, I lift up my soul.
PSALM 86:4 NKJV

The psalmist buried a nugget in this verse, showing us the source of joy and how to be joyful. All we have to do is ask, then look to God to "rejoice our soul."

So often we get stuck in frustration, depression, ingratitude, or anger. We go about our days feeling defeated, without the hope and joy the scriptures promise us. But have we asked our Lord for joy? Have we lifted our soul to Him? Psalm 16:11 (NKJV) tells us, "In Your presence is fullness of joy." When we draw near to God, confessing our sin and our need of Him, we are met by His mercy, His forgiveness, His perfect love that casts out all fear. In the presence of that love, our joy is found, regardless of our circumstances. He is a father. He desires to love and care for His children.

Just as we want our children to come to us when they hurt, our heavenly Father longs to hear your voice crying out to Him. Sure, He already knows your need; but He also knows there is benefit for each of us in the confession, in crying out to Him. When we hear ourselves verbally lifting our souls to Him, we are reminded of our need of Him. Confession is good for the soul.

Father, help me to lift my soul to You, the source of joy. Only You can make me to rejoice. Forgive my pride that keeps me from confessing my sins. Draw me into Your loving presence where there is fullness of joy.

DAY 300
What's in Your Heart?

Delight thyself also in the LORD: and he
shall give thee the desires of thine heart.
PSALM 37:4 KJV

What is it that you most desire? Is it a successful career or large bank account? Do you wish for someone with whom you can share romantic dinners or scenic bike rides? It really doesn't matter. What does matter is that you are fully committed to God. When that is the case, the desires in your heart will be the ones He places there. He will grant them because they honor Him.

Too many times we look at God's promises as some sort of magic formula. We fail to realize that His promises have more to do with our own relationship with Him. It begins with a heart's desire to live your life in a way that pleases God. Only then will fulfillment of His promises take place.

The promise in Psalm 37:4 isn't intended for personal gain—although that is sometimes a side benefit. It is meant to glorify God. God wants to give you the desires of your heart when they line up with His perfect plan. As you delight in Him, His desires will become your desires, and you will be greatly blessed.

Lord, I know You want to give me the desires of my heart.
Help me live in a way that makes this possible.

DAY 301
Equipped for the Task

[May God] equip you with everything good for doing his
will, and may he work in us what is pleasing to him.
HEBREWS 13:21 NIV

God knew Paul the apostle would face hard times in his life. This distinguished, well-educated Pharisee went through an intensive training period for more than seven years, living obscurely in his hometown. God equipped Paul because He knew the price he would pay for following Christ: lashed five times, beaten three times with rods, stoned once, shipwrecked three times, adrift alone in the sea a night and day, robbed, rejected by his own countrymen, hungry, cold, naked, and resigned to a relentless thorn in his flesh. Through it all, many Gentiles came to know Jesus.

Hopefully, we aren't being equipped for a rigorous life like Paul's. But whatever He's called us to do, He will give what we need to accomplish it. You may not feel you are equipped, but God keeps His Word. Scripture plainly states He's given you everything good for carrying out His work. When you are discouraged in ministry and you want to quit, remember He promises to work in you what pleases Him. The Spirit empowers us, making us competent for our tasks.

Lord, help me to draw on Your resources that I might be fully
equipped for accomplishing Your tasks. Work in and through
me to touch the lives of others as only You can do. Amen.

DAY 302
All You Need

For your Maker is your husband—the LORD Almighty is his name—the Holy One of Israel is your Redeemer; he is called the God of all the earth.

ISAIAH 54:5 NIV

Are you without? Do you find yourself longing for a certain relationship in your life? Maybe you never knew your earthly father and there is a void in your heart for a daddy. Perhaps you are single and longing for a mate, or married, but your mate seems absent even though he is there with you. Do you wish for a child? Is your relationship with your mother or sister or friend constantly draining you?

God is the great "I Am." He is all things that we need. He is our maker. He is our husband. He is the Lord Almighty, the Holy One, the Redeemer, the God of all the earth—and these are just the names found in one verse of scripture.

God is the Good Shepherd, your Provider, your Protector, your Comforter, your Defender, your Friend.

He is not a god made of stone or metal. He is not unreachable. He is present. He is near, as close as you will let Him be, and He will meet your needs as no earthly relationship can. Seek the fullness of God in your life. Call on Him as your Prince of Peace and your King of Glory. He is all that you need—at all times—in all ways.

Oh, Father, be close to me. Fill the empty spots in my heart.
Be my husband, my redeemer, and my best friend. Amen.

DAY 303

A Clear Focus

Hope deferred makes the heart sick,
but a longing fulfilled is a tree of life.
PROVERBS 13:12 NIV

We all have dreams and a desire to pursue them. But then life gets busy, and we become distracted with the choices we have to make on a daily basis. Do you go right or left, choose this way or that? Too much too fast is overwhelming, and looking for balance can leave us lost, not knowing which way to turn. The best way to gain your balance is to stop moving and refocus.

Jesus is your hope! He stands a short distance away bidding you to take a walk on water—a step of faith toward Him. Disregarding the distractions can be hard, but the rough waters can become silent as you turn your eyes, your thoughts, and your emotions on Him.

You can tackle the tough things as you maintain your focus on Jesus. Let Him direct you over the rough waters of life, overcoming each obstacle one at a time. Don't look at the big picture in the midst of the storm, but focus on the one thing you can do at the moment to help your immediate situation—one step at a time.

Lord, help me not to concentrate on the distractions, but to keep
my focus on which step to take next in order to reach You. Amen.

DAY 304

The Purpose of My Life

I long for your salvation, LORD, and your law gives me delight.
Let me live that I may praise you, and may your laws sustain me.
PSALM 119:174–175 NIV

We each have so many plans and goals and dreams for our lives, but our main mission should be to live each day to please God. Our purpose here on earth is to worship the God who created us and calls us His children.

Praise and worship isn't just about singing songs to God every Sunday morning. Praise and worship should be an everyday activity. Praise is about putting God first in our lives. It's about doing our daily tasks in a way that honors Him.

Can you really do laundry to please God? Can you really go to work to please God? Can you really pay the bills and make dinner to please God? The answer is a resounding *yes!* Doing all the mundane tasks of everyday life with gratitude and praise in your heart for all that He has done for you is living a life of praise. As you worship God through your day-to-day life, He makes clear His plans, goals, and dreams for you.

Dear Father, let me live my life to praise You.
Let that be my desire each day. Amen.

DAY 305
No Matter What

Sometimes being thankful seems almost impossible. How can I be thankful when I'm working as hard as I can and I'm still unable to pay off all my debt? How can I be thankful when my car dies, my water pump breaks, or my wallet is stolen? How can I be thankful when my parents split up or my boyfriend breaks my heart or my children refuse to behave?

Living in today's world is difficult, and we often experience hardships that make being thankful extremely difficult. When Paul wrote this verse, however, you can bet that he did not write it lightly. He knew what it was to experience hardships and suffering. But Paul also knew the wonderful power and blessing that comes from having a relationship with Christ.

Jesus enables us to be thankful, and Jesus is the cause of our thankfulness. *No matter what happens,* we know that Jesus has given up His life to save ours. He has sacrificed Himself on the cross so that we may live life to the fullest. And while "to the fullest" means that we will experience pain as well as joy, we must *always* be thankful—regardless of our circumstances—for the love that we experience in Christ Jesus.

Dear Lord, thank You for Your love. Please let me be thankful, even in
the midst of hardships. You have blessed me beyond measure. Amen.

DAY 306
Abide in the Vine

"I am the vine; you are the branches. If you remain in me and I in you,
you will bear much fruit; apart from me you can do nothing."
JOHN 15:5 NIV

Fruit is the tangible evidence of life. Only live plants can produce fruit. Nourishment travels from the roots to the branches, sustaining the fruit. Jesus refers to Himself as the vine and to us as branches. Unless we are attached to the vine, we are not receiving spiritual nourishment. We become grafted into the vine by faith in Jesus Christ as Lord and Savior. His power then flows through us, producing spiritual fruit.

The fruit we bear is consistent with His character. Just as apple trees bear apples, we bear spiritual fruit that reflects Him. Spiritual fruit consists of God's qualities: love, joy, peace, patience, kindness, goodness, faithfulness, gentleness, and self-control. The Fruit of the Spirit cannot be grown by our own efforts. We must remain in the vine.

How do we abide in Him? We acknowledge that our spiritual sustenance comes from the Lord. We spend time with Him. We seek His will and wisdom. We are obedient and follow where He leads. When we remain attached to Him, spiritual fruit will be the evidence of His life within us. Abide in the vine and be fruitful!

Dear Lord, help me abide in You so that I may produce
fruit as a witness to Your life within me. Amen.

DAY 307

God Cares for You

"Consider how the wild flowers grow. They do not labor or spin. Yet I tell you, not even Solomon in all his splendor was dressed like one of these. If that is how God clothes the grass of the field, which is here today, and tomorrow is thrown into the fire, how much more will he clothe you—you of little faith!"

LUKE 12:27–28 NIV

Take a look at God's creation. He has created this world with such intricate detail. He designed every tree, the majestic mountains, a glorious sun, and a mysterious moon. Each animal has been given unique markings, parts, and sounds. Consider the long-necked giraffe, the massive elephant, the graceful swan, and the perfectly striped zebra!

If God makes the flowers, each type unique and beautiful, and if He sends the rain and sun to meet their needs, will He not care for you as well?

He made you. What the Father makes, He loves. And that which He loves, He cares for. We were made in His image. Humans are dearer to God than any of His other creations. Rest in Him. Trust Him. Just as He cares for the birds of the air and the flowers of the meadows, God is in the business of taking care of His sons and daughters. Let Him take care of you.

Father, I am amazed by Your creation. Remind me that I am Your treasured child. Take care of me today as only You can do. Amen.

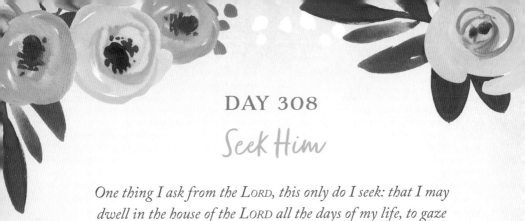

DAY 308
Seek Him

One thing I ask from the LORD, this only do I seek: that I may dwell in the house of the LORD all the days of my life, to gaze on the beauty of the LORD and to seek him in his temple.
PSALM 27:4 NIV

David understood what it takes to dwell with God. He continually gazed at His beauty. At the time he composed this psalm, David was living on the run, not in the lavish palace of a king. He was finding beauty and richness in the starkest of environments, stripped of amenities.

Do we seek God's beauty in our environment, which is not quite so bleak? Isn't His beauty reflected in the smiling toddler in the grocery store line? What about the elderly married couple's hand-holding throughout the church service? Don't these reflect our Creator?

When we bite into an apple—crisp, sweet, and naturally packaged for freshness—or observe the grace and agility of a dancer or listen to the intoxicating notes of a flute, don't they reveal more about God? Where did it all originate? Whose power and creativity is behind it all? Life reveals glimpses of His power and awesomeness. These everyday things draw us into His presence where we can praise Him, enjoying His beauty and greatness all the days of our life.

Magnificent Creator, Your greatness and beauty surround me. May my eyes gaze at You, seeking You, that I might dwell in Your presence continually. Amen.

DAY 309

Justice and Mercy

*"We know that we don't deserve a hearing
from you. Our appeal is to your compassion."*
DANIEL 9:18 MSG

Being merciful is not as popular as being just. There are plenty of commercials and billboards for law firms saying they'll "get you what you deserve." And the phrase, "It's not fair!" is never far from our lips. Sometimes we have a good idea of what we deserve, but most of the time we think we deserve more than we actually do.

As Christians, we must resist the temptation to think and talk about the ways in which our lives are not fair. Instead, we should remember the words of Daniel and humble ourselves before the God of creation. The world tries to tell us that we deserve to be treated well; we deserve money, success, and possessions; we deserve happiness and an easy life. But Daniel knew the world's sense of justice was not God's justice.

We do not deserve help from God. We don't *deserve* anything from God. But our God is merciful and loving, and He delights in us. God helps us, listens to us, and *loves* us because He is merciful. Praise Him for His mercy today!

*Dear Lord, thank You for Your mercy. Thank You for Your love.
Teach me to humble myself before You and look for Your
mercy rather than for the world's justice. Amen.*

DAY 310
Sacrificial Love

For God so loved the world, that he gave. . .
JOHN 3:16 KJV

Every mother understands sacrifice. We sit on dusty bleachers in 95-degree heat in anticipation of our child's moment up to bat. Crammed between screaming parents, we cheer on our homegrown Michael Jordan. We struggle with an unbridled umbrella and flyaway blanket to repel the cold, pelting rain and whipping wind just to watch our soccer star kick a muddy ball downfield.

For some of us, sports are foreign. But as moms, it doesn't matter if we confuse a hole in one with a slam dunk; we support, love, and cheer our kids on. It matters little if we have to rush from job to gym or if we sit for hours on hard benches. Love impels us to do so.

God's love is similar. Today's scripture declares that God loved us so much that He gave. That included so much more than weathering the elements or laundering smelly socks and grimy uniforms. He gave more than His time, efforts, and care. He gave His Son's life. And His love continues. He's never too busy to attend to our needs, and He isn't irritated when we absorb hours of His time.

Someone commented, "We are shaped and fashioned by what we love." God's love for us fashioned Him in the shape of a cruel cross. That's sacrificial love.

Father, amid the daily demands of motherhood,
remind me of what You did for me. Amen.

DAY 311
Comfort in Sadness

You've kept track of my every toss and turn through the sleepless nights,
each tear entered in your ledger, each ache written in your book.
PSALM 56:8 MSG

In heaven there will be no more sadness. Tears will be a thing of the past. For now, we live in a fallen world. There are heartaches and disappointments. Some of us are more prone to crying than others, but all of us have cause to weep at times.

Call out to God when you find yourself tossing and turning at night, or when tears drench your pillow. He is a God who sees, a God who knows. He is your "Abba" Father, your daddy.

It hurts the Father's heart when you cry, but He sees the big picture. God knows that gut-wrenching trials create perseverance in His beloved daughter and that perseverance results in strong character.

Do you ever wonder if God has forgotten you and left you to fend for yourself? Rest assured that He has not left you even for one moment. He is your Good Shepherd, and you are His lamb. When you go astray, He spends every day and every night calling after you. If you are a believer, then you know your Good Shepherd's voice.

Shhhh. . .listen. . .He is whispering a message of comfort even now.

Father, remind me that You are a God who sees my pain.
Jesus, I thank You that You gave up Your life for me. Holy
Spirit, comfort me in my times of deep sadness. Amen.

DAY 312

Standards of Success

"Worship and serve him with your whole heart and a willing mind. For the LORD sees every heart and knows every plan and thought. If you seek him, you will find him."
1 CHRONICLES 28:9 NLT

God's view of success is vastly different than the world's. God asks that we give ourselves to Him in worship. We find our success in earnestly seeking after God and following His commands.

On the other hand, the world says that we must have a good job, make lots of money, buy the newest toys, and focus on making ourselves happy. The world does not care how we accomplish these things. If we have to be superficial, fine. If we have to tell a lie here or there, no problem. If we have to pretend to be something we are not, who cares?

God cares. God sees our hearts and knows our motives—good or bad. The world's mindset looks to the tangible elements of success. A good car, a nice job, and big house indicate success, regardless of how we obtained them. On the other hand, God's focus is on our journey. We may not live in the biggest house on the block, and we may not even own a car, but those things are not important to God. Instead, worshipping and serving God with our whole hearts, being genuine and sincere, and willingly seeking God are the aspects of success in God's eyes.

Dear Lord, teach me to seek after You willingly, with sincere motives. Please help me focus on pleasing You rather than seeking success by worldly standards. Amen.

DAY 313

Feeling Pressed?

By his divine power, God has given us
everything we need for living a godly life.
2 PETER 1:3 NLT

People need you—your family, your friends. Adding their needs to your commitments at school or work can sometimes be too much. Maybe your boss demands extra hours on a project, or your sister needs you to help her with a family birthday party.

People pulling you here and there can have you going in circles. Somehow you keep pushing forward, not always sure where the strength comes from, but thankful in the end that you made it through the day.

In those situations you're not just stretching your physical body to the limit, but your mind and emotions as well. Stress can make you feel like a grape in a winepress. But there is good news. God has given you everything you need, but you must choose to use the wisdom He has provided. Don't be afraid to say no when you feel you just can't add one more thing to your to-do list. Limit your commitments, ask someone to take notes for you in a meeting you can't make, or carpool with someone who shares your child's extracurricular activity.

Alleviate the pressure where you can and then know that His power will make up for the rest.

Lord, help me to do what I can do; and I'll trust You
to do for me those things that I can't do. Amen.

DAY 314

Hard Times

He comes alongside us when we go through hard times, and before you know it, he brings us alongside someone else who is going through hard times so that we can be there for that person just as God was there for us.

2 CORINTHIANS 1:4 MSG

Hard times are bound to come. Don't let that discourage you. God says that in this world we will have trouble (John 16:33), but to take heart because He has overcome the world!

If you are in the middle of something rough right now, remember that God is always there to comfort you. You may feel that you are at the end of your ability to cope, but that is where God likes to meet us. He is close to the brokenhearted. If you have just experienced something difficult, reflect on what God wants to teach you from that.

Try journaling the things that God has taught you so that you can remember all that He has done for and through you. You can share these memories with someone later on. Don't forget that God uses all of our trials for good, to make us more like Christ and to help those around us in their time of need.

Lord, You are the God of comfort. Please help me lean on You during hard times, and help me be a blessing to someone else. Amen.

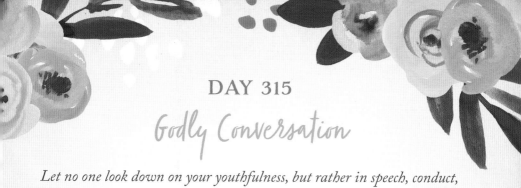

DAY 315

Godly Conversation

Let no one look down on your youthfulness, but rather in speech, conduct,
love, faith and purity, show yourself an example of those who believe.
1 TIMOTHY 4:12 NASB

God hears the conversations of His children—no matter how young or old. As we spend time together and speak with one another, our Father cares about our conversations and wants them to bless and enrich the lives of those who participate.

Conversations peppered with faith and purity, as directed in 1 Timothy 4, are in stark contrast to the ungodly chatter of the world today. The world is darkened by complaints against God, cynicism, unbelief, and gossip—none of which honor God. His heart aches when we use words to tear others down rather than speak truth that encourages.

He wants us to build one another up with the words we use. True Christ-centered fellowship happens when everyone involved is encouraged and strengthened in their faith. And we must always remember that unbelievers watch and listen, always looking to find Christ in the lives of those of us who profess His name. Let's share God's faithfulness, goodness, and love, because our conversations have an impact in the lives of everyone we reach.

Jesus, please touch my lips and allow nothing dishonorable
to pass through them. Guide me and give me grace and
discernment in my conversations so that they would always
be pleasing to You and give glory to Your name. Amen.

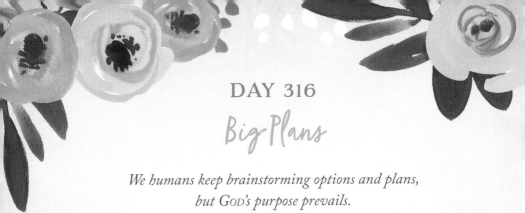

DAY 316

Big Plans

We humans keep brainstorming options and plans,
but GOD's purpose prevails.
PROVERBS 19:21 MSG

This young woman had a plan. She wanted a North Carolina man to marry, so a small college nestled in a mountain cove was just the place for her. Florida would no longer be her home—just the gorgeous Smoky Mountains. Her man? A wavy- and dark-haired athletic type, business major; she had him pictured.

Well, who says God doesn't have a sense of humor? This young woman went to that college, found that "man" who turned out to be hollow inside. God had a plan; it was to meld her heart to a man of strong godly character. A man specially selected for her. He wasn't from the mountains, but a Florida citrus grower she'd known since high school! They did marry and proved that God's plans are best.

We often worry, scheme, and strategize our lives away. And really, there is nothing wrong with planning and thinking ahead. But we must remember that God's ultimate purposes will prevail. We might not like that idea, hanging fiercely to our independence. But a loving God, who has all wisdom and power over all things, genuinely cares for us. His plans will not fail.

Father, You see the bigger picture. Your plan is best for me
even though at times I resist it. Help me to trust when things
aren't as I think they should be. Your will be done. Amen.

DAY 317
He Has Chosen You

*Therefore, as God's chosen people, holy and
dearly loved, clothe yourselves with compassion,
kindness, humility, gentleness and patience.*
COLOSSIANS 3:12 NIV

Four kids stood along the third-base line, kicking dust into the air.

"I'll take Abby," the first team captain said.

"Uhh. . .Simon," the second said.

The final two unclaimed girls glanced up at each other, both fearing they'd be the last one picked for the baseball game.

No matter how athletic, beautiful, popular, or smart you are, you've probably experienced a time when you were chosen last or overlooked entirely. Being left out is a big disappointment of life on earth.

The good news is that this disappointment isn't part of God's kingdom. Even when others forget about us, God doesn't. He has handpicked His beloved children now and forever. And this fact doesn't exclude others who haven't yet accepted Him; the truth is that Jesus died for *everyone*— every man, woman, and child who has ever and will ever live. The Father chooses us all. All we have to do is grab a glove and join the team.

*Father, thanks for choosing me. I don't deserve it, but You call
me Your beloved child. Help me to remember others who may feel
overlooked or unloved. Let Your love for them shine through me. Amen.*

DAY 318
Abiding Peace

He himself is our peace.
EPHESIANS 2:14 NIV

Powerful forces converge as a hurricane develops. Even though turbulent winds swirl uncontrollably, the calm eye, the center of the storm, remains unaffected by its surroundings. Regardless of the hurricane's magnitude, the eye always remains calm.

Have you ever experienced a hurricane—perhaps not a real one, but life circumstances that turned your world upside down? The winds of hardship were fiercely blowing. Your suffering felt like pelting rain. Experiencing havoc all around, you didn't know where to turn. Is peace possible in the midst of such turbulence?

Regardless of life's circumstances, hope and peace are available if Jesus is there. You do not have to succumb to getting buffeted and beaten by the storms of life. Seek refuge in the center of the storm. Run to the arms of Jesus, the Prince of Peace. Let Him wipe your tears and calm your fears. Like the eye of the hurricane, His presence brings peace and calmness. Move yourself closer. Desire to be in His presence. For He Himself is your peace. As you abide in His presence, peace will envelop you. The raging around you may not subside, but the churning of your heart will. You will find rest for your soul.

*Dear Lord, thank You for being our peace
in the midst of life's fiercest storms. Amen.*

DAY 319

Confidence

For I know that my redeemer liveth, and that he shall stand
at the latter day upon the earth: and though after my skin
worms destroy this body, yet in my flesh shall I see God.
JOB 19:25–26 KJV

What amazing hope we have! We serve a risen Savior.

It is hard to imagine how Job must have felt as he went through such a horrible situation—losing his family, his possessions, and even his health. Yet in all of his misery he said with confidence, "I *know* that my redeemer liveth." The irony of this is that Christ had not yet been born, much less had He completed His redemptive work. Still, Job's faith did not waver. He knew that one day he would stand before his redeemer in a perfected body.

Although we experience various difficulties throughout life, we can still look forward to the blessed future we have. No matter what our struggles are, our Lord controls.

Job had no idea what the purpose of his trial was, but he faced his troubles with confidence, knowing that ultimately he would emerge victorious. Too many times we view our own situations with self-pity rather than considering God's strength and trusting that His plan is perfect. What peace God offers when we finally cast our cares on Him and with great conviction declare, "I know that my redeemer liveth!"

O great Redeemer, in You I have confidence even when I don't
understand life's trials. Please help me to live victoriously.

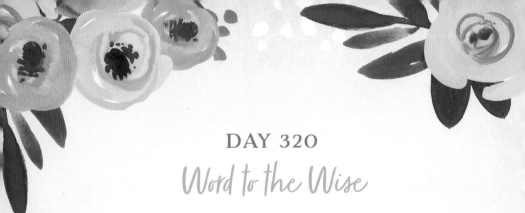

DAY 320
Word to the Wise

*If any of you lacks wisdom, he should ask God, who gives generously
to all without finding fault, and it will be given to him.*
JAMES 1:5 NIV

Wisdom should be our request as we seek God's face each day. We all need wisdom for the huge decisions: choosing a mate, picking the right college, which career path to take, or what ministries to pursue. But we also need wisdom for the smaller, day-to-day things as well: what to do in our spare time, how to spend this week's paycheck, or what relationships need attention.

God's Word tells us that He gives wisdom to all who ask—without finding fault. Ask and it will be given to you! However, the verse goes on to say that when you do ask the Lord for wisdom, trust that He will make good on His promise. If you find yourself asking for wisdom but doubting that God will really give it to you, confess that to the Lord and ask Him to change your mindset. Trust in the Lord and know that He is faithful to hear your prayers and answer according to His will.

*Father, forgive me for the times I have doubted You.
I ask for wisdom for the big decisions in my life but
also for daily wisdom. Help me to trust You more. Amen.*

DAY 321
The True Love

"Love one another; just as I have loved you."
JOHN 13:34 NASB

In a society that has distorted the concept of love, it's reassuring to know that God loves us with a deep, limitless love. He is, in fact, love itself. He gave His Son to die for people who didn't love Him in return. God the Father even had to turn His face from His Son when He died, as He took the sin of humankind upon Himself. What incredible love that is!

We Christians tell Jesus we love Him, and His response is, "I love you more." We cannot comprehend that kind of love, yet we are the recipients of it. And He loves us not because of anything we've done, but because of His goodness. First John 4:19 (KJV) says, "We love him, because he first loved us."

Jesus also commands us to love others in the same way that He loves us. We all have unlovable people in our lives. But Jesus doesn't see anyone as unlovable. Look at that difficult-to-love person through new eyes today and love her as God has loved you.

Heavenly Father, thank You for Your love for me. Forgive
me for not loving others in that same way. Give me the
ability to love others as You have instructed. Amen.

DAY 322

For Such a Time as This

"If you keep quiet at a time like this, deliverance and relief for the Jews will arise from some other place, but you and your relatives will die. Who knows if perhaps you were made queen for just such a time as this?"

ESTHER 4:14 NLT

Esther was between the proverbial rock and a hard place. If she approached the king without being invited, she risked losing her life. If she kept silent, she and her family would die. Her wise cousin Mordecai helped put the situation into perspective. He explained that God's plans and purposes would prevail—whether Esther cooperated or not. Esther merely had to choose whether she wanted to experience the joy of participating in God's plan of deliverance for the Jewish people.

Can you imagine the honor of being chosen to help God in this way? God has placed each of us on this earth for a purpose. When we cooperate with Him, we get to experience the blessing of being a part of His plans. If we choose not to participate, there will be consequences. Don't be mistaken—God's purposes will still unfold. But we won't get to be a part of it. Like Esther, the choice is ours. Will we cooperate with God or keep silent and miss out on our place in history?

Heavenly Father, thank You for placing me on earth at this time in history. Thank You for the opportunity to be a part of Your plan. Help me to choose to cooperate with You.

DAY 323
The Perfect Reflection

"Give careful thought to your ways."
HAGGAI 1:7 NIV

You probably know how it feels to have a bad hair day or a huge zit on your face. On days like these, we try to avoid the mirror. The last thing we want is to keep running into a reflection of ourselves when we look less than our best.

Our Christian lives often have a similar feel. Instead of facing our imperfections as followers of Christ, we work hard to avoid any mention of or allusion to them. God's command to give careful thought to our ways may fill us with dread because the reflection can be so unattractive.

As we give careful thought to our ways, we should first look back to where we have come from and reflect on God's work in our lives. We are on a journey. Sometimes the road is difficult; sometimes the road is easy. We must consider where we were when God found us and where we are now through His grace. Even more importantly, we must think about the ways our present actions, habits, and attitude toward God reflect our lives as Christians. Only when we are able to honestly assess our lives in Christ can we call on His name to help perfect our reflection.

Dear Lord, help me to look honestly at the ways I
live and make changes where necessary. Amen.

DAY 324

Contentment

The LORD is my shepherd, I lack nothing.
PSALM 23:1 NIV

Probably the most familiar passage in the Bible, the twenty-third Psalm is a picture of contentment. If the Lord is our shepherd, then we are His sheep. Sheep are fragile animals, easily lost and injured, and in need of constant care. They are vulnerable to predators, especially if separated from the flock, and need to be guarded and led to places of safety.

A shepherd spends all his time with his sheep. Theirs is a close relationship, and He is always guarding them. He is responsible for nourishment, rest, places of safety, and care for the injured. The sheep do not have to seek these things; it is the shepherd's job to know what they need and provide it.

Though it's not very flattering to be thought of as sheep, it does help to describe our relationship with God. Because we are sheep, with Christ as our shepherd, we do not have to worry, strive, want, or lack. We are never alone. As Philippians 4:19 (NKJV) says, "My God shall supply all your need according to His riches in glory by Christ Jesus."

*Lord, cause me to remember that I am a sheep and You are my shepherd.
In times of loneliness, anxiety, need, or pain, help me turn to You.*

DAY 325

Daily Choice

*"The thief comes only to steal and kill and destroy; I have
come that they may have life, and have it to the full."*

JOHN 10:10 NIV

Some days it seems the negative outweighs the positive. People demand
so much of our time. Bills demand so much of our money. Feelings of
inadequacy surface quickly. It all caves in around us—it's just too much!
But when God's words fall on our hearts, those thoughts of defeat are
shown for what they really are: lies that delight the enemy who wants to
destroy our souls.

But Christ comes to give life! Choosing life is an act of the will
blended with faith. We must daily make the decision to take hold of
the life Christ offers us. It's this Spirit-infused life that keeps us going;
our greatest efforts often come up short. Accepting this gift from Jesus
doesn't guarantee a perfect life; it doesn't even guarantee an easy life. But
Christ does promise to sustain us, support us, and provide a haven from
the storms of life in His loving arms.

*Giving Lord, help me daily choose You and the life You
want to give me. Give me eyes of faith to trust that
You will enable me to serve lovingly, as You do.*

DAY 326

Christ, My Identity

"The LORD your God is with you, the Mighty Warrior who saves.
He will take great delight in you; in his love he will no longer
rebuke you, but will rejoice over you with singing."
ZEPHANIAH 3:17 NIV

As women, we love to love. We tend to trust easily. If we are married, we expect our husbands to look after our children and us, to admire and desire us as wives, always to be our protectors. Even if we've never been married, most of us have dreamed of such relationships.

But when our expectations fall short—whatever the reason—our spirits shatter into a million little pieces. Often, we lose our identity. Any self-esteem we may once have had evaporates along with our dreams.

But God Himself, the maker of all creation, the very One who hung the stars in space and calls them by name, looks at each one of us with love. In His eyes are delight and joy. Because the Father has created us in His own image, He knows every hurt we feel—and He will quiet us with His love. He rejoices that we are His daughters and He delights in us—not because of anything we do but simply because we are His.

Lord Jesus, though I sometimes feel alone and without an identity,
I trust that You are with me. I ask that You will quiet my spirit with
Your mighty peace and allow me to know the depth of Your love for me.

DAY 327

Belly Laughs

*All the days of the afflicted are evil, but he
who is of a merry heart has a continual feast.*
PROVERBS 15:15 NKJV

Do you know how to relax? Have you built a time for laughter into your schedule?

Maybe that sounds silly and unimportant with the demands of life caving in on you. But it's not! In fact, relaxation and fun are vital to your health—and, by extension, the health of your family. We may face challenges, but as Proverbs reminds us, we can have a continual feast regardless of circumstances. Don't wait for laughter to find you—seek it out!

Find a comedy show to loosen up. Maybe get into a tickling match with the kids. Perhaps it's as simple as scheduling a popcorn and movie night with friends (or yourself!) to melt away the day's pressure.

A good laugh is health to our bones and gives our kids permission to lighten up too. Do it now—not when life is in perfect order. Others need to see us loosen up and enjoy ourselves now and then.

*Heavenly Father, You are a God of laughter and enjoyment.
Why does it seem frivolous to giggle with my children? Enable
me to have a continual feast regardless of my circumstances.*

Hurt by Others' Choices

God heard the boy crying. The angel of God called from
Heaven to Hagar, "What's wrong, Hagar? Don't be afraid.
God has heard the boy and knows the fix he's in."
GENESIS 21:17 MSG

A slave during early biblical times, Hagar had little say in her life decisions—others made them for her. Because of the infertility of her mistress, Sarah, Hagar became the concubine of Sarah's husband, Abraham, and gave birth to Ishmael.

At first, Hagar's hopes soared. Her son would become Abraham's heir, rich and powerful beyond her wildest dreams! However, the surprise appearance of Isaac, the late-life son of Sarah and Abraham, destroyed Hagar's fantasies of a wonderful future. Sarah wanted Hagar and Ishmael out of their lives. Abraham, though upset, loaded Hagar with water and food and told her to take Ishmael into the unforgiving desert.

When their water supply failed, Hagar laid her dehydrated son under a bush and walked away crying because she could not bear to watch Ishmael die. But God showed Hagar a well of water. Quickly she gave her child a drink. Both survived, and "God was on the boy's side as he grew up" (Genesis 21:20 MSG).

God is also on our side when we and our loved ones suffer because of others' choices. Even when we have lost hope, God's plan provides a way for us and those we love.

Heavenly Father, when my world seems out of control,
please help me love and trust You—even in the deserts of life.

DAY 329
Clap Your Hands!

*Clap your hands, all you nations; shout to God with cries of joy. For the
LORD Most High is awesome, the great King over all the earth. . . God
has ascended amid shouts of joy, the LORD amid the sounding of trumpets.
Sing praises to God, sing praises; sing praises to our King, sing praises.*
PSALM 47:1–2, 5–6 NIV

In 1931, German theologian Dietrich Bonhoeffer spent a year at a seminary in New York City. While there, he was introduced to a church in Harlem. Astounded, then delighted, at the emotion expressed in worship, he returned to Germany with recordings of Gospel music tucked in his suitcase. Bonhoeffer knew that the worship he observed was authentic and pleasing to God.

King David would have loved Gospel music! Many of the psalms were meant to be sung loudly and joyfully. David appointed four thousand professional musicians—playing cymbals, trumpets, rams' horns, tambourines, harps, and lyres—for temple worship. We can imagine they would have rocked the roofs off our modern-day church services!

Dancing was a part of worship in David's day too. David angered his wife Michal with his spontaneous dance in the street, as the Ark of the Covenant was returned to Jerusalem (1 Chronicles 15:29). The world, in David's viewpoint, couldn't contain the delight that God inspires. Neither could he!

How often do we worship God with our whole heart? Has God ever seen you burst forth in a song of praise? Has He witnessed you clapping your hands and lifting them up high? Let's try that today!

O Lord, great is Your name and worthy of praise!

DAY 330
A Pattern Worth Repeating

So know that the LORD your God is God, the faithful
God. He will keep his agreement of love for a thousand
lifetimes for people who love him and obey his commands.
DEUTERONOMY 7:9 NCV

We all know that patterns repeat in families, even to the "third and fourth generation" (Exodus 20:5 NIV.) We worry over negative patterns, like abuse and divorce, that have hurt our children the same way they hurt us. We long to replace those negative patterns with godly, joyful living.

God wants that for our families, as well. He encourages parents with a God-sized promise, the kind every mother wants for her family but thinks is impossible.

Think beyond a legacy for our grandchildren and great-grandchildren. God's vision extends far past that. He will show "love for *a thousand lifetimes*" (emphasis added). The idea of a "thousand lifetimes" boggles the mind. Taken literally, at twenty-five years times one thousand, it endures for twenty-five thousand years—longer than people have lived on the earth.

God takes our hands and says, "Love Me. Obey Me. I will show love to your family as long as you have descendants on the earth." And when we demonstrate our love for God by doing what He says, we guarantee His faithfulness and love to generations yet unborn, until the Lord returns to take us home.

That's a legacy worth passing on.

Heavenly Father, I praise You that You will be faithful to my children and
their children after them. I pray that they also will love You and obey You.

DAY 331
Perfect Prayers

In this manner, therefore, pray: Our Father in heaven.
MATTHEW 6:9 NKJV

How many messages have you heard on prayer? Have you ever come away thinking, *Did you hear how eloquently they prayed? How spiritual they sounded? No wonder God answers their prayers!*

Sometimes we take the straightforward and uncomplicated idea of prayer—the simple give and take of talking with God—and turn it into something hard. How many times have we made it a mere religious exercise, performed best by the "holy elite," rather than what it really is—conversation with God our Father.

Just pour out your heart to God. Share how your day went. Tell Him your dreams. Ask Him to search you and reveal areas of compromise. Thank Him for your lunch. Plead for your kids' well-being. Complain about your car. . . . Just talk with Him. Don't worry how impressive (or unimpressive!) you sound.

Talk with God while doing dishes, driving the car, folding laundry, eating lunch, or kneeling by your bed. Whenever, wherever, whatever—tell Him. He cares!

Don't allow this day to slip away without talking to your Father. No perfection required.

Father God, what a privilege it is to unburden my heart to You.
Teach me the beauty and simplicity of simply sharing my day with You.

DAY 332

Jesus' Wristwatch

So be careful how you live. Don't live like fools, but like those who are wise. Make the most of every opportunity in these evil days. Don't act thoughtlessly, but understand what the Lord wants you to do.
EPHESIANS 5:15–17 NLT

Time is money, they say. Society preaches the value of making good use of our time—and the expense of wasting it.

In the Bible, Ephesians 5 speaks of using every opportunity wisely. But even though scripture teaches the value of time, Jesus never wore a watch. He didn't view His opportunities within the bounds of earthly time.

Have you ever ended a day with guilt and regret over the growing black hole of work yet to be completed? Or do you feel peace at the end of your day, having walked in the presence of the Lord?

Satan wants to consume you with endless lists of meaningless tasks. Fight back! Concern yourself less with the items you can cross off your to-do list, and more with those things the Lord would have you spend your time and energy on. You can strive to be a great multitasker or workhorse—but it's more important and fulfilling to be an efficient laborer for the Lord.

Father, help me to see where You are working and join You there. Let me place my list of tasks aside as I seek Your will for me today. Then give me the ability to show myself grace over the things I do not get done.

DAY 333
Ladies in Waiting

I will wait for the Lord. . . . I will put my trust in him.
Isaiah 8:17 niv

Modern humans aren't good at waiting. In our fast-paced society, if you can't keep up, you'd better get out of the way. We have fast food, speed dialing, and jam-packed schedules that are impossible to keep. Instant gratification is the name of the game—and that attitude often affects our own families.

The Lord Jesus Christ doesn't care about instant gratification. Our right-now attitudes don't move Him. Maybe He finds the saying, "Give me patience, Lord, *right now*," humorous—but He rarely answers that particular prayer.

Do we want joy without accepting heartache? Peace without living through the stress? Patience without facing demands? God sees things differently. He's giving us the opportunity to learn through these delays, irritations, and struggles. What a wise God He is!

We need to learn the art of waiting on God. He will come through every time—but in *His* time, not ours. The wait may be hours or days, or it could be years. But God is always faithful to provide for us. It is when we learn to wait on Him that we will find joy, peace, and patience through the struggle.

Father, You know what I need, so I will wait. Help me be patient, knowing that You control my situation and that all good things come in Your time.

DAY 334

Anxieties

Casting all your care upon Him, for He cares for you.
1 PETER 5:7 NKJV

Because He cares for you. Not because you have to. Not because it's the "right" thing to do. Not because it's what you're supposed to do. No. Read it again. . . Because He cares for you. That's right, He cares for you!

Our Father isn't standing there with His hand on His hip, saying, "All right, spit it out, I don't have all day," or worse. . .holding His hands to His ears, saying, "Enough! You have way too many problems."

The New International Version puts it this way: "Cast all your anxiety on him because he cares for you" (1 Peter 5:7).

Because He cares for you. How humbling and emotionally overwhelming it is to realize that our Lord and God, Jesus Christ, actually wants us to unburden our hearts to Him. Not just because He knows that's what's best for us but simply because He cares. To know He isn't just informing us of one more requirement we have to meet. No. He asks each one of us to cast all our cares and anxieties on Him because He cares for us.

Father, I am overjoyed at Your concern for me. Thank You! Please teach me to cast my cares into Your arms. . .and leave them there.

DAY 335

Patience Is a Virtue

And not only so, but we glory in tribulations also:
knowing that tribulation worketh patience; and
patience, experience; and experience, hope.
ROMANS 5:3–4 KJV

"Teach me patience, Lord." There are very few more dangerous words a Christian can utter. Patience can only be taught through tribulation.

In your life, what is God using to teach you patience? A crying baby? Endless diapers? Sleepless nights? Calls from the school principal? Spilled milk? Nonstop questions? You fill in the blank.

Trials produce experiences from which we can learn. The growth that comes through trials teaches us that every unsavory moment in life will eventually pass—and that, through Christ, there is victory in the endurance. That wisdom is true hope.

Can you find hope in the midst of your tribulations today? Let the Holy Spirit help you navigate your day with the wisdom to see that "this too will pass." And when it does, patience, maturity, and most of all, hope, will be the reward.

Lord Jesus, help me to be like the apostle Paul, welcoming the tribulations
in my life as a means of becoming the person You've called me to be.
Let me learn from my experiences and grow to be more like You.

DAY 336
More Than Enough

*Let us not become weary in doing good, for at the
proper time we will reap a harvest if we do not give up.*
GALATIANS 6:9 NIV

How often do we become impatient and give up? We stand in line at the coffee shop and find ourselves behind an indecisive person. Frustrated, we give up—but before we get to our car, that person—coffee cup in hand—walks past. If we'd only waited another minute, we too could be sipping a steaming caramel latte.

Or maybe we have a dream that we can't seem to make a reality—and rather than trying "just one more time," we give up. A piece of who we are drifts away like a leaf on the sea.

The Word of God encourages us to keep going, to press on, to fight off weariness and never give up. Jesus Christ has a harvest for each of us, and He eagerly anticipates blessing us with it—but we have to trust Him and refuse to give in to weariness.

We can only imagine what that harvest might be because we know that God is the God of "immeasurably more than all we ask or imagine" (Ephesians 3:20 NIV). We can be recipients of His "immeasurably more" if we press on in the strength He provides.

When you're tired, keep going—and remember that, in His perfect timing, you will reap an unimaginable harvest.

*Father, You know that I'm tired and weary in this uphill
struggle. Fill me with Your strength so I can carry on.
I long to reap the harvest You have for me.*

This House Is Too Crowded

"Agreed," she replied. "Let it be as you say."
JOSHUA 2:21 NIV

Rahab and her family were crowded inside her tiny house situated on the walls of Jericho. They were waiting for those two Israeli spies to return with their army.

The spies had promised Rahab they would keep her safe from the coming siege. That's all she had to rely on—the word of spies. But Rahab had come to believe that the Israelites' God was the true God. She was willing to stake her life, as well as the life of her crowded household, on that belief.

Still, she faced an indeterminate wait—probably with irritable family members who doubted her story. On the day the spies had departed, Rahab had tied that scarlet cord outside her window, to tip them off to her house. Had the cord grown faded, like the patience of her family?

Where were the Israelites? What was taking them so long? Rahab could have no idea what was happening in the camp of the Israelites where, in obedience to God, Joshua had ordered all the men to be circumcised, in a day without anesthetics. Huge numbers of men, each one requiring time to heal!

Rahab didn't know any of that, but she still remained steadfast. Ultimately, she did see God act—saving herself and her family.

There are times when all we have to rely on is the Word of God. When that happens, remember Rahab's steadfastness! We can have confidence that His promises will come true: Let it be as He says.

*Lord, may my faith in Your Word benefit my family as
Rahab's faith in the spies' word helped hers. Help me
to remain steadfast regarding Your promises.*

DAY 338

Seasons of Life

*There is a time for everything, and a season for every activity
under the heavens: a time to be born and a time to die, a
time to plant and a time to uproot…a time to weep and a
time to laugh, a time to mourn and a time to dance.*
ECCLESIASTES 3:1–2, 4 NIV

There is a time for work and play, spending and saving, even for relationships and, perhaps marriage. Interestingly, the Bible is relatively silent about dating guidelines. Maybe that's because singles in biblical times didn't find themselves in consuming, intricate, even potentially dangerous situations like singles today.

Frivolous intimacy and temporary emotional attachments waste energy that God might want us to use elsewhere. God does want His children to have every good and perfect thing that He has planned for them—but in His time. Waiting patiently, until God's will becomes clear, ensures that the energy spent growing close to another person will be a building block for the future rather than a failure to add to the pile of regret.

Strive for such a close walk with the Father—in prayer and Bible study—that the seasons He has designated for you will reveal themselves clearly. Eventually, with faith in His perfect plan for you, the waiting will become an acceptable part of life, of reaching with confidence toward the future.

*Father, I trust in Your will, and I will wait until You lead me
forward in a relationship. Please make Your will clear to me in all
things. And please fill me with Your spirit so that I never feel alone.*

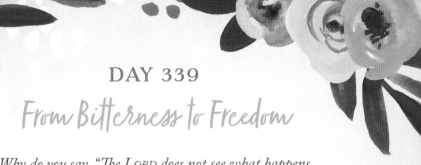

DAY 339
From Bitterness to Freedom

*Why do you say, "The LORD does not see what happens
to me; he does not care if I am treated fairly?"*
ISAIAH 40:27 NCV

Bitterness. . .even the sound of that word, when spoken aloud, conveys unpleasantness. And we as single mothers are particularly prone to this toxic form of resentment.

Though it's not always the case, the circumstances that brought us to our single parent status often create a deep root of bitterness in us. Perhaps we faced betrayal, deception, or broken promises. Financial struggles, the emotional sorrow of loneliness, losing hope over what might have been—so many things can lead to bitterness in our lives.

We know bitterness is wrong, and our friends tell us to let go. But it's not always that easy. Especially because, well. . .it can feel good to be the injured party. For many people, there's a strange satisfaction in being the "victim."

Bitterness, whether conscious or unconscious, is clearly not a biblical feeling. It eats at us emotionally, spiritually, and even physically. So what should we do?

Tell God how badly you hurt—then ask Him for the capacity to forgive. Allow God to be your vindicator. Place all of your mistreatment into His hands, because He cares. And He'll work things out in the end.

*Father, I admit I've been bitter at times as a single parent.
Enable me to forgive when I need to. I know that will set me free.*

DAY 340
The Gift of Receiving

*"In everything I did, I showed you that by this kind of hard work
we must help the weak, remembering the words the Lord Jesus
himself said: 'It is more blessed to give than to receive.' "*
ACTS 20:35 NIV

You probably already know that, like Jesus said, it is better to give to others than to receive for yourself. But what if everyone gave and no one received? That would be impossible, actually. In order for some to give, others have to receive. God designed it perfectly so that the body of Christ would work together and help one another.

Have you ever turned down help of any kind—tangible goods like money or groceries, or intangible things like babysitting or wise counsel—out of pride? Are you trying to keep a stiff upper lip to show the world how strong you are? Maybe you are fully capable of succeeding with no outside help. But in doing so, you might rob others of the joy of giving.

Next time someone offers help, consider graciously accepting the extended hand. By your willingness to receive, others might enjoy the blessings of giving.

*Lord, thank You for the times that You have sent help my way.
Please give me the wisdom and the grace to know when to accept
help from others—and even the courage to ask for it when I need it.*

DAY 341
Forgiven and Free

Blessed is the one whose transgressions are forgiven, whose sins are covered.
PSALM 32:1 NIV

Have you ever really pondered *freedom*? Every individual has a slightly different view of the concept. As women, we are free to vote and drive and earn a living. In western countries, we are free to walk down the street without hiding our faces; we are even free to abort babies and demand divorces. With many of our freedoms, however, come painful consequences.

God's Word shows that the freedom He offers is more far-reaching and eternally beneficial than our personal earthly freedoms we so often demand. When we find ourselves alone with children to feed, clothe, and love—and our children need so much more than we can give—God says we are free. When all we seem to receive from outsiders are glares and judgment, God says we are free. Whatever circumstances led us to this point in life—whether choices of our own or the choices of others—transgressions can be forgiven and we can find freedom. Freedom from judgment, guilt, past mistakes, and burdens.

Under God's umbrella, we are free to be who He created us to be. Nothing more, nothing less.

Father God, thank You for the freedom that comes from knowing You. You have forgiven my past and, even though I may live with consequences of that past, You say I am blessed. Thank You for the blessing of freedom that You give.

DAY 342

Waiting

Blessed are all who wait for him!
ISAIAH 30:18 NIV

Some studies indicate we spend a total of *three years* of our lives just waiting!

That may seem hard to believe. But consider a typical day, with a few minutes stopped at traffic signals, a half hour in the doctor's waiting room, more time yet in a bottlenecked check-out line at the grocery store.

Some of us can handle that waiting through a natural patience. Others? Forget it.

Yet waiting is an inevitable part of everyone's life. And it's a necessary part too. We wait nine months for a baby's birth. We wait for wounds to heal. We wait for our children to mature. And we wait for God to fulfill His promises.

Waiting for God to act is a familiar theme in scripture. Abraham and Sarah waited for a baby until a birth became humanly impossible. But it wasn't impossible to God. Joseph languished, unjustly accused, in Pharaoh's prison, while God ordained a far-reaching drought that would force Joseph's family to Egypt for survival. David spent years hiding from King Saul, but he matured into a wise and capable warrior during that time.

As frustrating as waiting can be, God is always at work on our behalf. Waiting time isn't wasted time. Whatever we might be waiting for—the salvation of our kids, provision for a physical need, a godly partner to help us with our parenting—we can wait with expectancy, trusting in God's timing.

By Your grace, Lord, help me to do the work You've called me to do and wait patiently for the good results You promise.

DAY 343
How Do I Love Thee?

This is what real love is: It is not our love for God; it is God's love
for us. He sent his Son to die in our place to take away our sins.
1 JOHN 4:10 NCV

If the word *love* were banned from popular music, radio stations and songwriters would go out of business. Even the Internet would shrink without this word, so key to human existence. All around the world, people search for someone to care. They chat with strangers, post videos, pay for profiles—anything to find the real love they crave.

Few prove successful—because we human beings are hard to love! Even our charity often wears a disguise. We give so we will receive attention, prestige, or assurance that other people will respect us. Some of us even think our little five-and-dime "love" will obtain a place for us in heaven, as if God were a headwaiter to be bribed.

The Bible tells us He does not *need* our love. He *is* love. God the Father, God the Son, and God the Spirit love each other in perfect eternal unity and joy. If God had done the logical thing, He would have wiped out us troublesome humans and created a new race, one that would worship Him without question.

But He would rather die than do that.

Oh, Lord, when I presume on Your love, please forgive me.
Open my eyes to Your magnificent generosity so I can worship
with my whole heart, in a way that pleases You.

DAY 344
One Chapter

"In the future, when your children ask you, 'What do these stones mean?' tell them that the flow of the Jordan was cut off before the ark of the covenant of the LORD. . . . These stones are to be a memorial to the people of Israel forever."
JOSHUA 4:6–7 NIV

Faith boils down to a willingness to trust God without knowing the end of the story. It means we trust the promises of God even though we don't know how He's going to work them out.

Centuries ago, Joshua faced that very issue of trusting God without knowing the outcome. God told him to march the Israelite soldiers around the city of Jericho in complete silence, once a day for six days. On the seventh day, they were to march around the city seven times. Then the priests were to blow their rams' horns and the soldiers to shout.

That's all the information Joshua had to conquer Jericho. But that's not the only chapter in this story. Joshua had a long history with God's interventions. He had seen God part the Red Sea for the wandering Israelites and had just witnessed another watery miracle as the Israelites walked through the Jordan River to reach Jericho. Joshua knew, by experience, that God was trustworthy.

When his army did what God had instructed, Joshua saw Jericho's walls come tumblin' down.

It's easy to focus on a single chapter in our story, and to forget God's many provisions. But the Lord wants us to keep the big picture in mind, remembering His answered prayers.

Is it worth starting a journal, like Joshua's stone monument, that will remind you and your kids of God's trustworthiness?

Lord, Your compassion has never failed me or my family. May I remember to praise You and thank You all the days of my life.

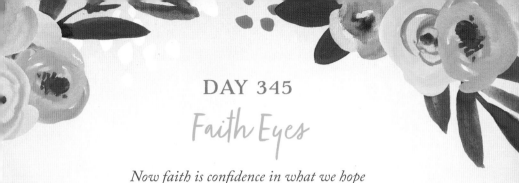

DAY 345

Faith Eyes

Now faith is confidence in what we hope
for and assurance about what we do not see.
HEBREWS 11:1 NIV

Think for a moment of things we can't see, but we know are there.

There's the wind, for one. Its effects are obvious, as golden grain sways to and fro or fall leaves blow into the sky. And there's gravity, which pulls our kids' cups—full of red Kool-Aid, usually—right to the floor.

It's the same with faith, as we simply believe in what do not see. God *says* He is faithful, and so His faithfulness exists. He gives us the signs of His unseen presence, and its effects surround us.

We read how the Israelites walked to the sea and, at Moses' command, the sea parted. They could have been killed—by the pursuing Egyptians or by the sea itself—but God made a safe way of escape for them.

What signs surround you, showing your God is real? Perhaps someone blessed you with money to pay a bill or purchase school supplies. Maybe your "guardian angel" caught your attention and helped you avoid a serious accident. Or perhaps your child prayed to accept the Lord.

Those are all signs of the faithfulness of God. Look around with your "faith eyes" and see the signs surrounding you.

God, I struggle to have faith. Show me where You have
been faithful so my faith can be strengthened. I know You
are faithful, but today I'm asking for a special sign that
You have not forgotten me. Thank You, Father.

Swing and Miss

And though she spoke to Joseph day after day,
he refused to go to bed with her or even be with her.
GENESIS 39:10 NIV

Hardships? Joseph knew them.

Sold into slavery by his brothers, he was carried off to a foreign land. By God's grace, Joseph gained an opportunity to manage the household of an Egyptian official named Potiphar. He was still a slave, but he had impressed Potiphar tremendously.

Joseph also impressed Potiphar's wife. She had a lusty eye for the "well-built and handsome" young man (Genesis 39:6 NIV), and she was determined to seduce him.

Was God tempting Joseph? Had the Lord set Joseph up to test his mettle? Maybe God was giving Joseph a chance to practice with temptation so he'd be more skilled at saying no when bigger temptations came later. You know—like a baseball player taking batting practice, hitting some balls, but occasionally swinging and missing.

That may seem logical, but scripture tells us God would *never* entice us to sin or fail. Since doing so would be contrary to His nature, He allows situations into our lives only for good. He wants us to succeed, each and every time. He wants us to hit a home run, by faith, every time we come to bat.

Joseph did. He told the woman, "How then could I do such a wicked thing and sin against God?" he said (Genesis 39:9 NIV). Then he ran! Let's learn from Joseph's example.

Lord, help me to see every circumstance in my life as ordained by
You for my welfare. Teach me to respond in faith, every time.

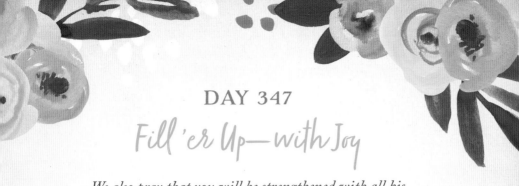

DAY 347

Fill 'er Up—with Joy

We also pray that you will be strengthened with all his
glorious power so you will have all the endurance and
patience you need. May you be filled with joy.
COLOSSIANS 1:11 NLT

We've all had days when we feel exhausted on every level, when we've drained our emotional gas tanks bone dry. As Paul prayed for the Christians of Colosse, we need a filling of God's strength so we can keep going—and rediscover *joy*.

But when can we find time to refill our tank in a life of constant work and worry? We don't have enough time for the rat race itself, let alone a pit stop. But if we don't refuel, we'll stall out—and be of no use to anyone.

That means we have to learn to make time for ourselves. We can explore things that give us a lift. Some things, like listening to a favorite song as we drift off to sleep, take no extra time. Others, like a bubble bath, may require minor adjustments to our schedule. Maybe we'll want to spend time in the garden or call a friend. There are any number of ways to recharge our spiritual batteries.

Every week—perhaps every day—we must set aside time to refill our tanks. The joy of the Lord will be our reward.

Lord of joy, we confess that we are tempted to work
until we fall apart. We pray that You will show us the
things that will give us the strength to go on.

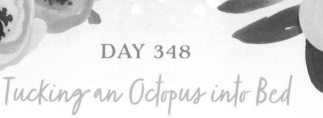

DAY 348
Tucking an Octopus into Bed

"Do not worry about your life, what you will eat or drink; or about
your body, what you will wear. . . . Can anyone of you by worrying
add a single hour to your life? . . . God clothes the grass of the field
. . .will he not much more clothe you—you of little faith?"
MATTHEW 6:25, 27, 30 NIV

Who among us doesn't struggle with anxiety?

Compare worry to trying to tuck an octopus into bed. One tentacle or another keeps popping out from under the covers. If we're not worried about one child, it's the other. If we're not worried about our kids, it's our aging parents. Or the orthodontist's bill. Or the funny sound under the hood of the car.

In the Bible, Jesus spoke much about worry. In a nutshell, He told us not to! Jesus never dismissed the untidy realities of daily life—He knew those troubles firsthand, having spent years as a carpenter in Nazareth, probably living hand-to-mouth as He helped to support His family.

But Jesus also knew that, without looking to God in faith, worry would leave us stuck in a wrestling match with the octopus. Only when we look to God to provide for our needs are we released from worry's grip. "Seek first his kingdom and his righteousness, and all these things will be given to you as well," Jesus promised (Matthew 6:33 NIV).

At that point, worry no longer has a hold on us. It is replaced by a liberating confidence in the power of God.

Lord, with Your help we can live our
daily life free from the grasp of worry.

DAY 349

Answered Prayer

Delight yourself in the Lord; and He
will give you the desires of your heart.
PSALM 37:4 NASB

Sometimes our heartfelt prayers receive a "yes" from God. Sometimes, it's a "no." At other times, we get back only a "not yet."

Have you heard anyone quote today's scripture, saying that God will give us the desires of our hearts? Some believe the verse means that a Christian can ask for anything—health, money, possessions, you name it—and get exactly what she wants. But this passage actually teaches something much deeper.

Note the first part of Psalm 37:4: "Delight yourself in the Lord." A woman who truly delights herself in the Lord will naturally have the desires of her heart—because her heart desires only God and His will. Our Father takes no pleasure in the things of this world—things that will all wither and die. Neither should we.

So what pleases God? He loves it when we witness for Him and live right. If those are things that we also truly desire, won't He grant us the "desires of our heart" and let us see people brought into the kingdom? Won't we have a life rich in spiritual growth?

Lord, please help me see where my desires are not in line
with Your will—so that the things that I pursue are
only and always according to Your own desires.

DAY 350
Dressed to the Nines

*Put on all of God's armor so that you will be able to
stand firm against all strategies of the devil.*
EPHESIANS 6:11 NLT

Have you ever left your house feeling as though you had forgotten something and weren't completely ready to face the world? Maybe you left home without putting on the belt that matches the dress you're wearing or traveled to an out-of-town conference without the proper shoes to wear. It may have been something as simple as forgetting to put on your watch or lipstick. Whatever the case may be, you feel underdressed and incomplete because of the missing item. You feel as if everyone is looking at you, which makes you feel self-conscious and keeps you from being your best on those days.

Paul wrote to the Ephesians, and to us, that it's important to put on the whole armor of God. This is our spiritual wardrobe. He lists the various pieces we should wear every day in order to stand against the devil and his tricks. We cannot afford to forget even one item. Why? Because the missing piece makes us vulnerable in that area. The enemy knows to attack us there. Each day, we must equip ourselves with the armor God has given us, from the breastplate of righteousness to the sword of the Spirit. Before you start your day, be sure you're fully dressed. Don't allow the devil to keep you from feeling confident and being at your best for God.

*Lord, help me to realize the importance of wearing the
armor You have provided and to never leave home without it.*

DAY 351
The Gift of Peace

"Peace I leave with you; my peace I give you. I do not give to you as the world gives. Do not let your hearts be troubled and do not be afraid."
JOHN 14:27 NIV

Watching the news every day is enough to make anyone uneasy and restless, especially if the news stories are happening nearby. People disappear every day, children are abused, and cities are torn apart by rioting and looting. There seems to be no end to the evil that abounds in every city and town across our country. How can anyone live in peace under those circumstances?

As Christians, we can have peace even in the face of all the tragedy happening around us. Jesus made a promise to His disciples and to us as well. He was going back to the Father, but He was giving us a priceless gift. He gave us His peace. The world can never give us the peace that Jesus gives. It's a peace that we, the recipients, can't even understand. It's too wonderful for our minds to grasp, but we know it comes from Him.

Whatever is happening in your world, Christ can give you peace. None of the problems you're facing are too big for Him, whether it's trouble in the city where you live or pain in your own home. He is saying to you, don't let your heart be troubled about these things, and don't be afraid.

Jesus, I ask for Your peace to fill my heart and mind.
Help me not to be afraid of the problems I'm facing.

DAY 352
Renewing the Mind

*Don't copy the behavior and customs of this world, but let God transform
you into a new person by changing the way you think. Then you will learn
to know God's will for you, which is good and pleasing and perfect.*
ROMANS 12:2 NLT

We are surrounded by technology that introduces us to new ideas all the
time. No matter what your choice of electronic device, you have the world
at your disposal. Sometimes the information isn't acceptable for Christians.
We may not have asked for these bits of information, but they invade our
world every day. No matter where we turn, evil is present on all sides. Paul
wrote to the Roman church telling them not to be conformed to the world
around them, but to allow God to transform them and renew their minds.
Can we as twenty-first-century Christians do the same? Yes, we can.

1. Don't allow yourself to view or read everything that comes across
the screen in front of you. If it appears suggestive or impure, it probably is.

2. Take time to read your Bible every day. Don't let the cyber world be
your only source of information. Hear what God has to say to you personally.

3. Ask God to renew your mind and show you what is profitable for
you as a Christian.

4. Don't accept something just because everyone else does it even if
it's "politically correct." Choose today to be transformed by the renewing
of your mind.

*Father, help me not to conform to the world's ideas. Renew my
mind and help me to know Your acceptable will for my life.*

DAY 353
Such as I Have

Then Peter said, "Silver and gold I do not have, but what I do have I give you: In the name of Jesus Christ of Nazareth, rise up and walk."
ACTS 3:6 NKJV

Have you ever been asked to fill a position for which you felt unqualified? Your first thought is to say no. Surely there is someone better qualified than you for the job. Satan doesn't make your decision any easier. He whispers negative thoughts into your ears. "You can't do that; you're not good at it." "Everyone's looking at you and thinking what a bad job you're doing." "You're making a mess of this. Let someone else do it." All of his thoughts are lies, of course. Maybe you aren't as experienced as the last person who had the job, but you're the one God chose. You may not have the abilities or talents of others, but you have something God can use.

When Peter and John approached the lame man at the gate of the temple, Peter didn't hesitate to tell him they didn't have any silver or gold for him. But he had something the man could use. He said, "What I do have I give you." God is looking for those who are willing to give what they do have. He knew before He called you what you could do, and He also has the ability to qualify you to do whatsoever He requires. Give God whatever You have and allow Him to use it.

Father, even when I feel ill-equipped to do what You ask of me, give me a willing heart. I believe You will give me the ability to do Your work! Amen.

DAY 354

Living Water

The woman said to him, "Sir, give me this water so that I won't
get thirsty and have to keep coming here to draw water."
JOHN 4:15 NIV

The Samaritan woman who came to draw water from Jacob's well didn't know she would meet Someone who would change her life drastically. Her life had been filled with relationships that didn't work. She may have felt worthless and used. That day may have started out like every other day in her life, but when she approached the well, Jesus was waiting. He asked her for a drink. When she questioned His reason, He in turn offered her water—living water. If she drank of it, she would never thirst again. She was all for never having to come to the well again to draw water, not realizing Jesus was offering her spiritual life, not a physical refreshment. As they talked, she found living water that gave her a new lease on life.

Some days our life can seem like one endless task after another; it exhibits a sameness that makes us weary. We thirst for something better or maybe just different. Maybe it's time for a trip to the well. As we come to Christ in prayer, seeking a much-needed drink, we will find Him waiting at the well, offering the same living water to each of us that He offered to the Samaritan woman. Are there any among us who don't need times of spiritual refreshing in our lives? Grab a bucket and go to the well. Jesus is waiting.

Jesus, help me to drink from Your well of
living water so I will never thirst again.

DAY 355
Restoring the Broken Pieces

*And the vessel that he made of clay was marred in the
hand of the potter; so he made it again into another
vessel, as it seemed good to the potter to make.*
JEREMIAH 18:4 NKJV

Some people enjoy restoring old furniture, giving it new life. They strip away the old finish that is scratched and ugly, sand the wood to a beautiful sheen, and cover it with a coat of new varnish or paint. Sometimes the old, worn fabric is replaced with a new piece of cloth. When it is finished, it is a "new" piece of furniture. But it doesn't happen overnight. It takes patient, loving care to get it just right.

Jeremiah went to the potter's house and saw the potter at work on a vessel of clay. While the potter was working on the piece, it became marred. The potter didn't toss the clay away but kept working, fashioning it into another vessel. God wants to restore lives scratched and marred by sin just as some restore furniture and the potter molds clay into usable vessels. No matter what has stained or disfigured our lives, God can mold us into the person He wants us to be. To become a usable vessel, we must allow the Potter to knead and work the clay. Even if we fall off the Potter's wheel by our own choice, He can pick us up and remold us into a new creation.

*Father, help me to stay on the Potter's wheel
until You are finished with me.*

DAY 356

Be Still

Be still, and know that I am God; I will be exalted
among the nations, I will be exalted in the earth!
PSALM 46:10 NKJV

A farmer's wife stepped outside into the blistering heat to take out the garbage. She couldn't wait to get back inside where it was cool. When she tried to open the door, it was locked. Panic seized her for a moment, but she realized there was nothing she could do about it. They lived miles from town and her husband wouldn't be home from work for a while. She looked around for a place to get out of the sun and spotted a large shade tree. She sat down under the tree and looked around. For the first time in a long time, she noticed the beauty of God's creation that surrounded her home. God's blessings were apparent everywhere she looked. By the time her husband arrived home, she felt rested and refreshed in spite of the heat. She realized God had probably been trying to get her attention for some time. She just hadn't been listening. It had taken getting locked out of her house to make her stop and listen.

Has God been trying to get your attention lately? If you're rushing around, buried in responsibilities and tasks you feel are important, what will it take for God to make you stop and listen to His voice? What will it take for you to "be still" and acknowledge Him?

Father, help me to slow down so I can hear You speaking to me.

DAY 357

Five Minutes of Glory

And whatever you do in word or deed, do all in the name of the Lord Jesus, giving thanks to God the Father through Him.
COLOSSIANS 3:17 NKJV

A local writers' group gives members a chance to share with the rest of the group their writing successes. They call this time "five minutes of glory." The author is allowed to stand in front of the group for five minutes to share what they've published recently. They are allowed to hold up a copy of the published work and share any information about the piece that they'd like. This five minutes is intended as a means of encouragement for those seeking publication or just beginning to write. It is not meant as a bragging session.

Sometimes as Christians, we forget to share "five minutes of glory" with others by telling them what God has done for us personally. We should never take credit for the blessings that come our way or do good deeds with the purpose of impressing others. Our time of sharing with others should give God full credit and serve as encouragement for others who may need a good word.

The next time God does something for you—either a blessing from Him or an ability He has given you to accomplish a task—share "five minutes of glory" with someone else. Just be sure all the glory goes to God.

Father, all glory be to You for the things You have accomplished in my life.

DAY 358
Praise to Be Raised

*My God, I cry out by day, but you do not answer, by night,
but I find no rest. . . . To you they cried out and were
saved; in you they trusted and were not put to shame.*
PSALM 22:2, 5 NIV

Life isn't easy. We've heard many platitudes meant to encourage us. Being a complainer is not attractive. You need to find the silver lining in every cloud. If life gives you lemons, make lemonade. Smile even when it hurts.

Most of us try to begin our day by thanking God for our blessings before we face our challenges. But when we feel despair, is it acceptable to complain or do we need to bury those emotions? The Bible recounts times when people cried out to the Lord, times when they voiced their complaints. In Psalm 22 we're told that Christ poured out His soul to His heavenly Father throughout His sufferings. If we follow Christ's example, we can take our complaints to God in prayer as long as we, like Christ, also acknowledge our love for and trust in God.

If we just complain to others, we won't solve our problems. If we praise God and trust Him to stand with us during our trials, He will raise us up to handle our problems. Maybe we need to replace those old platitudes with this one: Complain and remain, or praise to be raised.

*Lord, thank You for listening to my complaints and
saving me from my sins. Even during my struggles
I will praise You as my God and Savior. Amen.*

DAY 359

Love One Another

Greet one another with a kiss of love.
Peace to all of you who are in Christ.
1 PETER 5:14 NIV

Our capacity for love is unlimited. If we ever wonder how much love one person can shower on others, we need only to consider the love between a parent and a child. There is scientific evidence that when a baby is born a hormonal process occurs for both parents that ensures parental love for the new life. If it were truly just a matter of some unseen chemical that causes parents to offer unconditional-love-for-life, how then can we experience that same type of love for an adopted child or a grandchild? How does it happen that we have dear friends we love even though we don't always "like" them?

How? Love is a choice. We choose to give and receive love. As Christians, we must heed God's command to love one another. In 1 Peter we read that we are to greet one another with love.

As when you were a child and shared valentines with your friends, think today of those you love as God loves you. Reach out and show them your love. It can be as simple as a call, text, or email saying, "I love you." Today is a good day to ensure that your loved ones *know* that you love them, unconditionally.

Lord, thank You for all those You have given me to love.
Help me to show Your love as You have commanded. Amen.

DAY 360

Can't You Hear Him Whisper?

He says, "Be still, and know that I am God."
PSALM 46:10 NIV

Our society is so fast-paced there is little time to take care of our mental and physical health, let alone our spiritual health. We are beings created for eternity, and we are made in the image of a supernatural God, and yet paying attention to our spiritual journey gets put off and off and off.

Until something terrible happens. Like a financial crisis. Or infidelity in our marriage. Or bad news at the doctor's office. Or a death in the family. Then we do far more than pause. We go into a full-body panic mode, drenched in fear, racing around, grasping at anything and everything, desperate for answers. For peace.

But had we been in close fellowship with the Lord all along, we wouldn't be so frantic, our spirits so riddled with terror. What we need to do is to be still and know that He is God. Know that He is still in control, even though we think the bad news is in control. It's not. God is.

Life would be more peaceful, more focused, more infused with joy if we were already in the midst of communion with God when troubles come.

Can't you hear Him whisper to you, "Be still, and know that I am God"?

Lord, help me to want to spend time with You every day of my life—in fair weather as well as stormy. Amen.

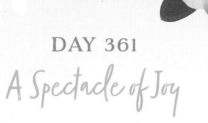

DAY 361
A Spectacle of Joy

*Wearing a linen ephod, David was dancing before the L*ORD
with all his might, while he and all Israel were bringing up the
*ark of the L*ORD *with shouts and the sound of trumpets. As the ark*
*of the L*ORD *was entering the City of David, Michal daughter of*
Saul watched from a window. And when she saw King David
*leaping and dancing before the L*ORD, *she despised him in her heart.*
2 SAMUEL 6:14–16 NIV

The world tells us how to live our lives—how to eat, communicate, love, sleep, grieve, and celebrate. But the problem is, the world's philosophies and values and viewpoints don't usually mesh with God's ways. In the book of 2 Samuel when David danced before the Lord, we sense that even though his wife Michal despised her husband's spectacle of utter joy, the Lord did not. David was celebrating with abandon—although not in the conventional ways perhaps—but he was indeed showing his passionate joy and profound thankfulness to God.

How easy it is to seek the approval of others. How tempting. But how unwise. Let us instead seek to satisfy God, to love Him, to joy in His presence. Life will then be more beautiful. Maybe not as the world describes beauty, but it will possess a loveliness in spirit from the Lord that the world cannot touch. That the world will puzzle over. That the world may even ponder and eventually desire.

Dear Lord, help me to seek Your approval and not the world's.
Show me how to praise You for Your goodness and mercy. Amen.

DAY 362

Deep in Our Hearts

For this God is our God for ever and ever;
he will be our guide even to the end.
PSALM 48:14 NIV

You turn a corner on a busy street, and suddenly you don't know where you are. You don't recognize the signs, the buildings, or the landmarks. You go back the way you came. You pause to think, to focus, trying not to panic. But it's no good. You know in your heart that you're off course, and you won't be able to find your way back without help.

And so it goes with our souls. We take many of the wrong paths in life. Then we backtrack. Then we take the wrong roads all over again. And again. Oh dear. We get scared, but we still want to go it alone. Or perhaps we reach out to the wrong people for help.

Still we search.

Deep in our hearts we know the truth, even if we spend a lifetime trying to deny it.

We're horribly lost.

We need someone to rescue us. We need the One who can take us by the heart and hand and give us a way out of our peril. Give us new life. And take us home where we belong.

There is only One who can be called on for that kind of mighty and supernatural rescue.

His name is Jesus.

Take heart. Your rescuer is here.

Lord, please set me free from sin and sadness. Let me walk on higher
ground with You by my side, for now and all eternity. Amen.

DAY 363

Itty Bitty Words

The words of the reckless pierce like swords,
but the tongue of the wise brings healing.
PROVERBS 12:18 NIV

Whoever started the childhood chant—"Sticks and stones may break my bones, but words will never hurt me"—lied. Plain and simple.

Words may seem itty bitty as they escape from our lips, but they have the power to make us cringe and cry and crumble into pieces. Pieces that may never come back together again the way they were meant to be.

Words can destroy a reputation. Break a tender heart. And a not-so-tender heart. Words can create an untold ripple effect of misery. And our words can grieve the Holy Spirit. Surely there is a better way to live. There is. It's with the power of the Holy Spirit. From the Psalms comes a wonderful daily heart-prayer: "May these words of my mouth and this meditation of my heart be pleasing in your sight, LORD, my Rock and my Redeemer" (Psalm 19:14 NIV).

Our words can heal, comfort, challenge, encourage, and inspire. It's our choice, every minute of every day, which kind of words we will use. Those that heal or those that hurt. Let us always speak truth, yes, but let us do it with tenderness. Not with a mindset that feeds our egos, but with a caring spirit that pleases God.

Holy Spirit, guide me in my thoughts, and may
my words be healing to all I meet. Amen.

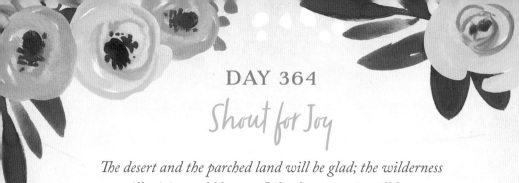

DAY 364

Shout for Joy

The desert and the parched land will be glad; the wilderness
will rejoice and blossom. Like the crocus, it will burst
into bloom; it will rejoice greatly and shout for joy.
ISAIAH 35:1–2 NIV

Is there any season as joyous as spring? The trees unfurl thousands of tiny juicy green flags to wave hello to the world. Flowers make that final push through the dark soil and stretch out their bedecked heads to embrace the sun-warmed air. Farmers plant seeds of promise into the brown, barren land—measuring out hope by the bushel.

You are human. You will go through times of sorrow and despair, times of suffering and boredom. You will work through long days and toss and turn through longer nights. You will worry and fret and stew. You will look around and see only gray.

But spring is our annual reminder that the story isn't over. It's never over. It starts up from page 1 again every year, ready to be filled with characters and plots and dialogue. No, the story won't always be happy and the characters won't all get along. But isn't it amazing that it happens at all? That our Creator God is willing to keep writing new chapters for us? And that He never runs out of ideas?

A new story every spring starts right before your eyes. Now that's something to shout about.

Dear Lord, thank You for Your endless creativity that brings
us so much grace and joy. Help me remember in the grayest
times that color is just an inch or so under my feet.

DAY 365

As Pure as Rainwater

Hatred stirs up conflict, but love covers over all wrongs.
PROVERBS 10:12 NIV

Have you ever seen a rain barrel filled after a good storm? That water is clean and refreshing. But if you take a big stick and whip up the contents, soon the dregs will rise and whirl. Suddenly what was clean is now a dirty mess. That visual is a good one for Proverbs 10:12, which reminds us that hatred stirs up old quarrels.

When we choose to hold on to grudges, then hatred seeps into our hearts. It's like we're carrying around a big stick, and we're more than ready to whip up some dregs by bringing up an argument from the past. This is a common way to live, but not a godly or healthy one.

What's the answer?

Love.

When we love others, we will overlook insults, whether they are intended or not. Does that seem like an impossible task using these feeble shells of ours?

It is impossible in our own humanness.

But with the supernatural power of the Holy Spirit, we can overcome this need to stir up trouble, and we can forgive freely and love abundantly—just as Christ has done for us. So let us come not with a big stick but with a spirit as refreshing and as pure as rainwater.

Holy Spirit, please take away any tendency in me to bicker, but instead make me into a woman who loves with my whole heart and who is an instrument of Your peace. Amen.

Scripture Index

THE OLD TESTAMENT

Proverbs

Ecclesiastes

Daily Inspiration for a Woman's Spirit!